MOON

OREGON HIKING

MATT WASTRADOWSKI

CONTENTS

OREGON HIKING REGIONS

1. **Portland and the Willamette Valley**
2. **Columbia River Gorge**
3. **Mount Hood**
4. **Oregon Coast**
5. **Bend and the Central Oregon Cascade**

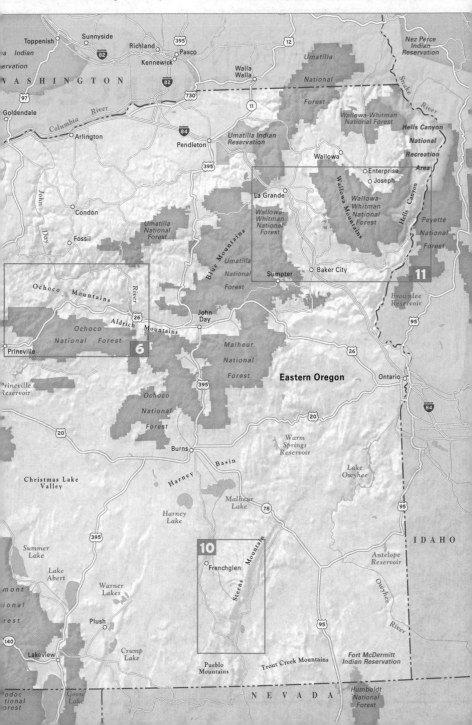

OREGON HIKING
TOP EXPERIENCES

1 Explore the Columbia River Gorge (page 57).

2 Take in Pacific Ocean views and spot marinelife (pages 119 and 128).

3 Hike around the state's highest peak (page 93).

4 Wander through fields of wildflowers (page 18).

5 Chase waterfalls (pages 16 and 20).

6 Discover fossils, dramatic rock formations, and the surreal Painted Hills at John Day Fossil Beds National Monument (pages 194 and 200).

7 Swim in mountain lakes (pages 260 and 263).

8 Follow trails through the urban forests of Portland (page 26).

9 Gaze into Crater Lake's dramatic blue depths (page 205).

10 Kick back with a post-hike beer (page 17).

HIT THE TRAIL

The secret's out: Oregon is a hiker's heaven. What makes it such a magical destination for the trail-bound is its surprising diversity of terrain.

It's famed for its lush greenery, exemplified by the Willamette Valley surrounding Portland. The waterfall-strewn Columbia River Gorge and the state's tallest peak, snowcapped Mount Hood, are world-class recreation destinations. The rugged Oregon Coast is speckled with crags, peaks, lighthouses, and viewpoints that reflect millennia of intense rains, frost-bitten winters, and never-ending windstorms. Along the spine of the Cascade Range running through the state, you'll find high-desert expanses and volcanic landscapes near Bend, not to mention Crater Lake, an isolated sapphire gem. The John Day Fossil Beds in central Oregon evidence more than 40 million years of changing climates, ecosystems, and natural evolution, as well as the Painted Hills, showcasing surreal layers of color. On the less-discovered eastern side of the state, you can wander the granite Wallowa Mountains and find authentic Oregon Trail wagon tracks in the Blue Mountains. Steens Mountain forms a natural wall hiding Oregon's driest point: the Alvord Desert. In between you can delight in wildflower-flecked meadows, swim in alpine lakes, and hop on a stretch of the Pacific Crest Trail.

It's possible to spend a lifetime discovering and rediscovering Oregon's landscape.

▼ LOWER MACLEAY TRAIL

HIKING GETAWAYS

Camping the Coast

With a mix of sea stacks, lighthouses, towering capes, tide pools, and beaches, the Pacific Northwest's coast offers classic adventure. Pick a hike and then pitch a tent nearby for the night, or string these suggestions together—they're listed north to south—to hop your way down the coast on a hiking-camping trip. Driving time between successive campgrounds ranges 0.75-3.25 hours.

Cannon Beach

The tent sites at **Saddle Mountain State Natural Area** promise a quiet respite from some of the region's more crowded campgrounds. Situated early along the **Saddle Mountain Trail,** you'll appreciate the proximity after climbing nearly 1,500 feet up the mountain's slopes.

Tillamook

Sitting on a sand spit between Netarts Bay and the Pacific Ocean, **Cape Lookout State Park** has a developed campground nestled in the heart of the Tillamook coast. Just a few miles south, you can hike to the tip of **Cape Lookout,** one of the best whale-watching spots on the entire Oregon Coast.

Yachats

The **Cape Perpetua Campground** makes a great base for exploring the area's natural beauty. Thor's Well, Spouting Horn, and "the best view on the Oregon Coast"—according to the U.S. Forest Service—are some of the many highlights along **Cape Perpetua**'s network of trails.

Florence

Embark on a magical hike to one of the coast's most iconic lighthouses—plus a beach—on the **Heceta Head to Hobbit Trail.** Less than a 30-minute drive south on U.S. 101 brings you to the campground at **Jessie M. Honeyman Memorial State Park,** set amid the Oregon Dunes.

Brookings

You don't have to go far to see one of the northernmost redwood groves on Earth—in fact, it's a short walk from your campsite at **Alfred A. Loeb State Park.** On the **River View Trail to Redwood Nature Trail,** you'll pass through a forest of Oregon myrtle before reaching the towering trees.

Day-Hiking the Pacific Crest Trail

The 2,650-mile Pacific Crest Trail (PCT) stretches from Mexico to Canada and is a dream trip for many backpackers. While thru-hikers take months to walk the entire trail, such an adventure isn't realistic for many. This doesn't mean you can't enjoy the famous route: Oregon is home to about 450 miles of it and offers numerous opportunities for day hikes, as well as nearby camping options.

▲ HECETA HEAD LIGHTHOUSE

Columbia River Gorge

The hike to **Dry Creek Falls** follows the PCT through patches of burned forest—damage done by the 2017 Eagle Creek Fire—before an offshoot trail detours to the base of the namesake falls. Camp about 8 miles east of the trailhead at **Wyeth Campground.**

Mount Hood

Ramona Falls, which tumbles over columns of basalt in a shady forest, is a popular destination, and on the hike you'll hop on and off the PCT. Spend the night about 10 miles southwest at **Tollgate Campground;** you're not far from U.S. 26, but the Zigzag River—which butts up against the campground's western edge—drowns out highway noise.

Bend and the Central Oregon Cascades

Hike part of the PCT on the way to **Little Belknap Crater.** You'll travel through a forest and emerge at the foot of a massive lava field with views of Cascade peaks. Camp 17 miles east at **Creekside Campground,** near downtown Sisters.

Ashland and the Rogue Valley

Hike the PCT through wildflower meadows and gain views of nearby peaks on **Mount Ashland.** Camp overnight just a few miles away at the **Mount Ashland Campground.**

Sky Lakes Wilderness and Klamath Basin

Follow the PCT on the **Brown Mountain Lava Flow** hike, which darts between verdant forests and eerie lava flows, all while delivering photo-worthy views of Mount McLoughlin. Sitting in the shadow of Mount McLoughlin about 5 miles north of the trailhead, **Fourmile Lake Campground** makes an ideal place to spend the night.

BEST BY SEASON

Spring

- **Tom McCall Point Trail:** Each spring, wildflowers dot the meadows leading to the summit of McCall Point, which affords views of Mount Hood and Mount Adams (page 88).
- **Cape Lookout:** Spy migrating gray whales from one of the best whale-watching spots along the Oregon Coast (page 128).
- **Lower Table Rock:** Hike to the pancake-flat summit of Lower Table Rock and admire its seasonal vernal pools and colorful wildflower displays before the summer heat arrives (page 234).

Summer

- **Opal Pool and Jawbone Flats Loop:** Follow this trail to a popular swimming hole and an old mining camp (page 44).
- **Cleetwood Cove and Wizard Island:** This two-parter is only accessible in summer, when you can take a trail down to Crater Lake's shore and then boat to a volcanic cinder cone for a hike to its summit (page 211).
- **Sky Lakes Basin via Cold Springs Trail:** Hike to some of the region's most popular swimming holes (page 260).

▾ OPAL POOL

▲ VIEW FROM THE PITTOCK MANSION IN WINTER

Fall

- **Trail of Ten Falls:** This trail's 10 waterfalls are even more impressive alongside vivid fall foliage displays (page 35).

- **Bagby Hot Springs:** With temperatures cooling and crowds dissipating, early fall is an ideal time to hike through old-growth forest to enjoy a soak in Oregon's most popular hot springs (page 41).

- **Misery Ridge-River Trail Loop:** After the summer crowds have simmered down at Smith Rock, enjoy a sunny hike up to one of the best viewpoints in Central Oregon (page 169).

Winter

- **Lower Macleay Trail to Pittock Mansion:** When the region's most popular hikes are socked in with snow and ice, this hike remains accessible, delivers a hearty workout, and offers stellar views of the downtown Portland skyline (page 26).

- **Mosier Plateau:** The Mosier Plateau's low elevation makes it a good winter hiking destination, and you also have a solid chance of spotting bald eagles overhead (page 85).

- **Cape Falcon:** Hike out to a windswept bluff overlooking the Pacific Ocean, where you might see migrating gray whales (page 119).

BEST WATERFALL HIKES

- **Trail of Ten Falls:** On this iconic hike you'll pass 10 waterfalls in less than 10 miles (page 35).
- **Latourell Falls Loop:** These scenic falls in the Columbia River Gorge cascade amid lichen-colored columnar basalt pillars (page 60).
- **Wahkeena Falls-Multnomah Falls Loop:** Bookend a hike with two of the most popular waterfalls in the Gorge (page 66).
- **Ramona Falls:** Hike to one of the most photographed waterfalls in the state, set in the shadow of Mount Hood (page 102).
- **Drift Creek Falls:** Cross a dramatic suspension bridge to this waterfall in the Oregon Coast Range (page 134).

▼ DRIFT CREEK FALLS

BEST BREW HIKES

In Oregon, you're never too far from a brewery. One of the joys of hiking is kicking back with a beer afterward. Here are some of the best trail-brewery pairings.

- **Lower Macleay Trail to Pittock Mansion, Portland and the Willamette Valley:** Pair some of Portland's best skyline views with one of the city's best breweries. After a hike up this trail inside city limits, head just a mile away to **Breakside Brewery,** which boasts a variety of hop-forward ales and crisp lagers (page 28). To try: Breakside IPA and Breakside Pilsner.
- **Cape Perpetua, Oregon Coast:** Hike a network of scenic trails and then refresh yourself afterward just a few miles north with a beer at **Yachats Brewing,** whose ales and lagers are named for local landmarks and incorporate locally and regionally sourced ingredients (page 140). To try: Thor's Well (IPA) and Log Dog Lager.
- **Tumalo Mountain, Bend and the Central Oregon Cascades:** This hike affords views of Mount Bachelor and its surroundings, and in nearby Bend you can unwind on the lawn at **Crux Fermentation Project** while soaking in more views of Cascade peaks, including the Three Sisters (page 174). To try: Cast Out (IPA) and PCT Porter.
- **Grizzly Peak, Ashland and the Rogue Valley:** Enjoy sweeping Rogue Valley views, Cascade peaks, and seasonal wildflowers, and then head into Ashland's **Caldera Brewing Company,** which boasts a tap list of 40 house-brewed beers (page 239). To try: Lawn Mower Lager and Pilot Rock Porter.
- **Hurricane Creek to Slick Rock Gorge, Wallowa Mountains and Blue Mointains:** Hike into the heart of the Wallowas amid a bucolic blend of alpine forests, crystal-clear rivers, and towering peaks. Afterward, in nearby Enterprise, enjoy sweeping views of the Wallowas from the outdoor bar at **Terminal Gravity Brewing** (page 296). To try: Terminal Gravity IPA and Terminal Gravity ESG.

▾ CRUX FERMENTATION PROJECT'S PCT PORTER

BEST WILDFLOWER HIKES

▲ WILDFLOWERS ALONG TOM MCALL POINT TRAIL

- **Tryon Creek State Natural Area Loop:** Trillium, tiger lily, and fireweed dot this trail in spring (page 32).

- **Tom McCall Point Trail:** Among the most popular wildflower hikes in the Columbia River Gorge, this trail hosts yellow balsamroot, purple grasswidow, and red paintbrush, plus views of Cascade peaks (page 88).

- **Elk Meadows:** Host to everything from purple lupine to white-fringed grass of Parnassus, this is one of the best wildflower-viewing spots on Mount Hood (page 108).

- **Lower Table Rock:** The flat summit of Lower Table Rock hosts numerous rare wildflowers, including the dwarf woolly meadowfoam—a plant found nowhere else on Earth (page 234).

- **Mount Ashland (via the Pacific Crest Trail):** Find some of the Rogue Valley's most breathtaking wildflower displays along this hike through hillside meadows (page 243).

BEST DOG-FRIENDLY HIKES

- **Lower Macleay Trail to Pittock Mansion:** Fido will appreciate the well-graded, well-maintained paths en route to Pittock Mansion, where you'll enjoy skyline views (page 26).

- **Lost Lake Butte:** Fit dogs and their owners will enjoy the steady ascent to postcard-worthy views of Mount Hood (page 96).

- **Cape Falcon:** What dog doesn't love a day at the beach? Pair your hike with off-leash fun at Short Sand Beach (page 119).

- **West Metolius River:** Horseback riders and mountain bikers aren't allowed on this mostly flat path, which means you and your four-legged friend have it all to yourselves (page 160).

- **Misery Ridge-River Trail Loop:** Pick up a cleanup bag near the Crooked River bridge and wander fascinating terrain with your pup (page 169).

▾ VIEW FROM THE TOP OF MISERY RIDGE

EASY WATERFALL WALKS

The Pacific Northwest's renowned precipitation makes it quintessential waterfall country, and many don't demand a thigh-burning workout to appreciate. Visit in the spring to see them flowing at full force.

BRIDAL VEIL FALLS

Distance/Duration: 1.4 miles round-trip, 45 minutes
Trailhead: between mileposts 28 and 29 on the Historic Columbia River Highway, Bridal Veil Falls State Scenic Viewpoint, Columbia River Gorge National Scenic Area

A pair of trails from the parking area showcase the best of the Columbia River Gorge without requiring much effort. The two-tiered falls here come from a creek that begins on nearby Larch Mountain. The upper loop trail shows off Gorge cliffs, along with springtime wildflowers, while the lower out-and-back trail descends to the base of Bridal Veil Falls. Keep an eye out for poison oak along this path.

HENLINE FALLS

Distance/Duration: 1.8 miles round-trip, 1 hour
Trailhead: roughly 18 miles northeast of Mehama on Forest Road 2209, Willamette National Forest

The path to Henline Falls starts in a forest of Douglas fir and hemlock, its undergrowth thick with ferns and, in spring, colorful wildflower displays. The out-and-back trail follows an old roadbed to a long-abandoned mine and climbs gently before ending at a small viewing area of the seemingly sheer wall of water. Keep left at two junctions along the way; the user-created trails off to the right don't head anywhere worthwhile.

PROXY FALLS

Distance/Duration: 1.5 miles round-trip, 45 minutes
Trailhead: roughly 10 miles southeast of Belknap Springs on Highway 242 (typically closed Nov.-June depending on snow; call 541/822-3381 for road info), Willamette National Forest

Just east of the McKenzie River, one stream cascades into two separate curtains of water—each dropping more than 200 feet—to form Proxy Falls. In turn, the water seeps into the porous lava rock at its base. This family-friendly loop affords views of both the upper and lower sections of Proxy Falls.

TOKETEE FALLS

Distance/Duration: 0.8 mile round-trip, 30 minutes
Trailhead: roughly 21 miles northwest of Diamond Lake on Forest Road 34, Willamette National Forest

Hike through an old-growth forest of Douglas fir and western red cedar alongside the North Umpqua River to a platform overlooking Toketee Falls, flanked by columnar basalt. The out-and-back trail includes nearly 200 steps.

WATSON FALLS

Distance/Duration: 0.8 mile round-trip, 30 minutes
Trailhead: roughly 19 miles northwest of Diamond Lake on Forest Road 37, Willamette National Forest

The path to Watson Falls—the third-highest waterfall in Oregon and the highest in southern Oregon—climbs through a forest of salal, Douglas fir, and vine maple before crossing a wooden bridge over Watson Creek. Just past the bridge, which affords spectacular views of the falls, a T-shaped junction offers two choices: Head left for a quick climb to the base of Watson Falls, or head right to complete a loop back to the trailhead.

▼ TOKETEE FALLS

PORTLAND AND THE WILLAMETTE VALLEY

Sixteen of Oregon's 20 largest cities sit within the Willamette Valley, making it the state's most populated region. But the area is also home to an abundance of verdant, peaceful landscapes, located conveniently close to the city centers. Portland offers easy retreats within its many green spaces, including 5,100-acre Forest Park, which hugs downtown and hosts miles of hiking trails. Near Salem, Oregon's largest state park draws crowds to its renowned waterfall hike. Elsewhere in the valley you'll find secluded hot springs and river walks, as well as summit hikes offering sweeping views of some of the region's most-beloved Cascade peaks.

▲ SAWMILL FALLS ON THE WAY TO OPAL POOL

▲ NORTH FALLS ON THE TRAIL OF TEN FALLS

◀ VIEW FROM MARYS PEAK

1 **Lower MacLeay Trail to Pittock Mansion**
DISTANCE: 6.4 miles round-trip
DURATION: 3 hours
EFFORT: Easy/moderate

2 **Marquam Trail to Council Crest**
DISTANCE: 3.9 miles round-trip
DURATION: 2 hours
EFFORT: Easy/moderate

3 **Tryon Creek State Natural Area Loop**
DISTANCE: 4.5 miles round-trip
DURATION: 2 hours
EFFORT: Easy

4 **Trail of Ten Falls**
DISTANCE: 9.3 miles round-trip
DURATION: 4.5 hours
EFFORT: Moderate/strenuous

5 **Table Rock**
DISTANCE: 8.2 miles round-trip
DURATION: 4 hours
EFFORT: Moderate

6 **Bagby Hot Springs**
DISTANCE: 3.3 miles round-trip
DURATION: 1.5 hours
EFFORT: Easy

7 **Opal Pool and Jawbone Flats Loop**
DISTANCE: 8.5 miles round-trip
DURATION: 4.5 hours
EFFORT: Moderate

8 **Battle Ax Mountain**
DISTANCE: 6.8 miles round-trip
DURATION: 3 hours
EFFORT: Moderate

9 **Marys Peak**
DISTANCE: 6.9 miles round-trip
DURATION: 3.5 hours
EFFORT: Moderate

10 **North Fork River Walk**
DISTANCE: 7 miles round-trip
DURATION: 3.5 hours
EFFORT: Easy/moderate

▼ VIEW FROM PITTOCK MANSION

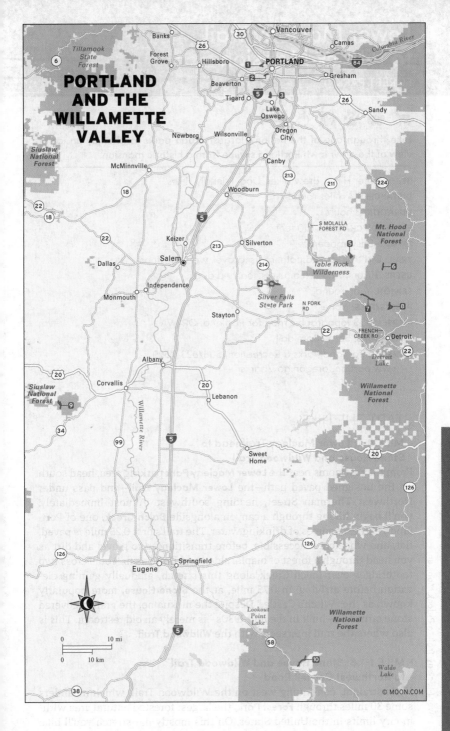

1

Lower Macleay Trail to Pittock Mansion

FOREST PARK

🦌 ❀ 🐾 🚶 ♿ 🚍

Hike through one of the nation's largest urban parks, and enjoy an iconic view of the downtown Portland skyline from a historic mansion.

BEST: Winter Hikes, Brew Hikes, Dog-Friendly Hikes
DISTANCE: 6.4 miles round-trip
DURATION: 3 hours
ELEVATION CHANGE: 1,010 feet
EFFORT: Easy/moderate
TRAIL: Dirt trail, paved path, roots, gravel, wooden steps
USERS: Hikers, wheelchiar users, leashed dogs
SEASON: Year-round
PASSES/FEES: None
MAPS: USGS topographic map for Portland, OR-WA
PARK HOURS: 5am-10pm daily
CONTACT: Portland Parks & Recreation, 503/823-7529, www.portlandoregon.gov/parks

START THE HIKE

▶ **MILE 0-1: Lower Macleay Trailhead to Stone House and Wildwood Trail**

From the restrooms near the **Lower Macleay Park** parking area, head south on the unsigned paved path—the **Lower Macleay Trail**—and pass under Northwest Thurman Street, heading southwest. Almost immediately, you'll begin hiking through a canyon alongside **Balch Creek,** one of Portland's earliest sources of drinking water. The trail's first 0.25 mile is paved, flat, and wheelchair-accessible, before transitioning to gravel and dirt as you head through a forest of maple, alder, and Douglas fir. You'll cross two footbridges over Balch Creek along this stretch, gradually gaining elevation before arriving, in 0.75 mile, at the **Stone House,** more popularly known as the "Witch's Castle." Despite the nickname, the graffiti-covered stone structure—built in the mid-1930s—is merely an old restroom. This is also where the trail intersects with the **Wildwood Trail.**

▶ **MILE 1-1.8: Stone House and Wildwood Trail to Northwest Cornell Road**

Head straight, continuing west on the Wildwood Trail, which meanders some 30 miles through **Forest Park,** the largest forested natural area within city limits in the United States. On this mostly flat stretch you'll hike through a forest of Douglas fir. In roughly 0.4 mile, you'll cross a footbridge over Balch Creek. Over the next 0.4 mile, you'll ascend a series of

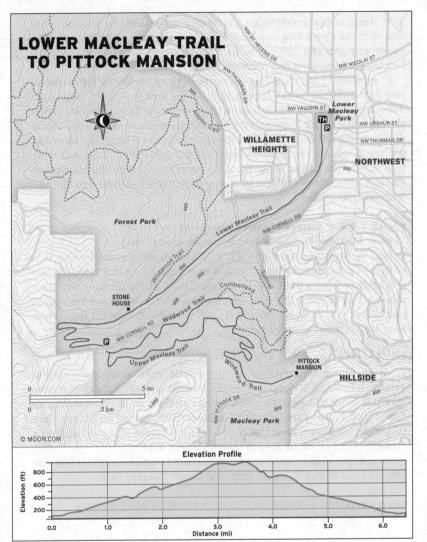

LOWER MACLEAY TRAIL TO PITTOCK MANSION

Elevation Profile

© MOON.COM

switchbacks out of the canyon and follow the trail east before arriving at Northwest Cornell Road. For a fun side trip, you could turn right on the road and walk an extra 0.1 mile to visit the **Portland Audubon Wildlife Care Center,** the oldest wildlife rehab facility in Oregon. Here you can view birds and owls that have been rehabilitated.

▶ **MILE 1.8–3.4: Northwest Cornell Road to Pittock Mansion Viewpoint (via Wildwood Trail)**

Cross the road, and ascend three switchbacks. In 100 feet, you'll arrive at an intersection with the Upper Macleay Trail, but turn left to remain on the Wildwood Trail for now. After 0.5 mile of steady ascent, you'll arrive at the first of several intersections in quick succession. Long story short: Follow the signs at each to remain on the Wildwood Trail. Roughly 0.3

mile after the first intersection, you might be confused by another junction with the Upper Macleay Trail. Don't take the hard right; instead, take the other righthand fork—up some wooden steps and alongside wooden fencing—to remain on the Wildwood Trail.

In another 0.5 mile, you'll arrive at the parking lot for the **Pittock Mansion** (503/823-3623, 10am-4pm daily Feb.-May and Sept.-Dec., 10am-5pm daily June-Labor Day, $8-12, free for children under 6), built in 1914 as the private home of the onetime publisher of the *Oregonian* newspaper. While there's an admission fee to enter the mansion, now a historical museum, it's free to wander the grounds. Head left through the parking lot to walk 0.25 mile to the easternmost point on the property. From this **viewpoint,** you'll catch some of the best glimpses of Portland's skyline and the surrounding mountains.

▶ **MILE 3.4–6.4: Pittock Mansion Viewpoint to Lower Macleay Trailhead (via Upper Macleay Trail)**

Return the way you came—but when you arrive again at the intersection with the **Upper Macleay Trail** after 0.75 mile, head left onto this trail. While it doesn't present a dramatically different view of the urban forest, it's a nice change of pace. The trail reconnects with the **Wildwood Trail** again just before you cross Northwest Cornell Road in another 0.5 mile. From here, return the way you came.

DIRECTIONS

From downtown Portland, head north on I-405 for 1.5 miles. Make a left at exit 3 to follow U.S. 30 west for 0.5 mile. Use either of the right two lanes to take the Vaughn Street exit, and continue straight on Northwest Vaughn Street for 0.4 mile. Turn left onto Northwest 27th Avenue for 1 block, then turn right onto Northwest Upshur Street for 3 blocks. The road ends at a turnaround and parking area in Lower Macleay Park.

It's also possible to reach the trailhead using Portland's TriMet bus system via lines 15 and 77, which stop near Lower Macleay Park.

GPS COORDINATES: 45.53585, –122.71249 / N45° 32.151' W122° 42.7494'

BEST NEARBY BREWS

Enjoy a pint at **Breakside Brewery** (1570 NW 22nd Ave., Portland, 503/444-7597, http://breakside.com, 11am-10pm Sun.-Thurs., 11am-11pm Fri.-Sat.). Breakside's flagship IPA has won numerous awards, but the brewery produces a well-rounded selection of flavorful crafts. From the trailhead, the 1-mile drive east takes 5 minutes via Northwest Thurman Street; you could also walk there in 20 minutes.

2

Marquam Trail to Council Crest

MARQUAM NATURE PARK

Head to one of the highest points in Portland city limits for sweeping views of downtown and nearby Cascade peaks.

DISTANCE: 3.9 miles round-trip

DURATION: 2 hours

ELEVATION CHANGE: 650 feet

EFFORT: Easy/moderate

TRAIL: Dirt trail, gravel, roadbed, roots, rocks

USERS: Hikers, leashed dogs

SEASON: Year-round

PASSES/FEES: None

MAPS: USGS topographic map for Portland, OR-WA; free trail map available at the trailhead

PARK HOURS: 5am-midnight daily

CONTACT: Portland Parks & Recreation, 503/823-7529, www.portlandoregon.gov/parks

START THE HIKE

Given this hike's accessibility and location so close to the city center, this trail is a popular after-work trek; you'll likely share it with runners and nearby residents, some of whose houses line the trail.

▶ **MILE 0-0.4: Shadyside Trail to Marquam Trail**

From the western edge of the parking lot, start hiking uphill—heading northwest—on the **Shadyside Trail,** following signs for the Marquam Trail and Council Crest. **Marquam Shelter,** to your right as you ascend, offers trail maps and interpretive information on the park through which you're hiking. After just 350 feet on the old roadbed, you'll come to a Y-shaped junction; ignore the trail heading downhill to your right, and continue uphill to the left to remain on the Shadyside Trail. Another junction, this one unsigned, arrives in another 150 feet; head left, continuing on the Shadyside Trail as it narrows and proceeds uphill. As you ascend, you'll see trillium blooms in spring, an ivy-covered forest floor, and a canopy of Douglas fir and bigleaf maple. In 0.3 mile you'll arrive at a T-junction; turn right onto the **Marquam Trail,** continuing uphill and following signs for the Council Crest summit.

▶ **MILE 0.4-1.6: Marquam Trail to Southwest Greenway Avenue**

In another 0.2 mile, head left at the T-junction to continue ascending the Marquam Trail toward the Council Crest summit; keep an eye out for barred owls, which nest in the area, amid the red cedar, western hemlock,

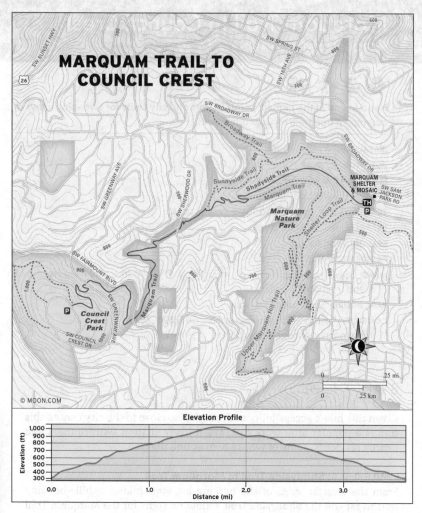

MARQUAM TRAIL TO COUNCIL CREST

Elevation Profile

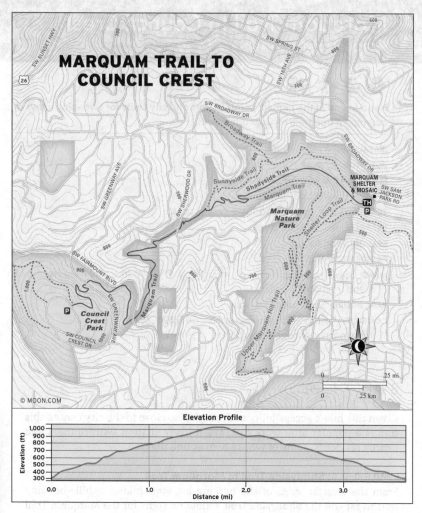

and Douglas fir lining Marquam Gulch, through which you've been hiking. Cross Southwest Sherwood Drive in 0.25 mile and pick up the trail across the road. Soon after, you'll come to an unsigned junction; cross the foot-bridge over the dry creek bed to the left, ignoring the trail to your right. Watch here for sword ferns and Oregon grape, the official state flower. In 0.5 mile, you'll cross Southwest Fairmont Boulevard and, in another 0.2 mile, Southwest Greenway Avenue.

▶ **MILE 1.6-1.95: Southwest Greenway Avenue to Council Crest Summit**
The trail starts leveling out here, as you begin circling the summit. After 0.25 mile, you'll arrive at an unsigned junction. If you head straight, the trail soon ends at an off-leash **dog park,** just below the summit. Head right at the unsigned junction and walk a couple hundred feet to another junc-tion, and then turn left. You'll leave the woods, cross Southwest Council Crest Drive, and continue on a paved path for about 0.1 mile to arrive at a plaza atop the **Council Crest summit**—1,073 feet above sea level. From here,

▲ MOUNT HOOD VIEW FROM THE SUMMIT OF COUNCIL CREST

you can peer into downtown Portland as well as spy the likes of Mount St. Helens, Mount Adams, and Mount Hood.

Return the way you came.

DIRECTIONS

From downtown Portland, head south on Southwest Broadway for 0.5 mile. Shortly after passing over I-405, take a right onto Southwest 6th Avenue, which becomes Southwest Terwilliger Boulevard and then Southwest Sam Jackson Park Road, for 0.5 mile. When you arrive at the U-shaped bend in the road, turn right into the parking area for Marquam Nature Park.

It's also possible to reach the trailhead using Portland's TriMet bus system via lines 8 and 68, which stop near the Marquam Trailhead.

GPS COORDINATES: 45.5028, –122.69174 / N45° 30.168′ W122° 41.5044′

BEST NEARBY BREWS

Head across the Willamette River for a pint at **Hopworks Urban Brewery** (2944 SE Powell Blvd., Portland, 503/232-4677, http://hopworks-beer.com, 11:30am-10pm Sun.-Thurs., 11:30am-11pm Fri.-Sat.). Hopworks is known for using organic, sustainably raised hops and grains in its wide variety of beers. From the trailhead, the 3-mile drive east takes 10 minutes via U.S. 26.

3

Tryon Creek
State Natural Area Loop

TRYON CREEK STATE NATURAL AREA

Find something to love about this trail all year long, from fall foliage displays to spring wildflowers and salmon runs, at the only Oregon state park located within a major city.

BEST: Wildflower Hikes

DISTANCE: 4.5 miles round-trip

DURATION: 2 hours

ELEVATION CHANGE: 350 feet

EFFORT: Easy

TRAIL: Dirt trail, paved path, gravel, roots, rocks

USERS: Hikers, leashed dogs, horseback riders (North Horse Loop and West Horse Loop only)

SEASON: Year-round

PASSES/FEES: None

MAPS: USGS topographic map for Lake Oswego, OR; free Tryon Creek Trail Map at the Nature Center

PARK HOURS: 7am-5pm daily January and November-December, 7am-6pm daily February, 7am-7pm daily March and October, 7am-8pm daily April and September, 7am-9pm daily May-August

CONTACT: Oregon State Parks, 503/636-9886, www.oregonstateparks.org

START THE HIKE

▶ **MILE 0-1.1: Nature Center to Cedar Trail**

Grab a trail map from the **Nature Center** just west of the parking lot, then head south from here on the **Old Main Trail,** passing a stone amphitheater along the way, to begin this clockwise loop. In just less than 0.2 mile, make a right onto the **Big Fir Trail.** You'll enter a second-growth Douglas fir forest before arriving at another junction in about 0.1 mile; turn left to remain on the Big Fir Trail and take heart that, while this trail is junction-heavy, it's exceptionally well signed. In 0.3 mile, continue straight to remain on the trail past an intersection with the Middle Creek Trail before arriving in a couple hundred feet at another junction; turn left here to hop back on the **Old Main Trail** for several hundred feet, when you'll meet up with and turn right onto the **Red Fox Trail.** Follow this trail for 0.4 mile, crossing **Red Fox Bridge** over **Tryon Creek** and ignoring an intersection with the South Creek Trail along the way; trillium, tiger lily, and fireweed are common along this stretch in spring.

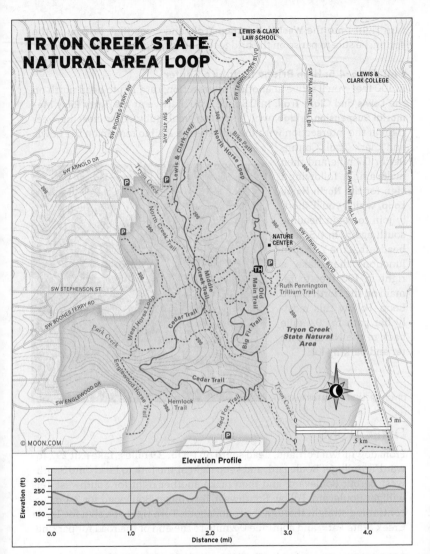

TRYON CREEK STATE NATURAL AREA LOOP

Elevation Profile

▶ **MILE 1.1–2.6: Cedar Trail to High Bridge**

Turn right onto the **Cedar Trail** and hike through the scenic cedar forest. Turn right to remain on the Cedar Trail at the junction with the Hemlock Trail, and cross **Park Creek** over **Bunk Bridge,** to begin looping back up north. Watch for a variety of wildlife in this area, including garter snakes, beavers, red foxes, coyotes, cougars, and several species of owl. In 1 mile, continue straight to remain on the Cedar Trail at a four-way intersection with the West Horse Loop—and then continue straight at another junction with this same trail in another 0.2 mile. Just past this second equestrian trail intersection—it can get confusing here—turn left onto the **Middle Creek Trail** to continue north, following the banks of Tryon Creek. The maple trees along this stretch put on dazzling foliage displays. In 0.3 mile, turn right onto the **West Horse Loop Trail,** and cross **High Bridge;** in the spring, be sure to pause on the bridge to look for salmon in the creek below.

▶ **MILE 2.6-4.5: High Bridge to Nature Center**
In 100 feet, you'll arrive at another intersection; turn left to head north on the **Lewis and Clark Trail.** In 0.3 mile, you'll arrive at the **Terry Riley Memorial Suspension Bridge,** which spans a small gully. After crossing, veer right at the intersection with the 4th Avenue Trail to remain on the Lewis and Clark Trail. Continue for 0.7 mile and then make a right, following a sign for the **North Horse Loop,** which you'll shortly join to begin heading south again. In 0.5 mile, head left at the Y-shaped junction, then take a right in 100 feet to remain on the North Horse Loop. Follow this mostly flat path for 0.4 mile back to the Nature Center and parking lot.

TRYON CREEK STATE NATURAL AREA ▶

DIRECTIONS

From downtown Portland, head south on I-5 for 2.9 miles. Take exit 297, toward Terwilliger Boulevard, and keep right at the fork to head onto Southwest Barbur Boulevard, and then make another right for Southwest Terwilliger Boulevard. Follow Southwest Terwilliger Boulevard for 2.4 miles, continuing straight through the roundabout. Turn right at a sign for Tryon Creek State Park, and continue 0.2 mile to the end of the road for parking.

GPS COORDINATES: 45.44117, -122.67605 / N45° 26.4702′ W122° 40.563′

BEST NEARBY BREWS
Sasquatch Brewing (6440 SW Capitol Hwy., Portland, 503/402-1999, http://sasquatchbrewery.com, 3pm-10pm Mon.-Thurs., noon-10pm Fri.-Sat., noon-9pm Sun.) is a cozy neighborhood pub that pairs a wide-ranging beer and cider selection with a seasonal food menu. From the trailhead, the 4-mile drive north takes 10 minutes via Southwest Terwilliger Boulevard.

On this iconic Oregon trail you'll hike to 10 waterfalls in less than 10 miles.

BEST: Fall Hikes, Waterfall Hikes

DISTANCE: 9.3 miles round-trip

DURATION: 4.5 hours

ELEVATION CHANGE: 890 feet

EFFORT: Moderate/strenuous

TRAIL: Dirt trail, paved path, gravel, rocks, roots, paved staircases

USERS: Hikers, leashed dogs (Rim and Upper North Falls Trails only)

SEASON: Year-round

PASSES/FEES: $5 day-use fee per vehicle

MAPS: USGS topographic map for Drake Crossing; free trail map available at the South Falls Lodge & Café and South Falls Nature Store in the South Falls day-use area

PARK HOURS: 8am-5pm daily November-January, 8am-6pm daily February, 8am-8pm daily March, 7am-9pm daily April-August, 7am-8pm daily September, 8am-7pm daily October

CONTACT: Oregon State Parks, 503/873-8681, www.oregonstateparks.org

START THE HIKE
The renowned waterfalls along this trail are most glorious in spring, and the fall foliage is also something to see.

▶ **MILE 0-1.2: South Falls Lodge to Lower South Falls**
At the South Falls day-use area, head west on the paved path just north of the **South Falls Lodge**—built in the 1930s by the Civilian Conservation Corps and today host to a small snack bar and restrooms—following a sign for the **Canyon Trail.** In 0.1 mile, turn right onto a gravel trail, following another sign for the Canyon Trail. Here you'll see your first waterfall on this clockwise loop trail: **South Falls,** dropping 177 feet, the second-tallest falls in the park. From here continue downhill, entering the canyon where you'll spend much of this hike and ignoring an offshoot trail to your right. In 0.25 mile, you'll pass behind South Falls and drop to the base of **South Fork Silver Creek;** you'll continue straight on the Canyon Trail from here, but take a moment to step onto the footbridge to your right for some of the best views of South Falls. Back on the Canyon Trail, you'll lose about 125 feet over the next 0.75 mile, hiking through a forest of fir and vine maple that puts on a colorful show every autumn, before arriving at **Lower South Falls.** Descend the paved staircase to walk behind the 93-foot falls.

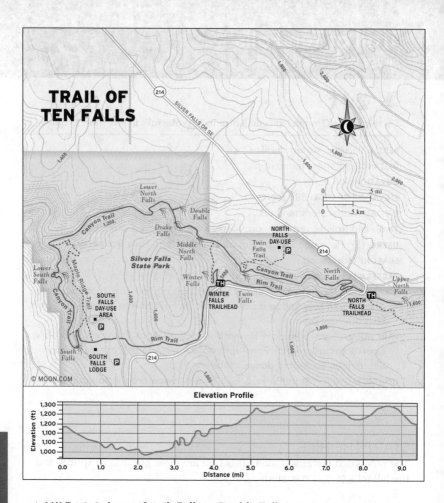

TRAIL OF TEN FALLS

Elevation Profile

▸ **MILE 1.2–3: Lower South Falls to Double Falls**

After a mostly flat 0.5-mile stretch you'll come to a junction; turn left and head downhill, going eastward. In another 1 mile, the 30-foot **Lower North Falls** comes into view; there's no one outstanding viewpoint for these falls, so admire them as you will and then continue another 0.1 mile, when you'll turn left for an approximately 0.2-mile round-trip jaunt to the base of 178-foot **Double Falls,** the tallest waterfall along the trail.

▸ **MILE 3–5: Double Falls to North Falls**

Back at the junction, turn left and continue on the loop, which will steadily ascend. In about 0.2 mile you'll arrive at a wooden platform overlooking the 27-foot **Drake Falls.** In another 0.2 mile you'll enjoy views of 106-foot **Middle North Falls;** you can also opt for a short spur to its base. In 0.1 mile is a junction with the Winter Trail; heading right onto the trail here would lop roughly 4 miles off your round-trip total, but continue straight to remain on the Canyon Trail. In another 0.5 mile, you'll come to another fork; head right for a view of the 31-foot **Twin Falls,** and follow the path as it rejoins the Canyon Trail. In 1 mile, you'll arrive at one of the most beautiful vantages along the whole loop, a cave-like path that takes you behind the majestic **North Falls,** which measures 136 feet tall. Have a seat on one of the benches behind the falls and enjoy.

▶ MILE 5–6.3: North Falls to Rim Trail

Continuing on, follow the trail as it curves behind the falls, ascending a staircase out of the canyon; proceed cautiously, as these steps can be slippery after rainfall and icy in winter. In 0.5 mile, you'll arrive at a T-shaped junction; turn left for an 0.8-mile round-trip spur trail to Upper North Falls, staying left again at another junction shortly on and following the **North Fork Silver Creek.** The spur ends at the base of the 65-foot **Upper North Falls.** Back at the T-shaped junction, head left onto the **Rim Trail,** which loops you back west.

▶ MILE 6.3–9.3: Rim Trail to South Falls Lodge

In 1.1 miles, you'll come upon the Winter Falls parking area; take a hard right to make the 0.5 mile out-and-back round-trip hike to the base of 134-foot **Winter Falls.** True to its name, Winter Falls is most dramatic in winter (and spring); at the height of summer, it resembles a leaky faucet. Back at the Winter Falls parking area, continue west on the Rim Trail. Along the way you'll intersect with a paved bike path; this can be confusing at various points, but don't worry: All these paths end at the South Falls day-use area where you began. In 1.2 miles, you'll arrive at a parking area with two painted lanes for pedestrians and cyclists; take the rightmost path for pedestrians to proceed onto a paved brick trail that ends, in another 0.2 mile, back at the South Falls Lodge.

DIRECTIONS

From Salem, head east on Highway 22 for 7.5 miles. Take exit 9, following a sign for Shaw and Aumsville. After looping to the south, turn right at the fork onto Shaw Highway SE, which becomes Brownell Drive Southeast and Highway 214, for 14.1 miles. After crossing a bridge and passing milepost 25, turn left at a sign for South Falls. Follow the road as it curves around toward the South Falls day-use area.

GPS COORDINATES: 44.87966, –122.65829 / N44° 52.7796′ W122° 39.4974′

BEST NEARBY BREWS

It only makes sense to pair your hike with a stop at **Silver Falls Brewery** (207 Jersey St., Silverton, 503/873-3022, http://silverfallsbrewery.com, 11:30am-9pm Mon. and Wed.-Thurs., 11:30am-10pm Fri.-Sat., 11:30am-8pm Sun.). It hosts a lineup of several classic styles—including an IPA, a porter, and a hefeweizen—alongside rotating seasonal selections. From the trailhead, the 16-mile drive north takes 25 minutes via Highway 214.

5

Table Rock
TABLE ROCK WILDERNESS

Hike through a dense conifer forest to the summit of Table Rock, where you'll enjoy views of famous Cascade peaks.

DISTANCE: 8.2 miles round-trip
DURATION: 4 hours
ELEVATION CHANGE: 1,620 feet
EFFORT: Moderate
TRAIL: Dirt trail, rocks, rock scramble, roadbed, roots
USERS: Hikers, leashed dogs, horseback riders (equestrian use discouraged through the boulder field)
SEASON: June–November
PASSES/FEES: None
MAPS: USGS topographic map for Rooster Rock, OR
CONTACT: Bureau of Land Management, 503/375-5646, www.blm.gov

START THE HIKE

▶ MILE 0-1.4: Table Rock Trailhead to Rockpile
From the parking area, find the **Table Rock Trailhead** just north of the restroom. On this early stretch, you'll follow an old roadbed through a forest of alder and vine maple. After 0.3 mile, the trail turns right into a new-growth forest, and you'll arrive at an unsigned junction with a steep, rocky social trail; continue straight ahead on the Table Rock Trail. After another 1.1 mile, the trail again turns right, becoming faint at times as you enter a forest of hemlock and fir; follow the logs and a strategically placed rockpile.

▶ MILE 1.4-3: Rockpile to Talus Slope
You'll hike in basically a large U-shape over the next 0.1 mile or so, when the trail becomes more legible again. In another 1.2 miles, you'll leave the forest to scramble through a **talus slope**—which can have patches of snow on it into July—beneath an impressive display of columnar basalt on Table Rock's northern face. The informal trail through this boulder field isn't immediately obvious, so scan ahead for lighter gray rocks—a by-product of regular use—and follow this more matted, navigable path for 0.3 mile before reentering the forest.

▶ MILE 3-4.1: Talus Slope to Table Rock Summit
In about 0.5 mile, you'll pass a **campsite** as the trail switchbacks and steadily ascends before arriving, in another 0.6 mile, at the **Table Rock summit**. Find an open area amid the pinemat manzanita, and savor the views: From here you can see Mount Hood, Mount Jefferson, and the Three Sisters,

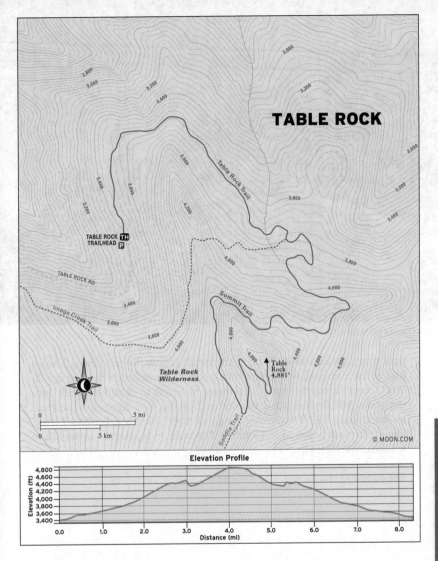

Elevation Profile

and, on a clear day, all the way north to Washington's Mount Rainier and south to California's Mount Shasta.

Return the way you came.

DIRECTIONS

From Oregon City, head south on Highway 213 for 9 miles, and turn left onto Union Mills Road. After 4.3 miles, turn right at a gas station to follow signs for Molalla and Woodburn on Highway 211 south. Turn left at a fork onto South Wright Road after 0.8 mile, and turn right onto South Feyrer Park Road in another 1.8 miles. Continue straight at the stop sign in 0.4 mile, when the road becomes South Dickie Prairie Road. Continue for 5.4 miles, then turn right to cross a bridge over the Molalla River, and immediately turn left onto South Molalla Forest Road. Soon after, you'll see

▲ THE FINAL APPROACH TO TABLE ROCK'S SUMMIT

your first sign for the Table Rock Trailhead. Follow the road for 11.2 miles and, at the Y-shaped fork just past milepost 11, continue left to head uphill. You'll come to another fork in 1.6 miles; head left to continue uphill onto the gravel Middle Fork Road. In another 2.7 miles, turn right onto the gravel Forest Road 7-3E-7, following a sign for the Table Rock Trailhead. Turn left at the next junction in 1.9 miles. The road ends after 2.4 miles at the trailhead parking area.

GPS COORDINATES: 44.976, –122.321 / N44° 58.56' W122° 19.26'

BEST NEARBY BREWS

Coin Toss Brewing (14214 Fir St., Suite H, Oregon City, 503/305-6220, www.cointossbrewing.com, 3pm-8pm Tues.-Fri., noon-8pm Sat., noon-6pm Sun.) offers brews in classic styles as well as a Heritage Series in which each beer is brewed from a historical recipe. From the trailhead, the 40-mile drive north takes 1.25 hours via Highways 211 and 213.

PORTLAND AND THE WILLAMETTE VALLEY

Table Rock

6

Bagby Hot Springs

MOUNT HOOD NATIONAL FOREST

Walk through an old-growth forest to one of the state's most popular hot springs.

BEST: Fall Hikes

DISTANCE: 3.3 miles round-trip

DURATION: 1.5 hours

ELEVATION CHANGE: 220 feet

EFFORT: Easy

TRAIL: Dirt trail

USERS: Hikers, leashed dogs, horseback riders

SEASON: June–October

PASSES/FEES: $5 fee to soak per person

MAPS: USGS topographic map for Bagby Hot Springs

CONTACT: Mount Hood National Forest, 503/630-6861, www.fs.usda.gov

START THE HIKE

Soaking at Bagby costs $5 per person. Purchase a wristband before setting out at the Ripplebrook Camp Store, which you'll pass on your way from Estacada, or at the trailhead; an attendant collects fees at the trailhead early spring-Labor Day, while a self-pay station is available Labor Day-early spring. While roads to the trail aren't maintained in winter, people with 4WD vehicles can still hike to Bagby if their vehicles can make it.

▶ **MILE 0-1.4: Bagby Hot Springs Trailhead to Wooden Bridge**

Head south from the parking area to start hiking from the **Bagby Hot Springs Trailhead** on a paved path. Almost immediately, you'll cross a footbridge over **Nohorn Creek** and continue along a dirt and gravel trail. This lush, gently graded out-and-back hike meanders through a towering old-growth forest of red cedar and Douglas fir along the **Hot Springs Fork** of the Collowash River. For a closer look at the river, you can follow a short, 50-foot spur trail off to your left after 0.6 mile. In another 0.8 mile, you'll cross a wooden bridge, near which you'll find another trail down to the riverbank. Keep an eye out for three-petaled trillium blooms in spring and vine maple—which turns vibrant shades of orange, yellow, and red—in autumn.

▶ **MILE 1.4-1.65: Wooden Bridge to Bagby Hot Springs**

While the trail continues on, you'll reach your destination in 0.25 mile: **Bagby Hot Springs.** Discovered in 1880 by local hunter Bob Bagby, the hot springs are perhaps the most popular in the state. A sign announces your arrival at the hot springs just past an old ranger cabin. The bathhouse to your right hosts one large tub, with room for up to six adults. A second bathhouse to your left hosts three individual tubs and one large tub in an open, communal setting. To soak, open the valve to let the hot water into your tub; it comes out of the springs a little too heated for comfort—120-138°F—so add buckets of cold water, available from a nearby tub, to reach your desired temperature. The open-air, wooden structures of Bagby allow you to gaze into the surrounding forest as you soak.

Abstain from using soaps, which can pollute nearby Peggy Creek. If others are waiting (a frequent occurrence, especially on summer weekends), limit your soak to 45 minutes.

When you're ready, dry off, get dressed, and return the way you came.

DIRECTIONS

From Estacada, head south on Highway 211, which becomes Highway 224, for 25.3 miles. Just past a sign for the Ripplebrook Campground—off to the left, at whose store you can purchase a Bagby soaking wristband (503/834-2322, 10am-5pm Sun.-Thurs, 10am-8pm Fri.-Sat.)—the road forks; head right onto Forest Road 46. After 3.7 miles, turn right at a one-lane ramp, following spray-painted directions on the roadway for Bagby Hot Springs, onto Forest Road 63. Continue for 3.5 miles, then turn right onto Bagby Road/Forest Road 70. Follow the road for 7 miles and then turn left, at a sign for the Bagby Recreation Site Trailhead, into the parking lot. If you're heading here out of season, the trail is open though the roads are not maintained; call the Clackamas River Ranger District (503/630-6861) for the latest conditions before setting out.

GPS COORDINATES: 44.95404, -122.17007 / N44° 57.2424' W122° 10.2042'

BAGBY HOT SPRINGS ▸

BEST NEARBY BREWS

Fearless Brewing Company (326 Broadway St., Estacada, 503/630-2337, www.fearless.beer, 4pm-9pm Wed.-Thurs., noon-10pm Fri.-Sat., noon-9pm Sun.) offers quality craft beer at the outskirts of the Mount Hood National Forest. Its flagship is the Fearless Scottish Ale, but the brewery offers a wide variety of easy-drinking styles. From the trailhead, the 39-mile drive north takes an hour via Highways 224 and 211.

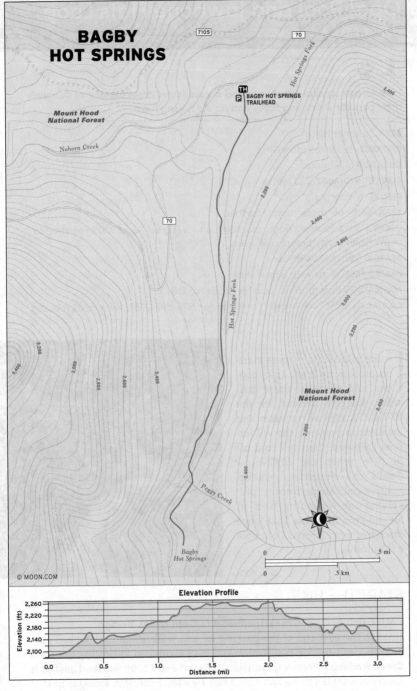

7

Opal Pool and Jawbone Flats Loop
OPAL CREEK WILDERNESS

Hike along a crystal-clear river and across scenic creeks to one of Oregon's most popular swimming holes and an old mining town.

BEST: Summer Hikes

DISTANCE: 8.5 miles round-trip

DURATION: 4.5 hours

ELEVATION CHANGE: 710 feet

EFFORT: Moderate

TRAIL: Dirt trail, roots, rocks, roadbed

USERS: Hikers, leashed dogs, mountain bikers (Forest Road 2209 roadbed to Jawbone Flats), horseback riders

SEASON: March–November

PASSES/FEES: Northwest Forest Pass

MAPS: USGS topographic map for Battle Ax, OR

CONTACT: Opal Creek Ancient Forest Center, 503/892-2782, www.opalcreek.org

OPAL POOL ▸

In the mid-1800s, miners started processing lead, zinc, copper, and silver in these hillsides. Loggers arrived in the 1970s. Decades of activism and lawsuits to preserve the wilderness followed; the work paid off in 1996, when the 20,827-acre Opal Creek Wilderness was formally established, forever preserving the remaining tract of an old-growth forest that once stretched from British Columbia to California.

START THE HIKE

▸ **MILE 0-0.5: Opal Creek Trailhead to Gold Creek Bridge**

Head to the east end of the parking lot and walk around the locked gate next to a self-service pay station and map signboard indicating the **Opal Creek Trailhead.** Follow the unsigned **Forest Road 2209 roadbed** east as it gently descends, flanked on either side by a thick forest of Douglas fir that predates Columbus's arrival in North America. Along the trail you'll hear the rushing **Little North Santiam River.** You'll lose about 50 feet of elevation

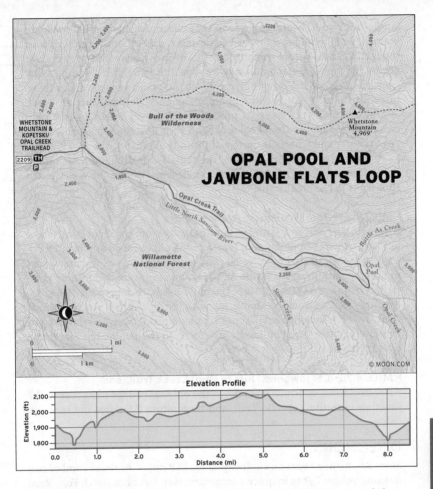

OPAL POOL AND
JAWBONE FLATS LOOP

Bull of the Woods
Wilderness

Whetstone
Mountain
4,969'

WHETSTONE
MOUNTAIN &
KOPETSKI/
OPAL CREEK
TRAILHEAD

2209

Opal Creek Trail

Little North Santiam River

Battle Ax Creek

Opal
Pool

Willamette
National Forest

Stony Creek

Opal Creek

0   1 mi
0   1 km

© MOON.COM

Elevation Profile

over the first 0.5 mile before crossing a bridge over **Gold Creek,** and then regain it as you head deeper into the old-growth forest.

▶ **MILE 0.5–2.4: Gold Creek Bridge to Merten Mill**
Roughly 1.7 miles past the bridge, you'll arrive at an unsigned Y-shaped junction; turn right off the roadbed to follow an unnamed **dirt trail.** You'll soon pass old tracks, axles, pipes, and other equipment; gold was found in the area in 1859, and these items were left behind when mining operations ceased in the 1950s. Just past the equipment—and after about 300 feet on the dirt trail—look for an unsigned spur to the right toward the river. Walk the 250 or so feet to a viewpoint of 30-foot **Sawmill Falls.** Back on the main trail, you'll shortly arrive at the site of **Merten Mill,** a former sawmill marked by a now-collapsed shed. As you continue east, the dirt trail reconnects with the old roadbed.

▶ **MILE 2.4–4.5: Merten Mill to Opal Pool**
In 0.3 mile, you'll reach a junction; turn right onto the **Kopetski Trail,** crossing a bridge over the river, and then turn left to proceed on the

single-track trail, beginning a loop that continues east. You'll navigate stumps, small boulders, downed cedar trees, and other overgrowth over the next 0.8 mile before reaching a series of **spur trails** offering easy river access for those interested in a swim. You'll then begin ascending away from the river, as Douglas fir gives way to thousand-year-old cedar trees. In about 0.9 mile, you'll come to an unsigned Y-shaped junction. Head left onto a rocky trail some 0.1 mile to a bridge over **Opal Creek.** As you cross the bridge, the **Opal Pool** will be to your left; the remarkable clarity of its emerald waters is quite a sight in the midst of the rocky gorge. In summer, the Opal Pool is one of the region's most popular swimming holes. If you'd like to take a dip, you can descend one of the short, rocky **spur trails** to the creek bank.

▶ **MILE 4.5-4.75: Opal Pool to Jawbone Flats**
After crossing the bridge and ascending away from the Opal Pool, take a left at the unsigned junction to return to the old **roadbed** and begin looping back west. In 0.25 mile, you'll pass more remnants of the area's past mining operations, cross **Battle Ax Creek,** and enter the old mining community of **Jawbone Flats.** Most of the buildings here date to the 1930s. Today, the onetime mining camp is home to the Opal Creek Ancient Forest Center, which includes cabin rentals, private residences, and outdoor education facilities. Most buildings are closed to the public, but hikers can wander the area.

▶ **MILE 4.75-8.5: Jawbone Flats to Opal Creek Trailhead**
After exploring, continue west down the old roadbed for 1.25 miles to the junction with the Kopetski Trail, and then return 2.5 miles the way you came.

DIRECTIONS

From Salem, head east on Highway 22 for 21.8 miles. At the second of two flashing yellow lights in quick succession, turn left onto North Fork Road and follow it for 15.4 miles, when the pavement ends. Continue for 5.6 miles as the road transitions to gravel and becomes Forest Road 2209. The road ends at the trailhead parking lot.

GPS COORDINATES: 44.85986, -122.26448 / N44° 51.5916′ W122° 15.8688′

BEST NEARBY BITES

Refuel with classic American comfort fare from **Poppa Al's Famous Hamburgers** (198 NE Santiam Blvd., Mill City, 503/897-2223, noon-9pm daily). The old-school restaurant serves sandwiches, soups, chili, milk shakes, and burgers, with buns baked fresh daily. From the trailhead, the 17-mile drive southeast takes just over an hour via North Fork Road and Highway 22.

Ascend rocky slopes and earn views of Elk Lake, Cascade peaks, and the scenic Bull of the Woods Wilderness in every direction.

DISTANCE: 6.8 miles round-trip
DURATION: 3 hours
ELEVATION CHANGE: 1,580 feet
EFFORT: Moderate
TRAIL: Dirt trail, stream crossings, rocks, roots, roadbed
USERS: Hikers, leashed dogs, horseback riders
SEASON: June-October
PASSES/FEES: None
MAPS: USGS topographic map for Mother Lode Mountain
CONTACT: Willamette National Forest, 503/854-3366, www.fs.usda.gov

START THE HIKE

▶ MILE 0-1.2: Forest Road 4697 to Elk Lake Clearing
From the junction with Elk Lake Campground on **Forest Road 4697,** walk 0.4 mile west up the gently graded road, turning right at a post indicating the start of **Trail #544.** On the first stretch of this counterclockwise loop trail, you'll ascend steadily northward through a forest of Douglas fir and vine maple, switchbacking twice before arriving after 0.8 mile at a small **clearing** with views of Elk Lake below.

▶ MILE 1.2-2.4: Elk Lake Clearing to Battle Ax Mountain Trail
In 0.5 mile, proceed cautiously through some scree. You'll encounter a bit more in another 0.3 mile as you cross a large **rockslide.** In between the rocky stretches, keep an eye out for bear grass and monkey flower, both of which bloom in spring and remain through early summer. After 0.4 mile, you'll arrive at an X-shaped junction, where you'll make a hard left onto the unsigned **Battle Ax Mountain Trail** to head uphill and begin looping back south.

▶ MILE 2.4-3.7: Battle Ax Mountain Trail to Battle Ax Mountain Summit
The hike intensifies here—you still have 770 feet of elevation gain to go before the summit—as you ascend a western ridge. The forest of hemlock and pinemat manzanita gives way to narrow ledges and scree as you near the summit, which may be challenging for those with a fear of heights. Roughly 1.1 miles past the junction, you'll arrive at a clearing, and then, in 0.2 mile, the **Battle Ax Mountain summit,** marked by concrete pilings—the lone remnants of an old fire lookout. Elk Lake sits nearly 2,000 feet

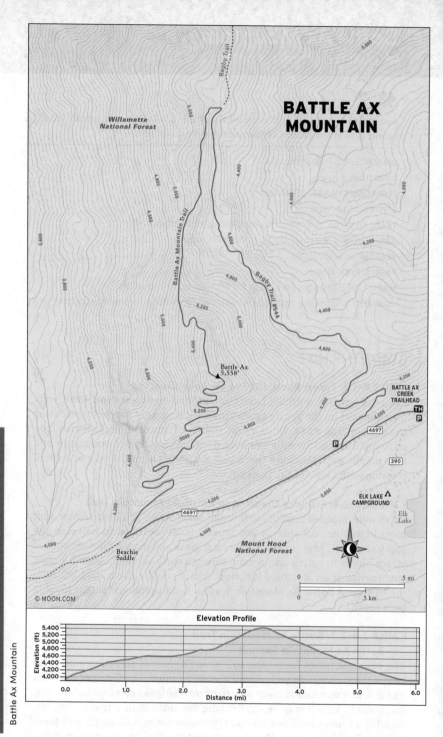

below, and this vantage point also affords dramatic views of the Bull of the Woods Wilderness, marked by steep ridges and old-growth forest. On a clear day, Mount Jefferson, Three Fingered Jack, the Three Sisters, and several other Cascade peaks are visible.

▶ **MILE 3.7–6.8: Battle Ax Mountain Summit to Forest Road 4697**
Pick up the Battle Ax Mountain Trail just past the summit and start descending the lightly traveled path—which can appear faint at times amid the overgrowth—via switchbacks before reentering the forest. After descending gradually for 1.8 miles, you'll arrive at an unsigned junction with **Forest Road 4697**; turn left onto the old roadbed, and head steadily downhill. After 0.9 mile, you'll pass the trailhead on your left. Continue another 0.4 mile along the road to return to your vehicle.

DIRECTIONS

The final few miles to this trailhead are infamously rutted and bumpy—the potholes all seem to have potholes—so a high-clearance vehicle is strongly recommended. Whatever you do, take it slow.

From the town of Detroit, head north on Breitenbush Road, following signs for Breitenbush, Elk Lake, and Olallie Lake. Continue for 4.4 miles, then turn left onto paved Forest Road 4696. Follow the road for 0.7 mile, then turn left onto gravel Forest Road 4697. After a miserable 4.7 miles on this rutted, potholed road, turn left at a Y-junction marked only by a nondescript post. Drive another 2 mostly flat miles to a junction with Elk Lake Campground. Your best bet is to park along the road near this junction, or head downhill and park at Elk Lake Campground in 0.4 mile.

GPS COORDINATES: 44.82521, –122.125 / N44° 49.5126′ W122° 7.5′

ELK LAKE ▶

BEST NEARBY BITES

Pizza? Barbecue? You can enjoy both at **Connor's BBQ** (195 Detroit Ave., Detroit, 503/913-1040, noon-9pm daily). Highlights include a giant plate of pulled pork nachos and meat-forward pies. From the trailhead, the 13-mile drive south takes 40 minutes via Forest Road 4697 and Breitenbush Road.

Hike through springtime wildflower displays to the highest point in the Oregon Coast Range for spectacular panoramic views.

DISTANCE: 6.9 miles round-trip

DURATION: 3.5 hours

ELEVATION CHANGE: 1,640 feet

EFFORT: Moderate

TRAIL: Dirt trail, roots, rocks, paved road, old roadbed

USERS: Hikers, leashed dogs, mountain bikers (East Ridge, North Ridge, and Tie Trails May 15–Oct. 15), horseback riders

SEASON: April–November

PASSES/FEES: Northwest Forest Pass

MAPS: USGS topographic map for Alsea, OR; Siuslaw National Forest website; free trail maps available at trailhead

CONTACT: Siuslaw National Forest, 541/750-7000, www.fs.usda.gov

START THE HIKE

▶ **MILE 0-2.8: East Ridge Trailhead to Summit Loop Trail**

Head to the northwest corner of the parking area—directly across the road from the restrooms—and start at the **East Ridge Trailhead.** Cross unsigned Forest Road 2005 after 0.1 mile and ascend gradually northward through lush old-growth Douglas fir forest, ferns, and clovers. You'll arrive, after 1.1 miles, at a Y-shaped junction just past a wooden bench; turn left to remain on the East Ridge Trail, continuing to ascend steadily on the pleasant grade. In 1.25 miles, you'll arrive at another junction; take a hard left to head south on the **Summit Trail** and ascend a series of short switchbacks that lead to an east-facing meadow in 0.15 mile—and your first views. To your left are the Oregon Coast Range foothills and the Willamette Valley. Cross unsigned **Marys Peak Road** in 0.2 mile, following a sign for the **Summit Loop Trail** back into the forest.

▶ **MILE 2.8-3: Summit Loop Trail to Marys Peak Summit**

In 200 feet, head left at the Y-shaped junction, following a sign for the Marys Peak summit. You'll soon leave the forest and enter a meadow teeming with grasshoppers. In another 0.2 mile, the dirt trail ends at the gravel Marys Peak Road, a fenced-in collection of radio equipment, and a picnic table on the **Marys Peak summit.** At 4,097 feet, this is the highest point in the Oregon Coast Range. The 360-degree views encompass the Pacific Ocean and Cascade peaks, from Washington's Mount Rainier in the north to Diamond Peak in southern Oregon, and Mount Hood, Mount Jefferson, the Three Sisters, Mount Bachelor, and more in between.

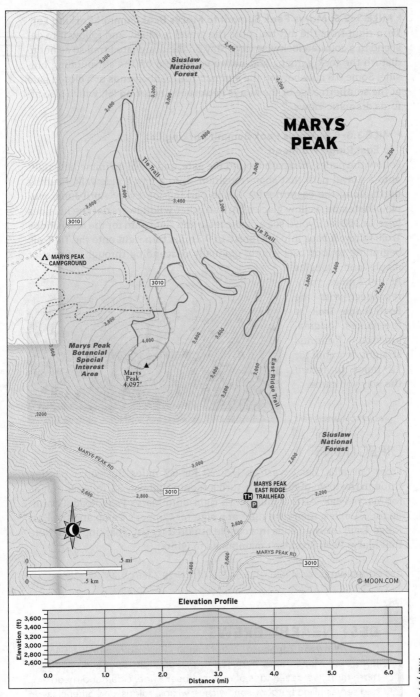

Elevation Profile

▶ **MILE 3-3.6: Marys Peak Summit to Marys Peak Summit Parking Lot**
Turn right from the dirt trail onto the gravel roadbed, and follow it to descend in a counterclockwise loop. Stay on the designated trail so as not to disturb the rock gardens and native vegetation on the surrounding hillside. Some 0.6 mile beyond the summit, the roadbed ends at a closed gate at the southern edge of the **Marys Peak summit parking lot,** which also affords dramatic views.

▶ **MILE 3.6-6.9: Marys Peak Summit Parking Lot
to East Ridge Trailhead**
Follow the pedestrian path around the gate, and make an immediate right onto a gravel path that soon transitions into a paved sidewalk, heading north along the eastern edge of the parking lot. Every April-June, purple penstemon, yellow glacier lily, and other wildflowers dot the hillsides here. In 300 feet, you'll see a picnic table and signboard for the **North Ridge Trail;** follow it back into the forest. In 0.7 mile, turn right onto the **Tie Trail,** beginning to loop back south, gradually descending through a forest of maple and Douglas fir. In 1.3 miles, you'll reconnect with the **East Ridge Trail** at the hike's original junction. Continue straight downhill for 1.2 miles to return the way you came.

VIEW FROM MARYS PEAK ▶

DIRECTIONS

From Corvallis, head west on U.S. 20 for 6.2 miles. Just after passing through the town of Philomath, turn left onto Highway 34, following signs for Marys Peak. After 9 miles, turn right onto Marys Peak Road. Continue for 5.4 miles, then turn right at a sign for Conner's Camp and the East Ridge Trail; the road ends in a couple hundred feet at a parking area. Note that Marys Peak Road isn't maintained in winter.

GPS COORDINATES: 44.49561, -123.54298 / N44° 29.7366' W123° 32.5788'

BEST NEARBY BREWS

Nearby **Vinwood Taphouse** (1736 Main St., Philomath, 541/307-0457, 11am-9pm Mon.-Thurs., 11am-10pm Fri.-Sat., 11am-8pm Sun.) boasts more than two dozen taps of regional beer, wine, cider, and mead—and serves filling burgers, sandwiches, wraps, salads, and other classic American fare. From the trailhead, the 15.5-mile drive east takes 30 minutes via Marys Peak Road and Highway 34.

Walk through a bucolic forest alongside a river offering opportunities for summertime swimming and sunbathing.

DISTANCE: 7 miles round-trip
DURATION: 3.5 hours
ELEVATION CHANGE: 340 feet
EFFORT: Easy/moderate
TRAIL: Dirt trail, rocks, exposed roots, roadbed
USERS: Hikers, leashed dogs, mountain bikers, horseback riders
SEASON: Year-round
PASSES/FEES: None
MAPS: USGS topographic map for Westfir East
CONTACT: Willamette National Forest, 541/782-2283, www.fs.usda.gov

O ne of the many joys of this trail is the opportunities it presents for year-round recreation. Its low elevation makes it suitable for a quiet winter hike, rhododendron blooms add a splash of pink in the spring, summertime brings the chance to cool off in the river, and the vine maple dazzles with reds, oranges, and yellows in fall.

START THE HIKE
As you hike, keep an eye out for poison oak, which tends to crowd the trail, as well as cyclists; this region is a renowned mountain biking destination.

▶ **MILE 0-0.7: Trailhead to Concrete Piling**
Just past the Office Covered Bridge, park your car, walk to the northeast edge of the parking lot, and begin at the sign marked, simply, "**Trail.**" Follow the unmarked roadbed under a railroad bridge for just over 0.1 mile before turning right onto the **North Fork Trail.** This dirt trail is a simple out-and-back along the western side of the **North Fork of the Middle Fork of the Willamette River.** The trail soon narrows, crowded by dandelions and ferns, and the river provides an ambient soundtrack as you walk through a forest of hemlock, alder, Douglas fir, and salal, as well as rhododendron in spring. Continue straight at an unsigned junction in 0.5 mile, ignoring a trail that turns sharply left. In another 0.1 mile, you'll notice a **concrete piling** to your right. It's all that's left of an old millpond that was part of a logging operation based in the nearby town of Westfir from the 1920s to the 1980s.

▶ **MILE 0.7-1.4: Concrete Piling to Spur Trail**
In 0.7 mile, you'll see a slight drop-off to your right; this quick **spur trail** ends at the river's shore and offers the chance to cool off in warm weather

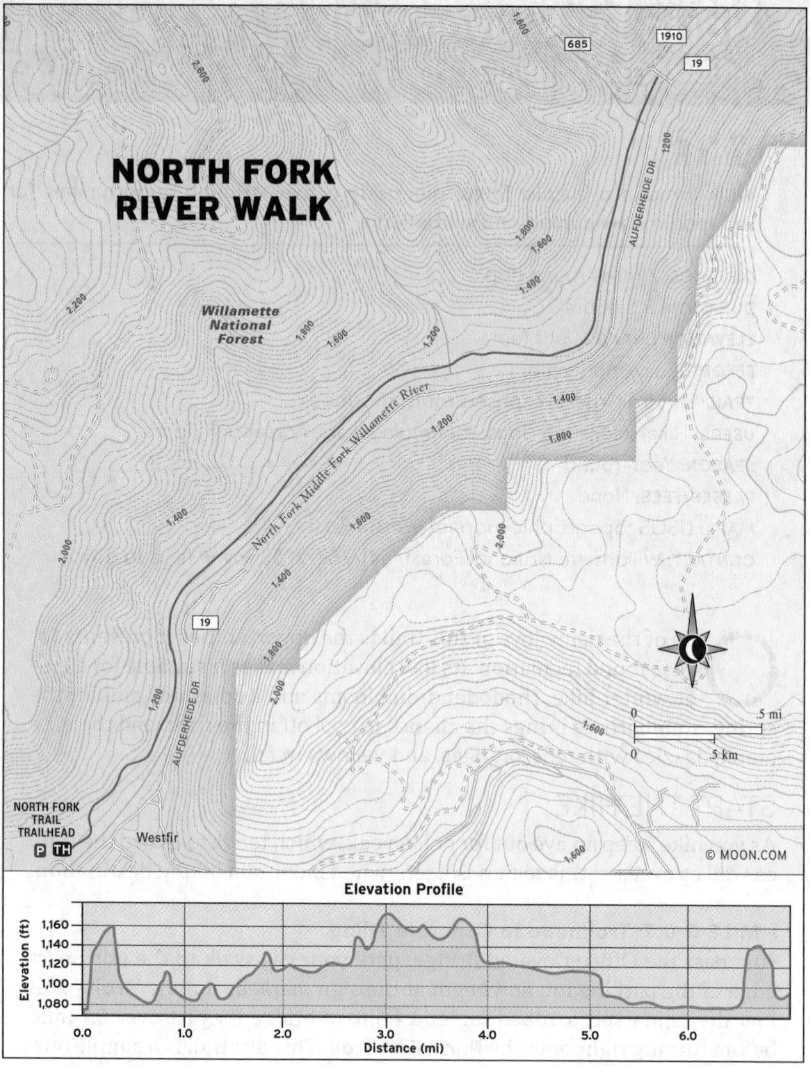

NORTH FORK RIVER WALK

685 · 1910 · 19

Willamette National Forest

AUFDERHEIDE DR

North Fork Middle Fork Willamette River

19

AUFDERHEIDE DR

NORTH FORK TRAIL TRAILHEAD

Westfir

0 — .5 mi
0 — .5 km

© MOON.COM

Elevation Profile

Elevation (ft): 1,080 / 1,100 / 1,120 / 1,140 / 1,160

Distance (mi): 0.0 · 1.0 · 2.0 · 3.0 · 4.0 · 5.0 · 6.0

or, in chilly weather, cast your line for rainbow and cutthroat trout. At any time of year, you can appreciate the water's stunning clarity.

▶ **MILE 1.4-3.5: Spur Trail to Forest Roads 685 and 1910**

Another 1 mile farther on, keep an eye out for another short **spur trail** to your right that ends at a large, flat rock, perfect for sunbathing riverside. After another 1 mile, you'll arrive at an intersection with **Forest Roads 685 and 1910.** The trail continues on across the street, but this is a fine turn-around spot.

Relax in the shade and enjoy a snack before returning the way you came.

If you didn't do so before embarking on the trail, spend a few minutes exploring the **Office Covered Bridge** before taking off. It's the longest

▲ OFFICE COVERED BRIDGE

covered bridge in Oregon, at 180 feet. The original span was built in 1924—and subsequently replaced in the 1940s—and there's a protected pedestrian pathway through it.

DIRECTIONS

From Eugene, head east on Highway 58 for 38 miles. Turn left onto Westfir Road, following signs for Westfir and the Office Covered Bridge, for 0.5 mile. Turn left at the T-shaped junction to remain on the road for 1.8 miles, following it along the river as it becomes North Fork Road. Turn left to cross the Office Covered Bridge and enter the trailhead parking area.

GPS COORDINATES: 43.75909, -122.49601 / N43° 45.5454' W122° 29.7606'

BEST NEARBY BREWS

Unwind with a pint at **The 3 Legged Crane Pub and Brewhouse** (48329 E. 1st St., Oakridge, 541/782-2024, noon-8pm Sun.-Tues. and Thurs., noon-10pm Fri.-Sat. Nov.-Apr.; noon-9pm Sun.-Wed., noon-10pm Thurs., noon-11pm Fri.-Sat. May-Oct.). Most of its beers are casked rather than kegged, and served at specific cellar temperatures for an authentic British pub experience. From the trailhead, the 4-mile drive west takes 7 minutes via Westoak Road.

PORTLAND AND THE WILLAMETTE VALLEY

North Fork River Walk

NEARBY CAMPGROUNDS

NAME	DESCRIPTION	FACILITIES	SEASON	FEE
Silver Falls State Park	campground in Oregon's largest state park	91 tent and electrical sites, 14 cabins, restrooms	year-round	$19-53
Silver Falls Hwy. SE, Sublimity, 503/873-8681, www.oregonstateparks.org				
Bagby Campground	basic campground near the Collawash River	15 tent sites, restrooms	year-round	$18
Bagby Rd./Forest Rd. 70, Estacada, 503/668-1700, www.fs.usda.gov				
Shady Cove Campground	quiet campground along the Little North Santiam River	12 nonelectric sites, restrooms	year-round	$8
Forest Rd. 2207, Gates, 503/854-3366, www.fs.usda.gov				
Detroit Lake State Recreation Area	popular campground on Detroit Lake	267 full-hookup, electrical, and tent sites, restrooms	year-round	$19-31
Hwy. 22, Detroit, 503/854-3346, www.oregonstateparks.org				
Breitenbush Campground	quiet campground along the Breitenbush River	30 nonelectric sites, restrooms	May-September	$18
Forest Rd. 46, Detroit, 503/854-3366, www.fs.usda.gov				

COLUMBIA RIVER GORGE

Roughly 15,000 years ago, the first of several floods—part of a larger event later dubbed the Missoula Floods—swept through the Columbia River and carved out one of the region's most iconic natural features: the Columbia River Gorge. Some 80 miles long and up to 4,000 feet deep, the river canyon cuts through the Cascades and forms the boundary between Washington and Oregon. Trails on both sides of the Gorge draw nature lovers with their dramatic beauty. The National Scenic Area comprises old-growth forests, spectacular waterfalls, and iconic bluffs and ridges, making it one of the Pacific Northwest's most popular hiking destinations, even after the 2017 Eagle Creek Fire burned nearly 50,000 acres on the Oregon side.

▲ FOOTBRIDGE ON LARCH MOUNTAIN

▲ MOUNT HOOD FROM MCCALL POINT

1 **Latourell Falls Loop**
DISTANCE: 3.1 miles round-trip
DURATION: 1.5 hours
EFFORT: Easy/moderate

2 **Angel's Rest**
DISTANCE: 4.9 miles round-trip
DURATION: 2.5 hours
EFFORT: Moderate

3 **Wahkeena Falls-Multnomah Falls Loop**
DISTANCE: 5.9 miles round-trip
DURATION: 3 hours
EFFORT: Moderate

4 **Larch Mountain Crater Loop**
DISTANCE: 7.1 miles round-trip
DURATION: 3.5 hours
EFFORT: Easy/moderate

5 **Beacon Rock**
DISTANCE: 2 miles round-trip
DURATION: 1 hour
EFFORT: Easy/moderate

6 **Dry Creek Falls**
DISTANCE: 5 miles round-trip
DURATION: 2.5 hours
EFFORT: Moderate

7 **Dog Mountain**
DISTANCE: 6.9 miles round-trip
DURATION: 4 hours
EFFORT: Moderate/strenuous

8 **Coyote Wall (Labyrinth Loop)**
DISTANCE: 6.3 miles round-trip
DURATION: 3.5 hours
EFFORT: Easy/moderate

9 **Mosier Plateau**
DISTANCE: 3.7 miles round-trip
DURATION: 1.5 hours
EFFORT: Easy/moderate

10 **Tom McCall Point Trail**
DISTANCE: 3.8 miles round-trip
DURATION: 2 hours
EFFORT: Easy/moderate

▾ VIEW FROM DOG MOUNTAIN

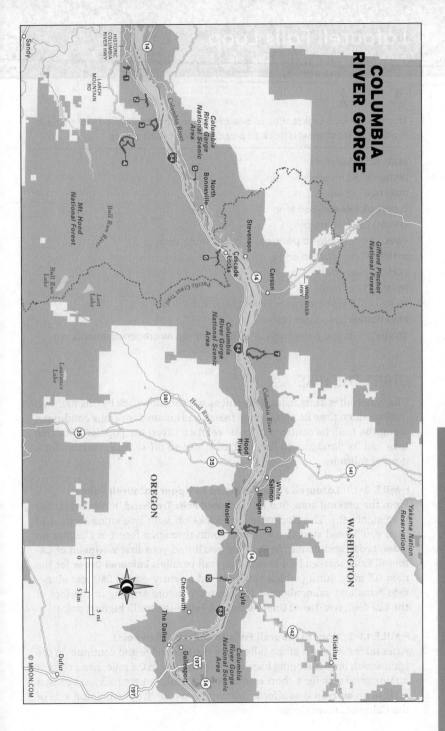

COLUMBIA
RIVER GORGE

COLUMBIA RIVER GORGE

This breezy loop crescendos at one of the most photographed waterfalls in the Gorge, set against a backdrop of columnar basalt pillars.

BEST: Waterfall Hikes
DISTANCE: 3.1 miles round-trip
DURATION: 1.5 hours
ELEVATION CHANGE: 880 feet
EFFORT: Easy/moderate
TRAIL: Dirt trail, paved path, roots, rocks, stone steps
USERS: Hikers, leashed dogs
SEASON: Year-round
PASSES/FEES: None
MAPS: USGS topographic map for Bridal Veil, OR-WA
PARK HOURS: 6am-10pm daily
CONTACT: Oregon State Parks, 503/695-2261, www.oregonstateparks.org

START THE HIKE

The waterfall is at its most powerful as winter snowpack begins melting, during which time its splash may freeze and create dangerous conditions along the trail; be cautious in cold weather. Given the popularity of this hike and its proximity to Portland, consider an off-season weekday for a dose of solitude.

▶ **MILE 0-1.1: Latourell Falls Trailhead to Upper Latourell Falls**
From the parking area, find the **Latourell Falls Trailhead,** indicated by the map signboard. The clockwise loop kicks off with five stone steps, and then you'll head steeply uphill and south through a forest of Douglas fir, alder, cedar, and maple. At 0.3 mile you'll find your first **viewpoint** of Latourell Falls, marked by a bench. The trail parallels **Latourell Creek** for the next 0.8 mile, during which you'll ascend a gently graded 280 feet alongside ferns and salmonberries (in summer), before arriving at the foot of the 120-foot, two-tiered **Upper Latourell Falls**—the trail's highest point.

▶ **MILE 1.1-2: Upper Latourell Falls to Outcrop Viewpoint**
After taking in views of the falls, cross the footbridge and continue on the trail, which begins looping back north from here. In 0.8 mile, head right at an unsigned fork for a short **spur trail.** This path can get rocky at times; it ends at an **outcrop** that affords dramatic views of the Washington side of the Columbia River Gorge.

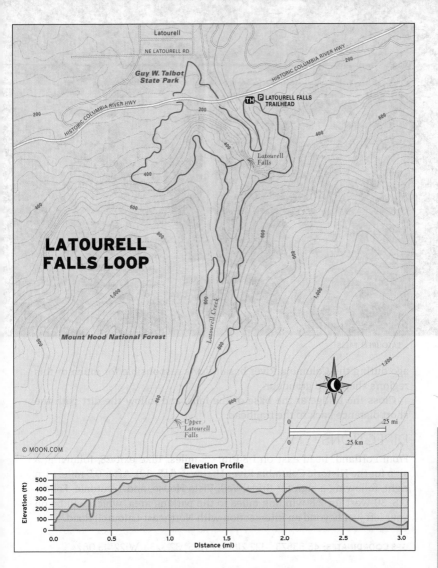

LATOURELL FALLS LOOP

Latourell

NE LATOURELL RD

Guy W. Talbot State Park

HISTORIC COLUMBIA RIVER HWY

HISTORIC COLUMBIA RIVER HWY

TH P LATOURELL FALLS TRAILHEAD

Latourell Falls

Latourell Creek

Mount Hood National Forest

Upper Latourell Falls

© MOON.COM

0   .25 mi
0   .25 km

Elevation Profile

Elevation (ft) / Distance (mi)

▶ **MILE 2–3.1: Outcrop Viewpoint to Latourell Falls and Trailhead**

Back on the main trail, you'll climb gently for the next 0.25 mile before steadily descending back toward the Columbia River. Cross the Historic Columbia River Highway in another 0.6 mile, and pick up the unmarked trail on the north side of the road. Take a sharp left onto the paved path at the first unsigned intersection almost immediately after crossing the highway. The trail descends a small stone staircase and immediately forks; turn right to head east, following a sign for the Loop Trail and Base of Lower Falls and passing some shaded picnic benches to your left. The paved path curves back south and continues under the highway, once again paralleling Latourell Creek. After 0.2 mile, you'll arrive at the misty base of photogenic **Latourell Falls,** which tumbles 200 feet amid lichen-colored columnar basalt pillars—created more than 10 million years

▲ LATOURELL FALLS

ago during the Columbia River basalt flows responsible for much of this region's shape and grandeur.

Cross the bridge at the base of the falls, and follow the dirt path the short distance back to the trailhead.

DIRECTIONS

From Portland, head east on I-84 for 25 miles. Take exit 28, following a sign for the Historic Columbia River Highway (U.S. 30). After 0.5 mile, turn right, following a sign for Bridal Veil, Vista House, and Troutdale. Follow U.S. 30 west for 2.8 winding miles to the parking area, which will be on your left just beyond an intersection with Northeast Latourell Road.

GPS COORDINATES: 45.53873, –122.21804 / N45° 32.3238′ W122° 13.0824′

BEST NEARBY BREWS

Built in 1911 as the Multnomah County poor farm, today **McMenamins Edgefield** (2126 SW Halsey St., Troutdale, 503/669-8610, www.mcmenamins.com, hours vary by individual venue) is a hotel and part of the McMenamins regional chain, which is known for refurbishing historic properties while adding a modern sense of whimsy. This property hosts numerous bars and restaurants serving McMenamins' libations from its on-site brewery, winery, and distillery, not to mention a popular concert venue and two par-3 golf courses. From the trailhead, the 16-mile drive west takes 25 minutes via the Historic Columbia River Highway and I-84.

Hike through a wildfire-scarred landscape and past waterfalls to arrive at the summit of an exposed bluff offering spectacular views of the Columbia River Gorge.

DISTANCE: 4.9 miles round-trip
DURATION: 2.5 hours
ELEVATION CHANGE: 1,300 feet
EFFORT: Moderate
TRAIL: Dirt trail, rock scrambles, roots
USERS: Hikers, leashed dogs
SEASON: Year-round
PASSES/FEES: None
MAPS: USGS topographic map for Bridal Veil, OR-WA
PARK HOURS: 6am-10pm daily
CONTACT: Columbia River Gorge National Scenic Area, 541/308-1700, www.fs.usda.gov

START THE HIKE

Damaged by the Eagle Creek Fire, this trail reopened after months of restoration and has quickly regained its popularity; make this a midweek hike in the off-season if you can to avoid crowds.

▶ **MILE 0-0.6: Angel's Rest Trailhead to Upper Coopey Falls**
From the main parking area, head south to cross the Historic Columbia River Highway and find the **Angel's Rest Trailhead.** In a couple of hundred feet, you'll arrive at an unsigned, Y-shaped junction; head left to continue uphill. Here you'll see several burned tree trunks, evidence of the Eagle Creek Fire, though for the most part this early stretch comprises dense forest including ferns, old-growth trees, and white trillium blossoms in early spring. For the first 0.4 mile, you'll steadily ascend a gentle slope to arrive at the top of 150-foot **Coopey Falls.** After another 0.1 mile along the trail, you'll cross a bridge over **Coopey Creek** and, almost immediately, find a short spur trail to your left offering views of the 35-foot **Upper Coopey Falls.**

▶ **MILE 0.6-2.1: Upper Coopey Falls to Rockslide**
Back on the main trail, the hike begins to intensify, gaining 300 feet before arriving, in another 0.6 mile, at Eagle Creek Fire-devastated forest; from here to the summit, the greenery gradually gives way to downed logs, snags, and blackened tree trunks. After another 0.5 mile, you're almost entirely surrounded by toothpick-like snags littering the hillsides (much

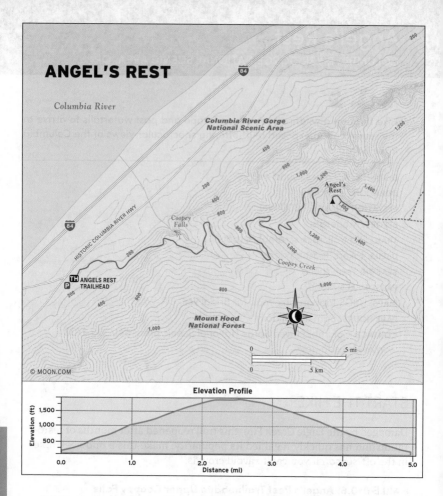

ANGEL'S REST

Columbia River

Columbia River Gorge
National Scenic Area

Angel's Rest

Coopey Falls

Coopey Creek

ANGELS REST TRAILHEAD

Mount Hood National Forest

HISTORIC COLUMBIA RIVER HWY

0   .5 mi
0   .5 km

© MOON.COM

Elevation Profile

of this area burned in a 1991 wildfire as well). As you switchback up the slopes—with the summit of Angel's Rest now visible to the east—you'll see several shortcuts filled in with rocks and spur trails blocked off with logs; stay on the established trail at all times, as there's a high risk of falling trees, uneven ground, and erosion as the area recovers. In roughly 0.4 mile, you'll arrive at a 150-foot-long rockslide that can be slippery after rainfall.

▶ **MILE 2.1–2.45: Rockslide to Angel's Rest Summit**
After another 0.25 mile of steep climbing, you'll arrive at an unsigned Y-junction. Continue straight to head north, and delicately climb a 15-foot rock scramble. As soon as you navigate this tricky stretch, you'll arrive at the **Angel's Rest summit,** featuring epic views: To the east, you'll see Beacon Rock, Hamilton Mountain, and some charred forests; to the west is the Vista House, built in 1916 as a rest stop for travelers on the Historic Columbia River Highway, on the basalt promontory of Crown Point.

Return the way you came.

▲ UPPER COOPEY FALLS

DIRECTIONS

From Portland, head east on I-84 east for 25 miles. Take exit 28, following a sign for the Historic Columbia River Highway (U.S. 30). You'll arrive at the main parking area to your right after 0.5 mile, just beyond a sign for Bridal Veil, Vista House, and Troutdale. Additional parking is also available farther west along the Historic Columbia River Highway.

GPS COORDINATES: 45.56022, -122.17264 / N45° 33.6132' W122° 10.3584'

BEST NEARBY BREWS

Choose among a well-rounded selection of balanced beers at **Migration Brewing** (18188 NE Wilkes Rd., Portland, 971-274-3770, http://migrationbrewing.com, 11am-9pm Sun.-Thurs., 11am-10pm Fri.-Sat.). Its lineup includes a mix of lagers, barrel-aged beers, and hop-forward IPAs and pale ales. From the trailhead, the 16-mile drive west takes 17 minutes via I-84.

Angel's Rest

3

Wahkeena Falls–Multnomah Falls Loop

COLUMBIA RIVER GORGE NATIONAL SCENIC AREA, OR

Enjoy dense, old-growth forest and plenty of waterfalls along this loop, including iconic Multnomah Falls—the tallest in Oregon.

BEST: Waterfall Hikes

DISTANCE: 5.9 miles round-trip

DURATION: 3 hours

ELEVATION CHANGE: 1,670 feet

EFFORT: Moderate

TRAIL: Dirt trail, paved path, stream crossings, rocks, gravel

USERS: Hikers, leashed dogs

SEASON: Year-round, but trail may be icy or snowy winter–early spring

PASSES/FEES: None

MAPS: USGS topographic map for Multnomah Falls, OR-WA; free trail maps available at the U.S. Forest Service information center inside Multnomah Falls Lodge

CONTACT: Columbia River Gorge National Scenic Area, 541/308-1700, www.fs.usda.gov

The loop between Wahkeena Falls and Multnomah Falls is one of the most popular hikes in Oregon—no surprise, given that Multnomah Falls is among the state's biggest tourist draws.

START THE HIKE

Plan to share portions of this trail with scores of fellow hikers; consider saving this hike for a weekday if possible, or start before 9am.

▶ MILE 0–0.8: Multnomah Falls Lodge to Wahkeena Falls

From the parking lot, follow the pedestrian crosswalk south under I-84, crossing Multnomah Creek and the Historic Columbia River Highway, to the plaza in front of **Multnomah Falls Lodge,** which has a snack stand and restrooms; you can also grab a free trail map inside. Pause to appreciate views of **Multnomah Falls** from here now or at the end of the hike. From the lodge head west to begin the counterclockwise loop along the shoulder of the **Historic Columbia River Highway.** After 0.1 mile, take a slight left onto the **Return Trail.** This mostly flat dirt and gravel path parallels the highway and connects the parking areas at Multnomah and Wahkeena Falls (so you could start the hike from either end—but there's more parking at this trailhead). After 0.5 mile, you'll descend a short series of stone steps before coming to a junction; turn left to head west on the **unnamed paved path.** You'll shortly see a sign for Wahkeena Falls; proceed up the paved path, ascending through a forest of Douglas fir and hemlock. In 0.2

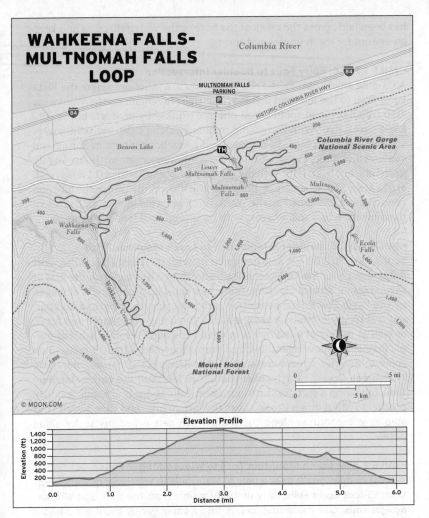

WAHKEENA FALLS-MULTNOMAH FALLS LOOP

Columbia River

MULTNOMAH FALLS PARKING

HISTORIC COLUMBIA RIVER HWY

Benson Lake

Columbia River Gorge National Scenic Area

Lower Multnomah Falls

Multnomah Falls

Multnomah Creek

Wahkeena Falls

Ecola Falls

Wahkeena Creek

Mount Hood National Forest

0   .5 mi
0   .5 km

© MOON.COM

Elevation Profile

mile, you'll emerge at the base of the upper tier of **Wahkeena Falls,** which cascades more 240 feet total and gets its name from the Yakama Nation's word for "most beautiful."

▸ MILE 0.8-1.4: Wahkeena Falls to Lemmons Viewpoint
The paved path switchbacks steeply uphill beyond the falls, arriving in 0.6 mile at a junction; turn right for a short spur trail to **Lemmons Viewpoint,** named for a firefighter who died nearby; it offers unfettered views of the Columbia River Gorge, including Beacon Rock and Hamilton Mountain to the east.

▸ MILE 1.4-1.7: Lemmons Viewpoint to Fairy Falls
Back at the junction, head south on the **Wahkeena Trail,** a dirt path that parallels **Wahkeena Creek** through a lush canyon before arriving, in 0.3 mile, at the base of **Fairy Falls.** Good news: This marks the end of the hardest part of the ascent, and the trail levels out from here. A wooden plank

has been laid across the creek at the base of the waterfall; cross and keep an eye out for ice in winter and spring.

▶ MILE 1.7–2.6: Fairy Falls to Boulder Intersection
A 0.1-mile amble past Fairy Falls brings you to a junction; ignore the Vista Point Trail to the left, and instead head right to remain on the Wahkeena Trail. You'll begin to spot burned-out tree trunks—by-products of the 2017 Eagle Creek Fire—with increasing frequency along here, but wildflowers including purple phlox, bear grass, and dandelions bloom in spring and summer along this stretch. In 0.4 mile is an intersection with the Angel's Rest Trail, but head left to remain on the Wahkeena Trail. In 0.4 mile you'll arrive at another junction; again ignore the Vista Point Trail to the left, and continue straight ahead on the Wahkeena Trail. This intersection is also a pleasant spot for a snack break, with its several boulders for sitting.

▶ MILE 2.6–3.5: Boulder Intersection to Larch Mountain Trail
Soon after you'll hit yet another junction, with the Devil's Rest Trail; veer left to remain on the Wahkeena Trail. Shortly you'll come upon the first of several minor stream crossings, and then enter an area heavily damaged by the Eagle Creek Fire; every tree along this stretch is burned and barren, but plenty of undergrowth remains, including vine maple and ferns, as well as variety of wildflowers in spring and early summer, such as purple foxglove, yellow tiger lilies, and purple fireweed. After 0.9 mile, you'll come to another stream crossing as you descend the canyon alongside **Multnomah Creek.** Shortly after you'll turn left onto the **Larch Mountain Trail,** following a sign for the Multnomah Falls Lodge and heading north, parallel to Multnomah Creek. Cross the last stream, and then watch your step as you continue along the trail, which gets especially rocky along here.

▶ MILE 3.5–4: Larch Mountain Trail to Wiesendanger Falls
After 0.25 mile, you'll pass a pair of waterfalls in relatively quick succession: 55-foot **Ecola Falls,** only partially visible from the trail, and **Wiesendanger Falls,** also cascading 55 feet into a small gorge. You'll get a better look at Wiesendanger Falls in another 0.2 mile when the trail switchbacks to its base; where the waterfall enters the creek makes a popular swimming hole in summer.

▶ MILE 4–4.7: Wiesendanger Falls to Multnomah Falls Viewpoint Spur
Another 0.1 mile past Wiesendanger Falls you'll pass **Dutchman Falls,** a series of three short waterfalls. In 0.3 mile, head left at the junction, following a sign for the **Multnomah Falls Viewpoint.** The 0.3-mile round-trip spur ends at a plaza at the top of Multnomah Falls; while you don't see much of the waterfall itself from here, it's worth the short side trip for its views of the Columbia River Gorge.

▶ MILE 4.7–5.9: Multnomah Falls Viewpoint Spur to Multnomah Falls Lodge
Back at the junction, turn left onto the Larch Mountain Trail, following the Multnomah Falls Lodge sign. You'll ascend briefly before descending via

▲ MULTNOMAH FALLS

11 paved switchbacks, crossing **Benson Bridge** near the base of **Multnomah Falls**; the 635-foot waterfall tumbles over basalt cliffs in two major steps and is among the most popular natural attractions in the Pacific Northwest, drawing more than two million visitors each year. After 1.2 miles, the trail levels out back at the Multnomah Falls Lodge.

DIRECTIONS

From Portland, head east on I-84 for 28.3 miles. Take exit 31—off to the left—and follow the signs for Multnomah Falls to arrive in the parking area.

The many parking areas near Multnomah Falls fill to capacity regularly, even on weekdays, so consider taking the **Columbia Gorge Express** (888/246-6420, http://columbiagorgeexpress.com), a shuttle between Portland and several popular destinations in the Gorge, including Multnomah Falls (US$7.50 round-trip). The shuttle departs Portland at the **Gateway Transit Center** (9900 NE Multnomah St., Portland), and the ride takes 35-45 minutes. Buses operate year-round, but check the website for the schedule because it varies seasonally.

GPS COORDINATES: 45.57769, -122.11719 / N45° 34.6614′ W122° 7.0314′

BEST NEARBY BITES

Enjoy an upscale meal at **Multnomah Falls Lodge** (53000 E. Historic Columbia River Hwy., Bridal Veil, 503/695-2376, www.multnomah-fallslodge.com, 8am-9pm daily). Located at the base of Multnomah Falls, its on-site restaurant offers fine Northwest-inspired cuisine.

4

Larch Mountain Crater Loop

COLUMBIA RIVER GORGE NATIONAL SCENIC AREA, OR

Hike into an eroded crater atop Larch Mountain—and enjoy jaw-dropping views of Mount Hood and other Cascade peaks.

DISTANCE: 7.1 miles round-trip
DURATION: 3.5 hours
ELEVATION CHANGE: 1,200 feet
EFFORT: Easy/moderate
TRAIL: Dirt trail, rocks, roots, stream crossings, paved path, stairs, roadside
USERS: Hikers, leashed dogs
SEASON: June–October
PASSES/FEES: Northwest Forest Pass
MAPS: USGS topographic map for Multnomah Falls, OR-WA
CONTACT: Columbia River Gorge National Scenic Area, 541/308-1700, www.fs.usda.gov

Larch Mountain is an extinct volcano near the western edge of the Columbia River Gorge. On this clockwise loop hike, you'll descend into a crater near the mountain's 4,055-foot peak.

START THE HIKE

▶ **MILE 0-2.1: Larch Mountain Trail to Multnomah Creek Way Trail**
Start hiking on the unsigned paved path—the **Larch Mountain Trail**—framed by two wooden posts at the northwestern edge of the parking lot. The path forks almost immediately; take the trail that heads slightly downhill to the left. It soon becomes a dirt trail and goes past a restroom. Old-growth Douglas fir and hemlock forest surrounds you. After about 0.2 mile you'll arrive at an unsigned T-shaped junction; head left to continue downhill. As you descend, vine maple, rhododendron, and summertime huckleberries flank the trail. You'll lose about 600 feet of elevation over the next 1.4 mile, at which point you'll arrive at an old roadbed and well-signed junction; cross the road to continue downhill on the Larch Mountain Trail. Enjoy the purple, bell-shaped foxglove along this stretch; it blooms in late spring and remains vibrant through midsummer. You'll come to a T-shaped junction in another 0.5 mile; head right to take the **Multnomah Creek Way Trail**.

▶ **MILE 2.1-5.2: Multnomah Creek Way Trail to Oneonta Trail**
The trail flattens out in 0.2 mile, where you'll cross **Multnomah Creek** on a wooden footbridge; this trickling creek feeds Multnomah Falls a few miles downstream. Red cedar and salmonberries grow along the trail here. Immediately after the bridge crossing, turn right to remain on the Multnomah Creek Way Trail and begin looping back south from where you came. You'll head into a marshy area, for a brief moment out from under the forest

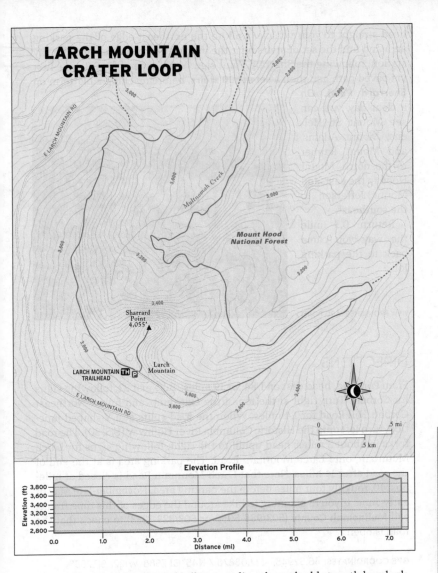

LARCH MOUNTAIN CRATER LOOP

Elevation Profile

canopy, and then begin gradually ascending through old-growth hemlock. The trail crosses numerous small, trickling streambeds over its next winding stretch, but the flow won't rise much above your boot sole. Along this stretch you'll find vibrant undergrowth and wildflowers in spring-summer, including twinflowers, noted for their Y-shaped stalks, and the three-petaled trillium. Some 2.9 miles beyond the Multnomah Creek crossing, you'll arrive at a T-shaped junction; turn right onto the **Oneonta Trail.**

▶ MILE 5.2–7.1: Oneonta Trail to Sherrard Point and Parking Lot

Steadily ascend the ridgeline; to your left is the **Bull Run Watershed,** the primary source of drinking water for the city of Portland. After 0.9 mile, the trail ends at **Larch Mountain Road;** turn right to head uphill, walking along its shoulder. The road ends, after 0.4 mile, at the parking area. Rather than head straight to your vehicle, walk to the northeast edge of the parking area and find the set of stairs near the information board/day-use fee pay station, following the Sherrard Point sign. You'll ascend for 0.3 mile, first via paved path and then a set of **100 stairs,** before reaching a platform on **Sherrard Point.** On a clear day, you can see Mount St. Helens, Mount Adams, and Mount Rainier to the north, Mount Hood to the east, and Mount Jefferson to the southeast.

Return 0.3 mile the way you came back to the parking lot.

VIEW FROM SHERRARD POINT ▶

DIRECTIONS

From Portland, head east on I-84 for 19 miles. Take exit 22, following signs for Corbett. Turn right at the top of the exit ramp, and follow Northeast Corbett Hill Road for 1.4 miles. When the road splits at a Y-shaped junction, turn left onto the Historic Columbia River Highway (U.S. 30). The road forks in about 2 miles; head uphill to the right, following signs for Larch Mountain, onto Larch Mountain Road. The parking area is at the end of the road after 14 miles. Note that Larch Mountain Road is closed at milepost 10, roughly four miles before the parking area, November-late May or early June. If you're planning to hike around the edges of this time frame, call **Multnomah County** (503/988-5050 or 503/823-3333) to check that the road is open.

GPS COORDINATES: 45.52948, –122.08878 / N45° 31.7688' W122° 5.3268'

BEST NEARBY BREWS

Located at the edge of Glendoveer Golf Course, **Von Ebert Brewing Glendoveer** (14021 NE Glisan St., Portland, 503/878-8708, http://glendoveer.vonebertbrewing.com, 11am-10pm Sun.-Thurs., 11am-11pm Fri.-Sat.) serves beers brewed on-site, as well as at its other location in Portland's Pearl District, alongside classic pub fare. From the trailhead, the 30-mile drive east takes 50 minutes via Larch Mountain Road and I-84.

5

Beacon Rock

BEACON ROCK STATE PARK, WA

Follow a shelf-like path blasted into the side of a towering monolith to a sweeping view of the Columbia River Gorge.

DISTANCE: 2 miles round-trip

DURATION: 1 hour

ELEVATION CHANGE: 650 feet

EFFORT: Easy/moderate

TRAIL: Dirt, wooden bridges, paved path

USERS: Hikers

SEASON: Year-round

PASSES/FEES: Discover Pass

MAPS: Green Trails Map 429 for Bonneville Dam

PARK HOURS: 8am-dusk daily

CONTACT: Washington State Parks, 509/427-8265, http://parks.state.wa.us

Rising above the Columbia River, Beacon Rock is the core of an ancient volcano. Lewis and Clark gave the rock its name when they camped here in 1805. Hiking to its top wouldn't be possible without the considerable efforts of Henry Jonathan Biddle, a wealthy engineer and geologist from Philadelphia who developed a love for the area and purchased Beacon Rock, saving it from demolition. From 1916 to 1918, Biddle and his friend Charles Johnson built a harrowing trail up the side of the rock. They blasted a 4-foot-wide path into the cliff and spanned narrow fissures with 22 wooden bridges and more than 100 concrete slabs.

START THE HIKE

▶ **MILE 0-1: Monolith West Side to Beacon Rock**

The path starts in the woods on the west side of the monolith and after a few bends passes through a **gate**. From there, 52 easy-to-manage **switchbacks** are packed into the 1 mile it takes reach the top. Handrails line the route, giving visitors a bit of comfort as they shift their attention between views of the Columbia River, the moss and

Beacon Rock

SWITCHBACKS ▶

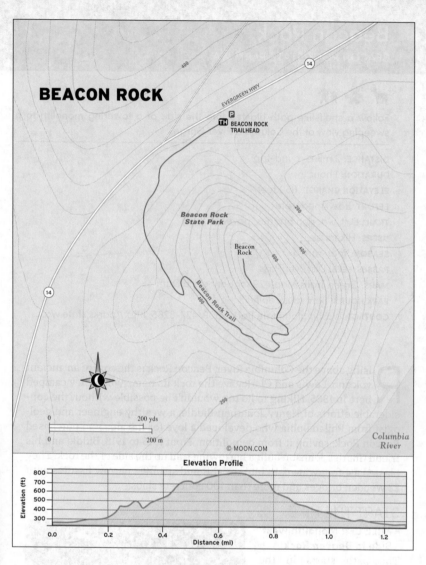

BEACON ROCK

Beacon Rock Trailhead

Beacon Rock State Park

Beacon Rock

Beacon Rock Trail

EVERGREEN HWY

14

14

Columbia
River

© MOON.COM

0   200 yds
0   200 m

Elevation Profile

Elevation (ft): 800, 700, 600, 500, 400, 300

Distance (mi): 0.0, 0.2, 0.4, 0.6, 0.8, 1.0, 1.2

lichen growing on the rock, and occasional wildflowers blooming in the crevices. Warblers, flycatchers, pigeons, hummingbirds, woodpeckers, and other birds frequent the area.

▶ MILE 1-2: Beacon Rock to Monolith West Side

Stone steps deliver you to the **top** (848 feet above sea level) and a view that stretches miles up and down the Columbia River Gorge. Ships motor up the river, and trains chug along the banks following the route the Lewis and Clark expedition pioneered two centuries ago. There's not much room at the top, so on nice days you might have to wait for an opportunity to stand at the railing and snap pictures of the Gorge.

After your turn, zigzag your way back to your car.

▲ TRAIL ALONG BEACON ROCK

DIRECTIONS

From I-205 in Vancouver, Washington, take exit 27 and merge onto Highway 14. Drive east for 28 miles. Beacon Rock and trailhead parking is on the right side of the road. Toilets are near the parking lot.

GPS COORDINATES: 45.628571, -122.022222 / N45° 37.7143' W122° 1.3333'

BEST NEARBY BITES

The riverside community of Stevenson, 8.5 miles (12 minutes) northeast of the trailhead via Highway 14, offers tasty post-hike options that include a salmon sandwich at the **Big River Grill** (192 2nd St., Stevenson, WA, 509/427-4888, www.thebigrivergrill.com, hours vary) and burgers and brews in the century-old saloon at **Clark & Lewie's Traveler's Rest Saloon & Grill** (130 SW Cascade Ave., Stevenson, WA, 509/219-0097, www.clarkandlewies.com, hours vary).

6

Dry Creek Falls

COLUMBIA RIVER GORGE NATIONAL SCENIC AREA, OR

Located just a couple of miles east of the Eagle Creek Fire's origin point, this trail offers some of the most gripping views of the devastation wrought by the wildfire—but it also shows signs of life, and concludes at a lovely waterfall.

DISTANCE: 5 miles round-trip

DURATION: 2.5 hours

ELEVATION CHANGE: 1,240 feet

EFFORT: Moderate

TRAIL: Dirt trail, roots, rocks, gravel roads

USERS: Hikers, leashed dogs, horseback riders

SEASON: Year-round

PASSES/FEES: Northwest Forest Pass

MAPS: USGS topographic maps for Bonneville Dam, OR-WA, and Carson, WA-OR

CONTACT: Columbia River Gorge National Scenic Area, 541/308-1700, www.fs.usda.gov

START THE HIKE

▶ **MILE 0-0.3: Bridge of the Gods Trailhead Parking to Eagle Creek Fire-Burned Forest**

From the southern edge of the **Bridge of the Gods Trailhead** parking area, walk south across the road leading to the Bridge of the Gods tollbooth, following a sign onto the **Pacific Crest Trail (PCT).** Walk 0.1 mile on the gently sloping trail, then turn right onto **Southwest Moody Avenue,** under I-84, heading uphill. After a few hundred feet, turn right onto the **unsigned gravel road,** following it for a couple of hundred feet before turning left to rejoin the **PCT.** In 0.1 mile you'll come upon Eagle Creek Fire-charred tree trunks, downed trees, and jagged snags lining the trail. But even with all the damage, signs of life are everywhere: You'll hear the occasional bird over nearby highway noise, and find ferns and raspberry bushes along the narrow trail.

▶ **MILE 0.3-1.3: Eagle Creek Fire-Burned Forest to Power Lines and PCT**

You'll gain 495 feet over the next 1 mile, steadily yet gently ascending, before arriving at a T-shaped intersection. Head right onto the **unnamed gravel road,** following a sign for the PCT, as the road curves uphill and ducks under a set of power lines. Just past the power lines, turn left, back onto the **PCT.**

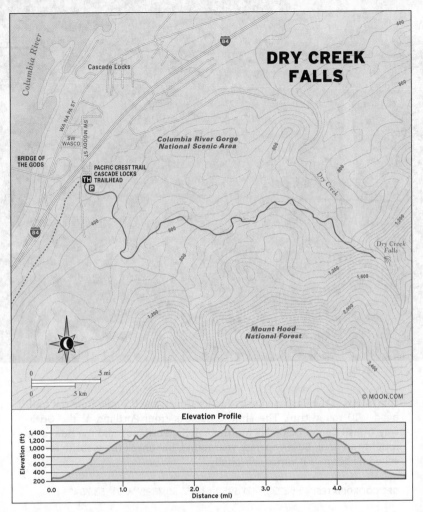

Elevation Profile

▶ MILE 1.3–2.5: Power Lines and PCT to Dry Creek Falls

Continue your gradual ascent through a forest of Douglas fir, vine maple, and hemlock for another 0.9 mile, at which point you'll arrive at a junction; make a hard right onto the wide **Dry Creek Falls Trail** for 0.3 mile. The trail ends at the base of **Dry Creek Falls,** a 75-foot plume in the heart of a narrow basalt canyon.

Return the way you came.

DIRECTIONS

From downtown Cascade Locks, head south on Wa Na Pa Street toward the Bridge of the Gods. Turn left at a sign for the Bridge of the Gods toll bridge, and follow the road as it loops around to the east. After a few hundred feet, turn right into a parking area at a sign for the Bridge of the Gods Trailhead in Toll House Park.

If you'd rather not drive and fight for parking at this popular trailhead, the **Columbia Gorge Express** (888/246-6420, http://columbiagorgeexpress.

▲ DRY CREEK FALLS

com) stops at the Cascade Locks Justice Court, just 0.5 mile from the trailhead ($10 round-trip). The shuttle departs from Portland at the **Gateway Transit Center** (9900 NE Multnomah St., Portland), and the ride takes roughly an hour. Buses operate year-round, but check the website for the schedule because it varies seasonally.

GPS COORDINATES: 45.66233, –121.8959 / N45° 39.7398′ W121° 53.754′

BEST NEARBY BITES

Enjoy hearty pizza and pub fare—and wash it down with a refreshing craft beer—at **Cascade Locks Ale House** (500 Wa Na Pa St., Cascade Locks, 541/374-9310, http://cascadelocksalehouse.com, noon-5pm Wed., noon-9pm Thurs.-Mon.). The pub serves pizza, sandwiches, and burgers alongside a selection of craft beer from Portland and the Columbia River Gorge. From the trailhead, the 0.5-mile drive takes 5 minutes via Wa Na Pa St.

COLUMBIA RIVER GORGE

Dry Creek Falls

Climb through colorful fields of wildflowers to a sweeping view of Mount Hood and the Columbia River Gorge.

BEST: Spring Hikes, Wildflower Hikes

DISTANCE: 6.9 miles round-trip

DURATION: 4 hours

ELEVATION CHANGE: 2,900 feet

EFFORT: Moderate/strenuous

TRAIL: Dirt, talus fields

USERS: Hikers, leashed dogs

SEASON: March–December

PASSES/FEES: Northwest Forest Pass, permit required March 31–July 1 ($1.50 per person)

MAPS: Green Trails Map 430 for Hood River, OR

CONTACT: Columbia River Gorge National Scenic Area, 541/308-1700, www.fs.usda.gov/crgnsa

Even if its slopes were barren and dusty, Dog Mountain's striking view of the Columbia River Gorge would draw a crowd. But they aren't. The upper mountain comes alive with color each spring as wildflowers bloom and hikers arrive by the busload. Springtime traffic is so heavy that in 2018 the Forest Service started requiring permits during the season, designed to encourage hikers to take public transportation and alleviate congestion at the trailhead. Permits are free for those riding the shuttle bus from Stevenson. Otherwise, buy a permit (www.recreation.gov) and arrive before sunrise for the best chance of staying ahead of the crowds.

START THE HIKE

▶ **MILE 0–0.6: Parking Lot to First Old Trail Junction**
From the 100-car parking lot, there are three options for making the 2,900-foot climb: Long but gradual (Augspurger Trail), shorter but steeper (the new Dog Mountain Trail), or even shorter and steeper (the old Dog Mountain Trail). Ascending on the new trail and returning via the Augspurger Trail makes an enjoyable loop with loads of inspiring scenery.

From the east end of the parking lot, follow the **new trail,** which tilts upward as heads east and arrives at a toilet in a matter of steps. Here, the real climbing commences, through a forest of Douglas fir. Trailside flora includes Oregon grape, snowberry, and poison oak. After 0.6 mile, pass the **old trail** on your left.

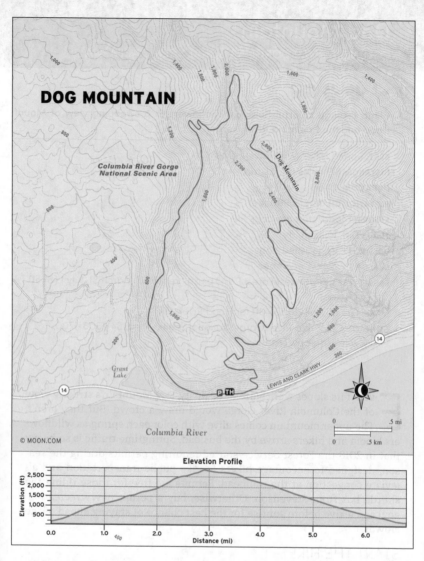

DOG MOUNTAIN

Columbia River Gorge
National Scenic Area

Dog Mountain

Grant Lake

Columbia River

© MOON.COM

Elevation Profile

▶ **MILE 0.6-2.1: First Old Trail Junction to Second Old Trail Junction**
After another 1.5 steep miles of hard work, pass the **upper junction with the old trail.** Views of the Gorge and the knowledge that the old trail is even steeper help distract you from the grind.

▶ **MILE 2.1-3: Second Old Trail Junction to**
  Columbia River Gorge Viewpoint
Push on for another steep 0.4 mile before finding yourself in vibrant **Puppy Dog Meadow.** Yellow balsamroot, scarlet paintbrush, purple lupine, red columbine: The kaleidoscope of colors coupled with views of Mount Hood and the Columbia River is so stunning some hikers choose to make this their destination. Look for a USGS survey disc on the trail before

continuing upward 0.3 mile, then turning right on a 0.2-mile **spur** that takes you to the high point and another breathtaking view of the Gorge.

▶ MILE 3–4.1: Columbia River Gorge Viewpoint to Augspurger Trail Junction

Wherever you choose to stop climbing, you can return the way you came or take the Old Trail shortcut. But to finish the loop retrace your steps on the spur and turn right to follow the **Dog-Augspurger Tie Trail** north along the ridge for 0.9 mile. At the junction with **Augspurger Trail,** turn left (right makes a 4-mile-each-way side trip to Augspurger Mountain)

▶ MILE 4.1–6.9: Augspurger Trail Junction to Parking Lot

Descend through the forest for about 0.8 mile before reaching the first of several **talus fields.** These rocky sections are easy to navigate if you watch your step, although I have seen hikers slowed enough by these stretches during evening hikes that they found themselves not finishing until after dark.

Expect more of the same for the final 2 miles to the car, with occasional views through the evergreens to Grant Lake. After all that work to get up Dog Mountain, this comparatively gradual descent is a knee's best friend.

DIRECTIONS

From I-205 in Vancouver, Washington, take exit 27 and merge on to Highway 14. Drive east for 47 miles. The well-marked Dog Mountain parking lot is on the left side of the road. A vault toilet is located near the trailhead.

Gorge TransLink (www.gorgetranslink.com) offers shuttle service to the busy trailhead 7:30am-4:30pm on weekends March 31-July 1. The $1-each-way service from the Skamania County Fairgrounds (710 SW Rock Creek Dr., Stevenson, WA) includes a Dog Mountain hiking permit and discounts at Stevenson businesses. Leashed dogs are permitted.

GPS COORDINATES: 45.699265, –121.708174 / N45° 41.9559' W121° 42.4904'

BEST NEARBY BREWS

Brewers stir every batch of beer by hand at **Walking Man Brewing** (240 SW 1st St., Stevenson, WA, 509/427-5520, www.walkingman-beer.com, 11:30am-9pm Wed.-Sun.) in Stevenson. The old-fashioned approach has served the two-decade-old, award-winning brewery well. Pizza, burgers, and salads supplement the beer selection. From the trailhead, the 9.5-mile drive west takes about 15 minutes via Highway 14.

Coyote Wall (Labyrinth Loop)
COLUMBIA RIVER GORGE NATIONAL SCENIC AREA, WA

🦌 ❋ 🏞 🐾

Link trails to visit fields of wildflowers, views of the Columbia River, and the edge of a basalt cliff.

BEST: Brew Hikes, Dog-Friendly Hikes
DISTANCE: 6.3 miles round-trip
DURATION: 3.5 hours
ELEVATION CHANGE: 1,200 feet
EFFORT: Easy/moderate
TRAIL: Dirt, rocks, paved and dirt road
USERS: Hikers, leashed dogs, off-leash dogs (July–Nov.), mountain bikers, horseback riders (May–Sept.)
SEASON: Year-round
PASSES/FEES: Northwest Forest Pass
MAPS: Green Trails Map 432S for Columbia River Gorge East; free maps at www.fs.usda.gov/crgnsa
CONTACT: Columbia River Gorge National Scenic Area, 541/308-1700, www.fs.usda.gov/crgnsa

When your hiking route is called "the Labyrinth," it's a good idea to double-check that you packed a good map. At Coyote Wall, for good measure, you might even snap a photo of the large map on the back of the trailhead kiosk or download a map from the Forest Service website (www.fs.usda.gov/crgnsa). With the Columbia River visible most of the way it's hard to stay lost, but a multitude of paths and sparse signage make it easy to wander off course.

START THE HIKE

▶ **MILE 0-0.4: Parking Lot East End to Trail Junction**
Starting at the east end of the parking lot beneath **Coyote Wall,** it's quickly evident why **Old Highway 8** was retired. The paved road is littered with huge rocks that fell from the basalt cliff. Look for jumping fish in Locke Lake, watch trains chug along the Columbia River, and gaze into Oregon as you walk the flat road. At 0.4 mile, pass a trail you'll use to finish the loop.

▶ **MILE 0.4-1.1: Trail Junction to Labyrinth Creek**
In another 0.3 mile, turn left on **Co7** (the Labyrinth Trail) and begin heading upward. Stay right at a junction a few steps up the hill, passing through a short rocky section. Pass a **small cave** in 0.3 mile and stay left at the intersection that follows. Check out a waterfall and cross **Labyrinth Creek** over the next 0.1 mile.

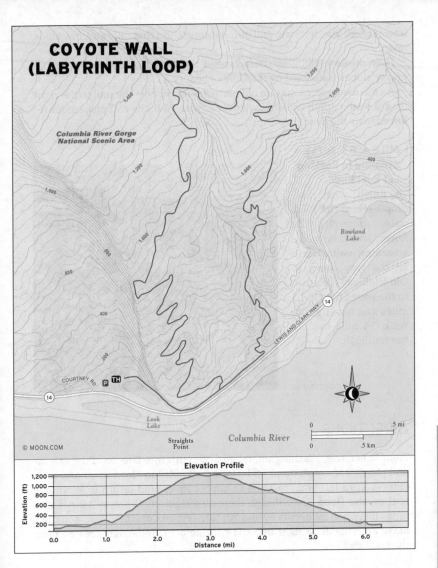

COYOTE WALL (LABYRINTH LOOP)

Columbia River Gorge National Scenic Area

Rowland Lake

LEWIS AND CLARK HWY

14

COURTNEY RD

14

Look Lake

Straights Point

Columbia River

© MOON.COM

0 — .5 mi
0 — .5 km

Elevation Profile

Elevation (ft)

1,200 / 1,000 / 800 / 600 / 400 / 200

0.0   1.0   2.0   3.0   4.0   5.0   6.0

Distance (mi)

Watch boats motor up and down the Columbia as Mount Hood rises above the panorama. In the spring, wildflowers add color to the slopes. Stay alert for rattlesnakes and poison oak.

▶ **MILE 1.1–2.5: Labyrinth Creek to Atwood Road**
Meander 0.7 mile beyond the **creek crossing** before turning left on **Co8** (Upper Labyrinth Trail) and walking another 0.7 mile (with some of the best views) to abandoned **Atwood Road.**

▶ **MILE 2.5–4.3: Atwood Road to the Syncline**
Turn left and follow the road 0.5 mile as it passes through a stand of trees, dips in and out of the Labyrinth Creek drainage, and arrives at a **three-way**

intersection. Stay left here and at the intersection that follows a few steps later.

Now on **Co4** (Old Jeep Trail), spend the next 1 mile descending the grassy slopes transfixed by the Gorge's beauty.

As the road approaches an old barbwire fence, take the trail to the right for a 0.3-mile uphill walk to look over Coyote Wall, the cliff sometimes referred to as the Syncline.

▸ **MILE 4.3–6.3: The Syncline to Parking Lot East End**

To finish your hike, drop back to the road, pass through the fence, and then make sweeping **switchbacks** all the way down to Old Highway 8. Return to the paved road in 1.3 miles and turn right to walk 0.4 mile back to the trailhead.

COYOTE WALL ▸

DIRECTIONS

From Vancouver, Washington, take I-205 south into Oregon. Take exit 22 and merge onto eastbound I-84. Drive 54.7 miles to Hood River and take exit 64. Turn left and cross the Columbia River (and return to Washington) on the Hood River Bridge then turn right on Highway 14. After 11 miles (between mileposts 69 and 70) turn left on Courtney Road and then make an immediate right into the parking area. Toilets are located near the trailhead.

GPS COORDINATES: 45.700604, –121.401706 / N45° 42.0362' W121° 24.1024'

BEST NEARBY BREWS

Burritos and brews await in White Salmon, less than 5 miles (less than 10 minutes) west of the trailhead via Highway 14. The food and beer are locally sourced at **Everybody's Brewing** (177 E. Jewett Blvd., 509/637-2774, www.everybodysbrewing.com, 11:30am–9:30pm Sun.-Thurs., 11:30am–10pm Fri.-Sat.), where the outdoor seating area includes views of Mount Hood.

Coyote Wall (Labyrinth Loop)

One of the newest trails in the Columbia River Gorge boasts waterfalls, wildflowers, and some of the region's best sunset views.

BEST: Winter Hikes
DISTANCE: 3.7 miles round-trip
DURATION: 1.5 hours
ELEVATION CHANGE: 560 feet
EFFORT: Easy/moderate
TRAIL: Dirt trail, gravel, roots, rocks, wooden steps
USERS: Hikers, leashed dogs
SEASON: Year-round
PASSES/FEES: None
MAPS: USGS topographic map for White Salmon, WA-OR
CONTACT: Friends of the Columbia Gorge, 541/386-5268, http://gorgefriends.org

This hike is a year-round gem, with bald eagles abundant in winter, more than 30 species of wildflower blooming each spring, Gorge breezes to keep you cool in summer, and fewer crowds than most Gorge hikes in the fall. Sunset views from the viewpoint on Mosier Plateau are stunning—just be sure to bring a flashlight for your return descent.

START THE HIKE

Note that ticks, rattlesnakes, and poison oak can be found along the trail, so long pants are strongly recommended, especially at the height of summer. Sensitive plants also line it, as does some private property; keep to the trail at all times.

▶ **MILE 0-0.3: Parking Area to Mosier Pioneer Cemetery**
From the parking area, head east for 0.2 mile along the **Historic Columbia River Highway** and cross **Mosier Bridge.** Just past the bridge you'll spot a bench on the south side of the highway, which is where the **Mosier Plateau Trail** begins. Some confusing unofficial trails converge near this early stretch, but head uphill on the well-maintained dirt trail and you'll be on the right track. In 0.1 mile, you'll arrive at **Mosier Pioneer Cemetery,** home to some of Mosier's earliest settlers.

▶ **MILE 0.3-1.3: Mosier Pioneer Cemetery to Mosier Viewpoint**
Continue up the gently graded trail through grassy fields, oak trees, and stands of ponderosa pine. After 0.25 mile, you'll find a **viewpoint** off to your right. Here you can see **Mosier Creek Falls** and, farther south, **Mosier Creek.** In another 0.25 mile, climb a set of wooden steps, the first of several while ascending Mosier Plateau. This stretch of trail is especially

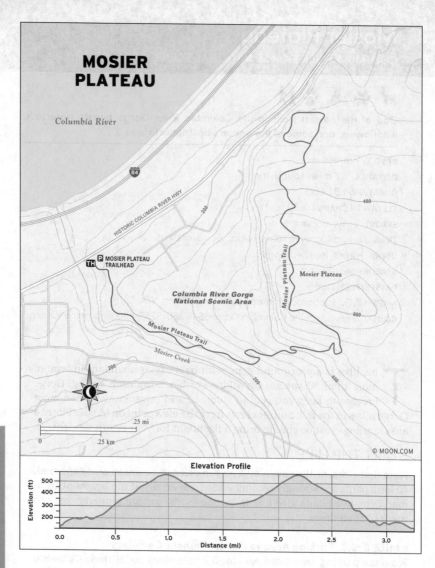

MOSIER PLATEAU

Columbia River

MOSIER PLATEAU TRAILHEAD

Columbia River Gorge National Scenic Area

Mosier Plateau Trail

Mosier Creek

Mosier Plateau Trail

Mosier Plateau

HISTORIC COLUMBIA RIVER HWY

© MOON.COM

0   .25 mi
0   .25 km

Elevation Profile

rich with wildflowers, including bighead clover, yellow arrowleaf balsamroot, and Columbia desert parsley, noted for its reddish-purple petals. In 0.5 mile, after steadily ascending an open hillside, you'll arrive at **Mosier viewpoint,** just below the summit of Mosier Plateau, from which you'll have views of Mosier, Hood River, and the Columbia River Gorge that are particularly spectacular during sunset.

▶ MILE 1.3-2: Mosier Viewpoint to Trail Loop

Continue on the trail, heading downhill for 0.4 mile. Yellow balsamroot and purple lupine bloom along this stretch each spring. Just beyond a concrete pad, once the site of a mobile home, you'll see a sign to your left indicating the **Trail Loop.** Follow the 0.25-mile loop for river views and a quiet respite just above the highway.

▲ MOSIER VIEWPOINT

▸ **MILE 2–3.7: Trail Loop to Parking Area**

After completing the loop to rejoin the main trail, return 1.7 miles the way you came.

DIRECTIONS

From Hood River, follow I-84 east for 5.5 miles. Take exit 69, following signs for Historic Columbia River Highway (U.S. 30) and Mosier. Follow the off-ramp for about 0.2 mile; at the first intersection, turn right to head south onto U.S. 30. Follow the road as it passes through the town of Mosier. After 0.3 mile, turn left onto a gravel driveway, following a sign for public parking. The road ends in a gravel parking area between the highway and railroad tracks.

GPS COORDINATES: 45.68478, –121.39391 / N45° 41.0868′ W121° 23.6346′

BEST NEARBY BREWS

Near the banks of the Columbia River, **pFriem Family Brewers** (707 Portway Ave., Suite 101, Hood River, 541/321-0490, www.pfriembeer. com, 11am–10pm daily) delivers a lineup of outstanding beers, including a heavy-hitting Belgian dark strong ale, a piney IPA, and a crisp pilsner. From the trailhead, the 7-mile drive west takes 10 minutes via I-84.

This trail traverses celebrated wildflower-strewn meadows and an oak savanna to a hillside boasting grand views of Mount Hood and the Columbia River Gorge.

BEST: Spring Hikes, Wildflower Hikes
DISTANCE: 3.8 miles round-trip
DURATION: 2 hours
ELEVATION CHANGE: 1,080 feet
EFFORT: Easy/moderate
TRAIL: Dirt trail, rocks, roots, stone staircase
USERS: Hikers
SEASON: March-October
PASSES/FEES: None
MAPS: USGS topographic map for Lyle, WA-OR
CONTACT: The Nature Conservancy, 503/802-8100, www.nature.org

McCall Point's location between the forested western part of the Gorge and the drier prairies and highlands of eastern Oregon make this fertile ground for wildflowers. The trail is maintained by The Nature Conservancy. Arrive at the height of wildflower season, and you'll likely encounter a docent along the path; these friendly volunteers are happy to help identify plant species and offer best practices for preventing further erosion.

START THE HIKE
Keep an eye out for poison oak, ticks, and rattlesnakes on this trail.

▶ **MILE 0-0.3: Tom McCall Point Trailhead to Viewpoint**
Start hiking from the **Tom McCall Point Trailhead** at the base of the turn-around at Rowena Crest, heading south through a meadow. If you're here May-June, this meadow offers your first glimpse of why McCall Point is among the most popular wildflower hikes in the Columbia River Gorge: purple lupine, shooting stars, and yellow balsamroot mingle in the grasses, splaying out in seemingly every direction. After 0.3 mile, stop at a **viewpoint** to your right for your first vistas of the eastern edge of the Columbia River Gorge; good as these views are, they only improve from here.

▶ **MILE 0.3-1.9: Viewpoint to McCall Point Summit**
Gently ascending, you'll briefly enter an oak grove in 0.7 mile. You might catch a glimpse here of a western meadowlark, Oregon's state bird. In another 0.2 mile, you'll climb a short stone staircase through another oak

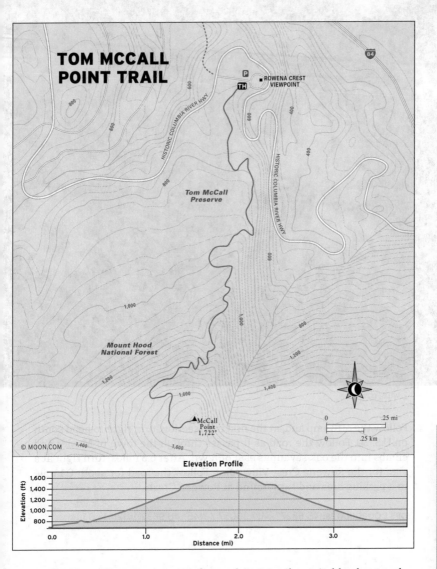

Elevation Profile

grove. The trail opens up soon after and, in 0.3 mile, switchbacks steeply through exposed hillsides. Mount Adams to the north, and wildflowers in every direction, soon come into view. Look for fields of prairie stars, foxglove, and more. You'll reach the **McCall Point summit** in 0.4 mile. The hillside meadow is awash in yellow balsamroot, clumps of purple grass widow, and red paintbrush, and affords gorgeous Gorge views including Mount Hood to the west and Mount Adams, Rowena Plateau, and the town of Lyle to the north.

Return the way you came.

DIRECTIONS

From Hood River, follow I-84 east for 5.5 miles. Take exit 69, following signs for the Historic Columbia River Highway (U.S. 30) and Mosier.

▲ WILDFLOWERS

Follow the off-ramp and, at the first intersection, turn right to head south on U.S. 30. Follow the road as it passes through the town of Mosier and climbs into the oak savannas east of town. After 6.6 miles, turn right at a sign for the Rowena Crest Viewpoint. Follow the road for about 0.1 mile to a parking area and turnaround at Rowena Crest.

GPS COORDINATES: 45.68272, -121.30057 / N45° 40.9632' W121° 18.0342'

BEST NEARBY BREWS
Full Sail Brewery (506 Columbia St., Hood River, 541/386-2247, http://fullsailbrewing.com, 11am-9pm daily) has been churning out quality craft beer in the heart of Hood River for more than 30 years. Full Sail prides itself on sustainable practices, and its pub patio delivers sweeping views of the Columbia River. From the trailhead, the 13-mile drive west takes 20 minutes via I-84.

NEARBY CAMPGROUNDS

NAME	DESCRIPTION	FACILITIES	SEASON	FEE
Ainsworth State Park	popular campground in the Columbia River Gorge	40 full-hookup sites, 6 walk-in tent sites, restrooms	March–October	$7-26
I-84, Cascade Locks, OR, 503/793-9885, www.oregonstateparks.org				
Beacon Rock State Park	4,464-acre park on the Columbia River with scenic trails	28 RV and tent sites, restrooms	year-round	$12-50
34841 Hwy. 14, Skamania, WA, 888/226-7688, www.washington.goingtocamp.com				
Skamania County Fairgrounds	fairgrounds that sometimes hosts events (call ahead)	60 RV and tent sites, restrooms	year-round	$20-25
710 SW Rock Creek Dr., Stevenson, WA, 509/427-3980, www.skamaniacounty.org				
Wyeth Campground	former Civilian Conservation Corps campsite	13 tent and RV sites, 3 group sites, restrooms	May–September	$20-30
Wyeth Rd., Cascade Locks, OR, 541/308-1700, www.fs.usda.gov				
Memaloose State Park	campground overlooks the Columbia River	43 full-hookup sites, 66 tent sites, restrooms	March–October	$19-31
I-84, Mosier, OR, 541/478-3008, www.oregonstateparks.org				
Maryhill State Park	park has more than 4,500 feet of waterfront on the Columbia River	70 RV and tent sites, restrooms	year-round	$12-50
50 U.S. 97, Goldendale, WA, 888/226-7688, www.washington.goingtocamp.com				

MOUNT HOOD

On a clear day, Mount Hood is nearly inescapable. The state's
tallest peak—at 11,250 feet—can be seen from Portland and
the Willamette Valley foothills, the Columbia River Gorge, and
the plains of eastern Oregon. Views of the mountain itself are
spectacular, but there's no better way to experience Mount
Hood's majesty than from its slopes. Its dozen glaciers remain
a defining feature and its forests unfurl in every direction like a
Christmas tree skirt. With panoramic views, colorful wildflower
displays, old-growth forest, lakes, rivers, and waterfalls, it's no
wonder Mount Hood is among the most popular destinations in
northwestern Oregon, an outdoor paradise popular even after
its bustling ski resorts have closed for the season.

▲ CROSSING THE SANDY RIVER ON THE RAMONA
FALLS TRAIL

▲ LOST LAKE BUTTE TRAIL

1 Lost Lake Butte
DISTANCE: 4.4 miles round-trip
DURATION: 2 hours
EFFORT: Easy/moderate

2 Vista Ridge to Owl Point
DISTANCE: 5.4 miles round-trip
DURATION: 2.5 hours
EFFORT: Easy/moderate

3 Ramona Falls
DISTANCE: 8.1 miles round-trip
DURATION: 4 hours
EFFORT: Moderate

4 Salmon River
DISTANCE: 8.2 miles round-trip
DURATION: 4.5 hours
EFFORT: Moderate

5 Elk Meadows
DISTANCE: 6.9 miles round-trip
DURATION: 3.5 hours
EFFORT: Easy/moderate

▾ SANDY RIVER AND MOUNT HOOD EN ROUTE TO RAMONA FALLS

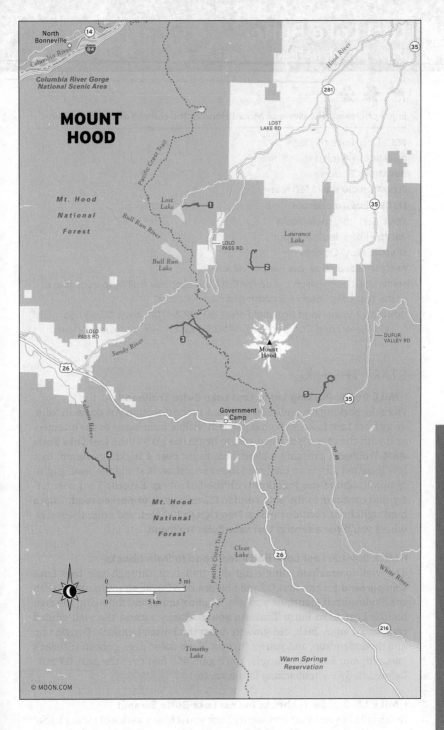

Lost Lake Butte
MOUNT HOOD NATIONAL FOREST

Enjoy photo-worthy views of Mount Hood at the summit of Lost Lake Butte.

BEST: Dog-Friendly Hikes
DISTANCE: 4.4 miles round-trip
DURATION: 2 hours
ELEVATION CHANGE: 1,180 feet
EFFORT: Easy/moderate
TRAIL: Dirt trail, roots, rocks
USERS: Hikers, leashed dogs
SEASON: May-October
PASSES/FEES: $9 day-use fee per vehicle
MAPS: USGS topographic map for Bull Run Lake; free trail map available at the Lost Lake Resort toll booth and general store
CONTACT: Mount Hood National Forest, 503/668-1700, www.fs.usda.gov; Lost Lake Resort and Campground, 541/386-6366, www.lostlakeresort.org

START THE HIKE

▶ **MILE 0-0.4: Parking Lot to Lost Lake Butte Trailhead**

From the parking lot, walk 300 feet back in the direction you drove in from, away from Lost Lake—which is partially visible from here—to the intersection with the Stop sign. Head east to begin the hike at the **Lost Lake Butte #616 Trailhead,** crossing a short boardwalk over a trickling stream. In a few hundred feet is an unsigned intersection; walk straight ahead, slightly uphill. Ignore the junction with the Lakeshore Express Trail soon after, and continue to the path's end in 0.2 mile at an **unmarked road.** Take a hard right here, continue past a Stop sign in 100 feet, and cross the street, where you'll see a second **Lost Lake Butte Trailhead.**

▶ **MILE 0.4-1.3: Lost Lake Butte Trailhead to Switchbacks**

The well-maintained, single-file dirt trail cuts through the **Lost Lake Campground** for the first 0.2 mile before arriving at an intersection with the Skyline Trail. Continue straight, heading uphill and following the sign for the Lost Lake Butte Trail. As you gradually ascend the well-graded trail, you'll enjoy lush, old-growth forest thick with hemlock, Douglas fir, and rhododendron, and you might spot black-tailed deer, gray and Steller's jays, chipmunks, and squirrels. You'll gain 450 feet over the next 0.7 mile before briefly switchbacking to the south.

▶ **MILE 1.3-2.2: Switchbacks to Lost Lake Butte Summit**

In 0.5 mile beyond that first switchback you'll hike a series of switchbacks toward the summit. The trail flattens out in 0.4 mile, after which you'll pass some stone steps—the remnants of a **fire lookout** that once stood

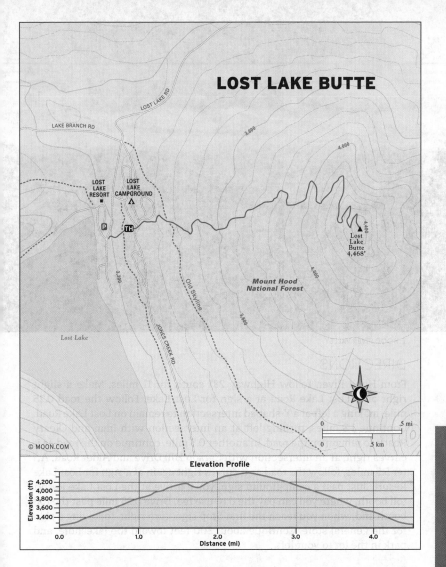

LOST LAKE BUTTE

LOST LAKE RD

LAKE BRANCH RD

3,600

4,000

LOST LAKE RESORT

LOST LAKE CAMPGROUND

P

TH

3,200

Old Skyline

JONES CREEK RD

Lost Lake

Mount Hood National Forest

4,000

4,000

Lost Lake Butte 4,468'

3,600

© MOON.COM

0 — .5 mi
0 — .5 km

Elevation Profile

Elevation (ft)
4,200
4,000
3,800
3,600
3,400

0.0   1.0   2.0   3.0   4.0
Distance (mi)

here—and arrive soon after at the **Lost Lake Butte summit,** in a clearing above the Hood River Valley. Mount Hood dominates the skyline to the southeast, towering over a patchwork of clear-cuts below, and Mount Adams rises over the Columbia River Gorge to the north. For a sense of Oregon's many ecosystems, look east toward the arid Columbia Plateau—a far cry from the verdant forest surrounding you.

Return the way you came.

If you have extra time, linger at **Lost Lake** before heading out. A level path hugs the lakeshore and boasts postcard-worthy views of Mount Hood. The Lost Lake Resort's general store sells snacks and souvenirs, and visitors can rent canoes, kayaks, and fishing poles. You'll also find all manner of wildflowers blooming near the lake well into June and July.

▲ HOOD RIVER VALLEY

DIRECTIONS

From Hood River, follow Highway 281 south for 11 miles. Make a slight right onto Lost Lake Road at a sign for Lost Lake. Follow the road 0.25 mile, making a left at a Y-shaped intersection to remain on Lost Lake Road. Continue 1.3 miles, turning left at an intersection with Imai and Oleary Roads to remain on the road. In another 0.5 mile, continue on the road as it curves right, at an intersection with Carson Hill Drive and Alder Road. After 5.5 miles, follow the road as it curves right again at a sign for Lost Lake Resort. Just past a campground sign, you'll arrive at the Lost Lake Resort toll booth, where you can pay the day-use fee. Drive 0.25 mile past the toll booth and, when you reach the first Stop sign, turn right, following a sign for the general store. Continue about 300 feet toward the lakeshore, and park in the lot to your left.

GPS COORDINATES: 45.49471, –121.81803 / N45° 29.6826′ W121° 49.0818′

BEST NEARBY BITES

Refuel with hearty fare at **Apple Valley BBQ** (4956 Baseline Dr., Parkdale, 541/352-3554, http://applevalleybbq.com, 11am–8pm Wed.-Sun.). The restaurant offers a full menu of barbecue classics, including a variety of sandwiches, ribs, and mac and cheese. From the trailhead, the 21-mile drive takes 45 minutes via Lost Lake Road and Highway 281.

MOUNT HOOD NATIONAL FOREST

Walk through wildflower meadows in the midst of a recovering forest, and enjoy unimpeded views of Mount Hood.

DISTANCE: 5.4 miles round-trip
DURATION: 2.5 hours
ELEVATION CHANGE: 580 feet
EFFORT: Easy/moderate
TRAIL: Dirt trail, rocks, roots
USERS: Hikers, leashed dogs
SEASON: July–October
PASSES/FEES: None; hikers must fill out and carry a self-issued wilderness permit (available along the trail)
MAPS: USGS topographic map for Mount Hood North
CONTACT: Mount Hood National Forest, 503/668-1700, www.fs.usda.gov

START THE HIKE

▶ **MILE 0-1.4: Vista Ridge Trailhead to Spur Trail**
The clearly marked **Vista Ridge Trail** starts at the southeastern edge of the parking lot. After hiking 0.2 mile through a fir forest, you'll arrive at a **wilderness permit station;** fill out a form and continue on the trail, which gets steep at times along this stretch. At a junction in another 0.25 mile, turn left to head north on the narrowing Vista Ridge Trail. It begins to flatten out as you walk through a recovering forest of fir and pine trees; here you'll see evidence of the Dollar Lake Fire, which burned more than 6,000 acres on Mount Hood's northern slopes in 2011 following a lightning strike. In 0.9 mile beyond the junction, you'll see a **spur trail** to your right; make the quick detour for your first view of Mount Hood.

▶ **MILE 1.4-2.4: Spur Trail to The Rockpile**
Back on the main trail, as you follow the ridgeline, you'll notice a handful of similar spurs; each is worth the quick side trip for improving views of Oregon's tallest peak. You'll arrive at a clearing after 0.6 mile; as the snow melts in summer, this meadow fills with purple lupine, red paintbrush, and other wildflowers. In 0.25 mile is an unsigned junction; continue straight for about 0.1 mile. A couple hundred feet on is another unsigned junction, denoted by a small rock cairn. Make a right, and walk 300 feet to **The Rockpile;** this talus slope is surrounded by huckleberry bushes at the height of summer and offers panoramic views of Mount Hood.

▶ **MILE 2.4-2.75: The Rockpile to Owl Point**

Return to the junction, and turn right to continue on the Vista Ridge Trail, walking through the forest of hemlock and subalpine fir. In 0.2 mile, turn right at the sign for Owl Point. Follow the trail for 0.15 mile to arrive at **Owl Point,** another jumble of talus and scree, boasting dramatic views of Mount Hood and the Hood River Valley; the best views come after careful climbing up the boulder piles before you. Hikers can sign a trail register stored in an old ammo box.

▶ **MILE 2.75-5.4: Owl Point to Vista Ridge Trailhead**

Head back to the junction, and return on the Vista Ridge Trail the way you came.

MOUNT HOOD ▶

DIRECTIONS

From Hood River, follow Highway 281 south for 11 miles. Make a slight right onto Lost Lake Road at a sign for Lost Lake. Follow the road 0.25 mile, making a left at a Y-shaped intersection to remain on Lost Lake Road. Continue 1.3 miles, turning left at an intersection with Imai and Oleary Roads to remain on the road. In another 0.5 mile, follow the road as it curves to the right, at an intersection with Carson Hill Drive and Alder Road. After 6 miles, make a left onto Forest Road 18, following a sign for Lolo Pass; the road becomes Forest Road 16 at an intersection with Lolo Pass Road. After 4 miles, turn left to remain on Forest Road 16 at an intersection with Stump Creek Road. Continue on, uphill, for 4.5 miles, then make a hard right onto Forest Road 1650 at the intersection. Follow the gravel road uphill for 3.5 miles; the parking area is at the end of the road.

GPS COORDINATES: 45.44292, -121.72913 / N45° 26.5752' W121° 43.7478'

BEST NEARBY BREWS

Wide-open views of Mount Hood are just the start at **Solera Brewery** (4945 Baseline Dr., Parkdale, 541/352-5500, www.solerabrewery. com, typically noon-10pm Thurs.-Tues. though hours can vary seasonally). Solera also offers a variety of small-batch beers and a solid line-up of barrel-aged offerings. From the trailhead, the 25.5-mile drive northeast takes 55 minutes via Lost Lake Road and Highway 281.

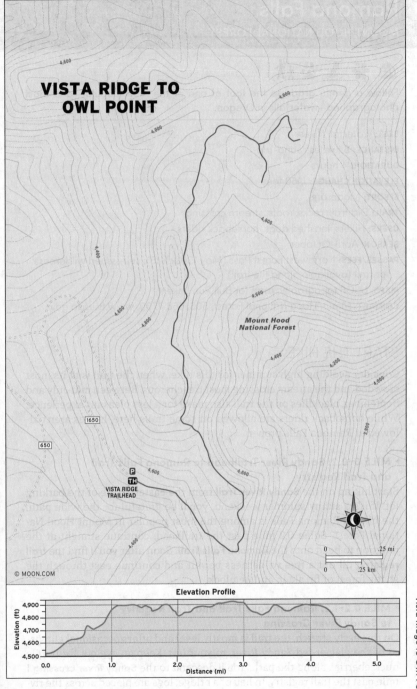

VISTA RIDGE TO
OWL POINT

4,600

4,800

4,400

4,800

4,800

*Mount Hood
National Forest*

4,600

4,400

4,200

4,000

4,600

1650

650

P

TH

VISTA RIDGE
TRAILHEAD

4,600

4,600

4,000

4,400

0   .25 mi

0   .25 km

© MOON.COM

Elevation Profile

Follow a gentle grade to the foot of one of the most popular—and most photographed—waterfalls in Oregon.

BEST: Waterfall Hikes
DISTANCE: 8.1 miles round-trip
DURATION: 4 hours
ELEVATION CHANGE: 1,180 feet
EFFORT: Moderate
TRAIL: Dirt trail, rocks, roots, stream crossing
USERS: Hikers, leashed dogs, horseback riders
SEASON: April–October
PASSES/FEES: Northwest Forest Pass (May 15–Oct. 15); self-issued wilderness permit (available along the trail)
MAPS: USGS topographic map for Bull Run Lake
CONTACT: Mount Hood National Forest, 503/668-1700, www.fs.usda.gov

START THE HIKE

Consider avoiding high summer for this hike, when the trail is at its most crowded and the stream crossing most treacherous. Between mid-July and September, blackflies on the trail also make for a less pleasant experience. While horseback riders are allowed on some trails here, horses aren't allowed at Ramona Falls proper.

▶ MILE 0–0.2: Sandy River Trailhead to Ramona Falls Trail and Trail Registry

Start hiking on the **Sandy River Trail** from the eastern edge of the parking lot. If it's a sunny summer weekend, you'll be grateful for the wide path; the hike to Ramona Falls is among the most popular in Mount Hood National Forest. Some 0.2 mile past the trailhead, continue straight at the junction to head onto the **Ramona Falls Trail.** Soon after you'll find the **trail registry;** fill out a free wilderness permit and continue east through the shady forest of fir, alder, and hemlock.

▶ MILE 0.2–1.2: Ramona Falls Trail and Trail Registry to Sandy River Crossing

On this early stretch, the trail is mostly level and offers occasional glimpses of the glacier-fed Sandy River, to your left. Keep an eye out for purple huckleberries along the path. You'll descend to the **Sandy River crossing** 1 mile past the trail registry. In lieu of a bridge, logs are placed across the river each summer to facilitate safe travels; hikers have died crossing this river, so be cautious, especially early in the summer and late in the day, when currents are strongest and swiftest.

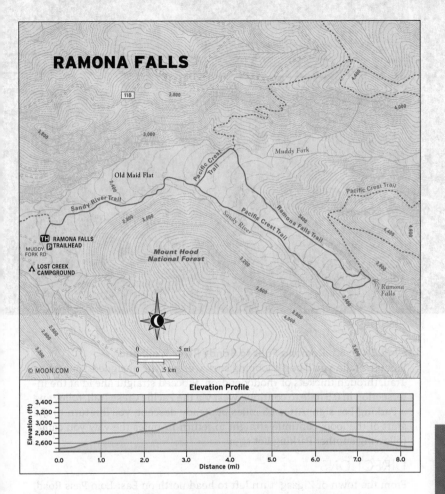

RAMONA FALLS

Elevation Profile

▶ **MILE 1.2–1.7: Sandy River Crossing to Pacific Crest Trail**

In 0.5 mile, you'll arrive at a junction; you could continue straight out-and-back for the quickest, most direct route to the waterfall—shaving 0.6 mile off the total mileage—but head left onto the **Pacific Crest Trail** for the more scenic, gradual route and to start a loop. (Horseback riders should continue straight, as horses aren't allowed on portions of the trail to the left.)

▶ **MILE 1.7–4.3: Pacific Crest Trail to Ramona Falls**

In 0.6 mile, head right at the T-shaped junction to follow the **Ramona Falls Trail** through thick pine forest. This stretch is sandy and less shady than previous sections on this hike, until the trail meets up with **Ramona Creek** in another 0.7 mile. From here, the trail parallels the creek through thick fir forest before arriving in another gently graded 1.3 miles at the 120-foot-tall **Ramona Falls,** impressive as it cascades over columns of basalt.

▲ RAMONA FALLS

▶ MILE 4.3–8.1: Ramona Falls to Sandy River Trailhead

From the falls, you'll begin looping back west via the unsigned Timberline Trail, through thickets of rhododendron. Proceed straight ahead at the intersection in 0.5 mile to continue west via the Pacific Crest Trail, following a Parking Lot sign. After 1.6 miles of steady descent, you'll return to the start of the loop; continue straight to return 1.7 miles the way you came, following another Parking Lot sign.

DIRECTIONS

From the town of Zigzag, turn left to head north on East Lolo Pass Road. Follow the road for 4.2 miles, and turn right onto paved Forest Road 1825, following the Trailheads and Campgrounds sign. After 0.7 mile, head right onto the Sandy River bridge. Continue 1.7 miles, and fork left onto Forest Road 100, following the Ramona Falls sign. The road ends, after a bumpy 0.4 mile, in a large gravel parking area at the end of the road.

GPS COORDINATES: 45.38676, –121.8318 / N45° 23.2056' W121° 49.908'

BEST NEARBY BREWS

Mt. Hood Brewing Co. (87304 E. Government Camp Loop, Government Camp, 503/272-3172, http://mthoodbrewing.com, 11am–10pm daily) serves IPAs, porters, stouts, and more, brewed from pure glacial water. From the trailhead, the 17.5-mile drive south takes 25 minutes via East Lolo Pass Road and Highway 26.

Salmon River

MOUNT HOOD NATIONAL FOREST

❀ 🐾 🚶

On this hike along the Salmon River, you'll find old-growth forest, popular swimming holes (bring a swimsuit), and expansive canyon views.

DISTANCE: 8.2 miles round-trip
DURATION: 4.5 hours
ELEVATION CHANGE: 1,280 feet
EFFORT: Moderate
TRAIL: Dirt trail, rocks, roots
USERS: Hikers, leashed dogs
SEASON: April-November
PASSES/FEES: Northwest Forest Pass (May 15-Oct. 15)
MAPS: USGS topographic map for Rhododendron
CONTACT: Mount Hood National Forest, 503/668-1700, www.fs.usda.gov

START THE HIKE

▸ **MILE 0-0.4: Salmon River Trailhead to Pools**
Start at the **Salmon River Trailhead** on the east side of the road near the parking areas, hiking alongside the Salmon River. After 0.4 mile of gentle climbing through old-growth Douglas fir—you'll spend most of this hike under thick canopy—you'll pass a series of small, sun-drenched **pools** that are nice for a dip in summer. This is also a popular stretch with anglers fishing for salmon and trout.

▸ **MILE 0.4-2: Pools to Rolling Riffle Campground**
Back in the forest, you'll almost imperceptibly ascend through the forest of thick Douglas firs— some with a diameter of 6-8 feet—and alongside nurse logs, downed trees that provide nutrients for plants and habitats for small wildlife. Keep an eye out for white, three-petaled trillium blooms April-May, as well as

SALMON RIVER ▸

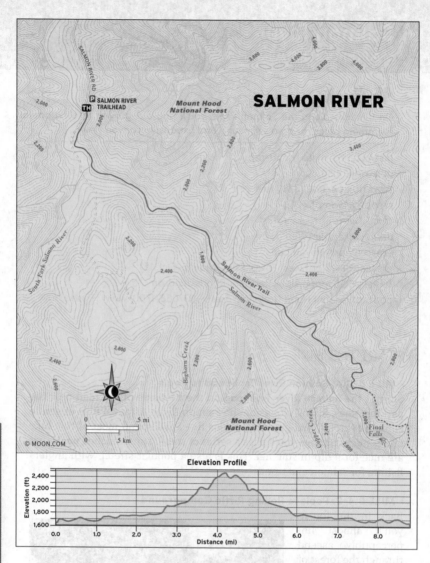

SALMON RIVER

Elevation Profile

huckleberries, which are ripe for picking and snacking June-August. Some 1.2 miles past the pools, you'll pass a few backcountry campsites and, in another 0.4 mile, a few more—these are popularly known as the **Rolling Riffle Campground.** Watch for short **spur trails** along this stretch, off to your right, which lead to the riverbank. If you're hiking with children, the campground makes a good turnaround point.

▸ **MILE 2-4.1: Rolling Riffle Campground to Salmon River Canyon Viewpoint**

The trail leaves the riverside 0.5 mile past the campground. Here you'll begin ascending in earnest, gaining more than 600 feet—sometimes gradually, sometimes steeply—before arriving in 1.5 miles at an unmarked 0.1-mile **spur trail.** Turn left onto the spur to ascend briefly, and then make an

MOUNT HOOD

Salmon River

▲ SALMON RIVER CANYON VIEWPOINT

immediate right; soon after, you'll arrive at the **Salmon River Canyon view-point,** indicated by a sign that says, "Camp Under Trees Not in Meadows." The meadow boasts sweeping views of the surrounding slopes, covered in old-growth Douglas fir. The trail continues on, but this viewpoint makes a fine turnaround point.

Return the way you came.

DIRECTIONS

From the town of Sandy, follow U.S. 26 east for 17 miles. Just past a sign for the Zigzag Ranger Station, turn right to head south on East Salmon River Road for 5 miles. The parking area—on both sides of the road—comes just before a bridge.

GPS COORDINATES: 45.27786, –121.93974 / N45° 16.6716' W121° 56.3844'

BEST NEARBY BITES

Refuel—or pick something up to go for your hike—at **Wraptitude** (67441 E. U.S. 26, Welches, 503/622-0893, http://wraptitude.com, 8am-8pm Mon.-Thurs., 7am-9pm Fri.-Sat.). The café specializes in wraps but also serves burgers, sandwiches, breakfast burritos, and salads. From the trailhead, the 6.5-mile drive northwest takes 15 minutes via East Salmon River Road and U.S. 26.

One of the best wildflower hikes on Mount Hood also delivers impressive views of Oregon's tallest peak.

BEST: Wildflower Hikes
DISTANCE: 6.9 miles round-trip
DURATION: 3.5 hours
ELEVATION CHANGE: 1,090 feet
EFFORT: Easy/moderate
TRAIL: Dirt trail, rocks, roots, stream crossings
USERS: Hikers, leashed dogs, horseback riders
SEASON: June-October
PASSES/FEES: Northwest Forest Pass (May 15–Oct. 15)
MAPS: USGS topographic map for Mount Hood South
CONTACT: Mount Hood National Forest, 503/668-1700, www.fs.usda.gov

START THE HIKE

▶ **MILE 0-1.4: Elk Meadows and Sahalie Falls Trailhead to Newton Creek Crossing**

Start hiking from the **Elk Meadows and Sahalie Falls Trailhead** at the north-western edge of the parking area to follow the **Sahalie Falls Trail,** which starts out mostly flat and heads through a hemlock and Douglas fir forest, with ripe huckleberries lining the way in summer. You'll arrive at a junction in 0.5 mile; continue straight onto the **Elk Meadows Trail,** crossing a footbridge over Clark Creek in 0.2 mile. Some 0.6 mile past Clark Creek is an intersection with the Newton Creek Trail, but continue straight to remain on the Elk Meadows Trail. In 0.1 mile you'll arrive at the **Newton Creek crossing;** logs are placed across the creek each summer, though the exact location varies year to year. Take care crossing, especially early in the season and late in the day, when currents are swifter.

▶ **MILE 1.4-2.8: Newton Creek Crossing to Perimeter Trail**

After the crossing, you'll hike through rocks and bushes before ascending a series of eight switchbacks over 1 mile, gaining 520 feet over this some-times steep stretch. Continue straight ahead on the Elk Meadows Trail at a junction 0.2 mile past the final switchback. In another 0.2 mile you'll reach another intersection with the **Perimeter Trail.**

▶ **MILE 2.8-3.5: Perimeter Trail to Elk Meadows Shelter**

Turn left onto the Perimeter Trail for a clockwise loop around Elk Mead-ows. The meadows are mostly obscured by the Douglas fir and noble fir forest, but you'll catch the occasional glimpse. In 0.3 mile you'll come to

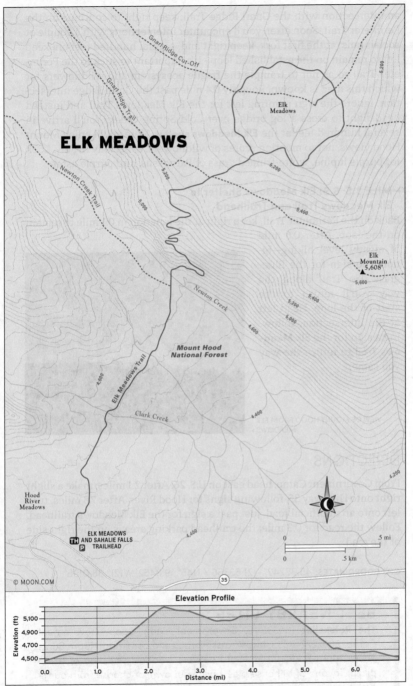

ELK MEADOWS

Elk Meadows

Gnarl Ridge Cut-Off

Gnarl Ridge Trail

Newton Creek Trail

Elk
Meadows

Elk
Mountain
5,608'

Newton Creek

Mount Hood
National Forest

Elk Meadows Trail

Clark Creek

Hood
River
Meadows

ELK MEADOWS
AND SAHALIE FALLS
TRAILHEAD

© MOON.COM

0 .5 mi

0 .5 km

35

Elevation Profile

Elevation (ft)

5,100
4,900
4,700
4,500

0.0   1.0   2.0   3.0   4.0   5.0   6.0

Distance (mi)

an intersection with the Gnarl Ridge Trail; keep right to continue on the Perimeter Trail. Soon after, you'll encounter intersections with a couple of social trails; at the first fork, keep right and, several hundred feet on, keep left to remain on the established loop—it's important to stick to the Perimeter Trail so as not to trample the fragile ecosystem and wildflowers for which this area is known. Roughly 0.4 mile past the Gnarl Ridge intersection, ignore the sign pointing left for the Elk Meadows Trail and instead head right to cross a log bridge over Cold Spring Creek. You'll arrive in several hundred feet at the **Elk Meadows shelter.** Here you'll enjoy Mount Hood views, not to mention scores of wildflowers, especially in July. Look for purple lupine, white-fringed grass of Parnassus, and purple aster.

▸ **MILE 3.5–6.9: Elk Meadows Shelter to Elk Meadows Trail and Trailhead**

Back on the Perimeter Trail, keep right at the junction in 0.1 mile to remain on the loop. After 0.6 mile of mostly level hiking—ignore the sign for the Bluegrass Tie Trail along the way—you'll return to the start of the loop. Head left at the intersection, following a sign for the **Elk Meadows Trail** to return the way you came.

VIEW OF MOUNT HOOD FROM ELK MEADOWS ▸

DIRECTIONS

From Government Camp, head east on U.S. 26. After 2.1 miles, make a slight right onto Highway 35, following signs for Hood River. After 7.8 miles, turn left onto an unofficial road, just past a sign for the Elk Meadows trailhead. Follow the road for 0.3 mile; the trailhead parking area is on the right side of the road.

GPS COORDINATES: 45.32242, –121.63366 / N45° 19.3452' W121° 38.0196'

BEST NEARBY BITES

The Ratskeller (88335 E. Government Camp Loop, Government Camp, 503/272-3635, http://ratskellerpizzeria.com, 11am–10pm Sun.–Thurs., 11am–midnight Fri.–Sat.) delivers a robust selection of filling pizza. Try one of 10 house pies, build your own, or choose from burgers, salads, wraps, calzones, and sandwiches. From the trailhead, the 11-mile drive west takes 15 minutes via Highway 35 and U.S. 26.

NEARBY CAMPGROUNDS

NAME	DESCRIPTION	FACILITIES	SEASON	FEE
Tollgate Campground	quiet campground on the Zigzag River	13 tent sites, 1 group site, restrooms	May–September	$22-42
U.S. 26, Welches, 503/668-1700, www.fs.usda.gov				
Lost Creek Campground	located conveniently close to Ramona Falls and the Sandy River	5 walk-up tent sites, 8 tent and RV sites, 2 yurts, restrooms	May–September	$21-35
Forest Rd. 1825, Welches, 503/668-1700, www.fs.usda.gov				
Lost Lake Resort and Campground	popular campground at Lost Lake	148 tent and group sites, 19 yurts, 7 cabins, 1 A-frame cabin, restrooms	May–October	$29-32 tent sites, $55-65 group sites, $85-155 yurts, $88-240 cabins, $195-210 A-frame cabin
9900 Lost Lake Rd., Hood River, 541/386-6366, www.lostlakeresort.org				
Trillium Lake Campground	busy campground on Trillium Lake	52 tent and RV sites, 5 group sites, restrooms	May–September	$22-90
U.S. 26, Government Camp, 503/668-1700, www.fs.usda.gov				
Hoodview Campground	charming campground on the shore of Timothy Lake	43 tent and RV sites, restrooms	May–September	$20
Forest Rd. 57, Government Camp, 503/668-1700, www.fs.usda.gov				

OREGON COAST

The Oregon Coast is famed for its scenic, rugged terrain. Its 360 miles encompass windswept bluffs and capes, temperate rain forests, inlets and spits, waterfalls, moss-covered crags, and the peaks of the Oregon Coast Range. Hikers enjoy hundreds of miles of trails traversing the dramatic terrain, enjoying no shortage of panoramic views, from the Pacific Ocean to sweeping old-growth forests. Just be sure to bring a rain jacket—the Oregon Coast is also known for rain.

▲ CAPE SEBASTIAN

▲ HECETA HEAD LIGHTHOUSE

◀ CAPE PERPETUA

1 **Saddle Mountain**
DISTANCE: 5.9 miles round-trip
DURATION: 3.5 hours
EFFORT: Moderate

2 **Cape Falcon**
DISTANCE: 5.8 miles round-trip
DURATION: 3 hours
EFFORT: Easy/moderate

3 **Neahkahnie Mountain**
DISTANCE: 5.9 miles round-trip
DURATION: 3 hours
EFFORT: Easy/moderate

4 **Kings Mountain**
DISTANCE: 5.4 miles round-trip
DURATION: 3 hours
EFFORT: Moderate

5 **Cape Lookout**
DISTANCE: 5.5 miles round-trip
DURATION: 2.5 hours
EFFORT: Moderate

6 **Cascade Head**
DISTANCE: 5.2 miles round-trip
DURATION: 2.5 hours
EFFORT: Easy/moderate

7 **Drift Creek Falls**
DISTANCE: 4.4 miles round-trip
DURATION: 2 hours
EFFORT: Easy/moderate

8 **Cape Perpetua**
DISTANCE: 5.8 miles round-trip
DURATION: 2.5 hours
EFFORT: Easy/moderate

9 **Heceta Head to Hobbit Trail**
DISTANCE: 5 miles round-trip
DURATION: 2.5 hours
EFFORT: Easy/moderate

10 **Cape Sebastian**
DISTANCE: 3.8 miles round-trip
DURATION: 2 hours
EFFORT: Easy/moderate

11 **River View Trail to Redwood Nature Trail**
DISTANCE: 3.3 miles round-trip
DURATION: 1.5 hours
EFFORT: Easy/moderate

▾ SADDLE MOUNTAIN TRAIL

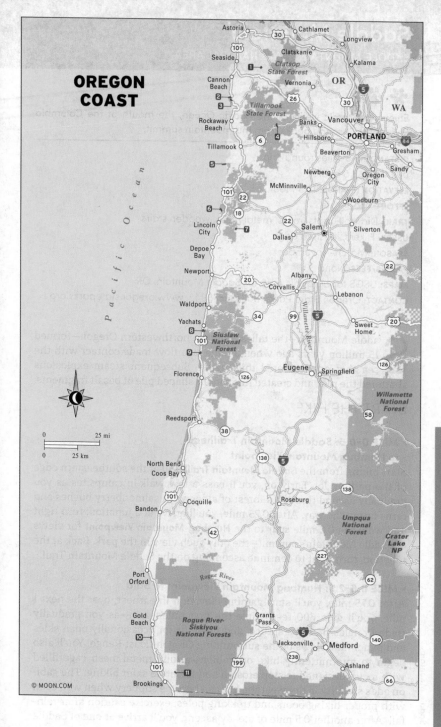

OREGON COAST

Astoria · **Cathlamet**
Clatskanie · **Longview**
Kalama
101 30
Seaside · Clatsop
State Forest
Cannon
Beach · **Vernonia**
26 **OR**
Tillamook **WA**
Rockaway State Forest
Beach · Banks **Vancouver**
6 · Hillsboro **PORTLAND**
Tillamook · Beaverton **Gresham**
34
Newberg Oregon **Sandy**
City
McMinnville Woodburn
101 22
Lincoln 18 22 **Salem** Silverton
City · Dallas
Depoe
Bay 22
Newport · Albany
20 Corvallis Lebanon
Waldport · 99
34 Sweet 20
Yachats Home
101 · Siuslaw 5
National 126
Forest
Florence · Eugene Springfield
126
Willamette
National
Forest
Reedsport · 58
38
138
North Bend 5
Coos Bay · Roseburg 138
101
Bandon · Coquille
42 Umpqua
National Crater
Forest Lake
227 NP
Port 62
Orford · Rogue River
140
Gold Rogue River- Grants
Beach · Siskiyou Pass
National Forests Jacksonville **Medford**
238
199 Ashland
10 66
11
Brookings

Pacific Ocean

0   25 mi
0   25 km

© MOON.COM

Enjoy panoramic views of the Pacific Ocean, the mouth of the Columbia River, and Cascade peaks from this mountain summit.

DISTANCE: 5.9 miles round-trip
DURATION: 3.5 hours
ELEVATION CHANGE: 1,430 feet
EFFORT: Moderate
TRAIL: Dirt trail, roots, rocks, metal mesh, wooden stairs
USERS: Hikers, leashed dogs
SEASON: March–November
PASSES/FEES: None
MAPS: USGS topographic map for Saddle Mountain, OR
CONTACT: Oregon State Parks, 503/368-5943, www.oregonstateparks.org

Saddle Mountain—the tallest point in northwestern Oregon—formed 15 million years ago when a large lava flow made contact with the sea that once covered this region. Subsequent steam explosions shattered the rock and created this saddle-shaped pile of basalt fragments.

START THE HIKE

▶ MILE 0–0.5: Saddle Mountain Trailhead to Humbug Mountain Viewpoint

Start hiking from the **Saddle Mountain Trailhead** at the southeastern edge of the parking lot. Early on, you'll pass a few walk-in campsites as you gradually ascend through a forest of alder, with salmonberry bushes and ferns lining the way. After 0.25 mile, you'll arrive at a junction; turn right and walk the 0.2-mile **spur** to the **Humbug Mountain Viewpoint** for views of Saddle Mountain's summit—the only such view in the park. Back at the junction, turn right to continue ascending on the Saddle Mountain Trail.

▶ MILE 0.5–2.9: Humbug Mountain Viewpoint to Bald

After 0.75 mile, you'll start gaining elevation in earnest; over the next 1 mile, you'll gain 600 feet—triple the first mile's gain—as you gradually trade Douglas fir, Sitka spruce, and noble fir for occasionally open skies and panoramic views of the surrounding Oregon Coast Range. You'll also begin to intermittently hike on gabion—a kind metal-mesh cage filled with rocks, designed to stop erosion and facilitate safer hiking. The gabion adds stability in dry weather, but can become slippery when wet, even with proper hiking boots and trekking poles; exercise caution after rainfall. After another 0.5 mile of steady ascent, you'll arrive at one of Saddle Mountain's famous grassy expanses, called **balds**. In spring, this area is covered in wildflowers; rosy plectritis and red paintbrush are just some of

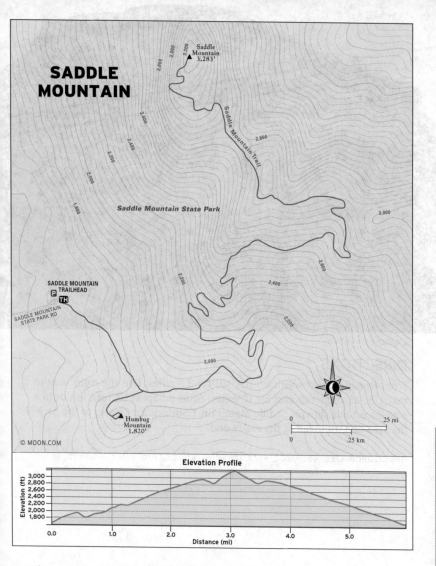

SADDLE MOUNTAIN

Saddle Mountain Trail

Saddle Mountain 3,283'

Saddle Mountain State Park

SADDLE MOUNTAIN TRAILHEAD
P
TH

SADDLE MOUNTAIN STATE PARK RD

Humbug Mountain 1,820'

© MOON.COM

0 .25 mi
0 .25 km

Elevation Profile

the varieties you'll encounter well into June-July. Note that picking wildflowers is prohibited.

▶ MILE 2.9–3.2: Bald to Saddle Mountain Summit

After descending briefly to cross the saddle—from which the mountain gets its name—you'll make your final push, mostly up steep stretches of gabion; the last 0.25 mile to the **Saddle Mountain summit** entails a rugged 275-foot ascent. A few cables offer support, but this stretch becomes especially treacherous after rainfall. Still, the summit views are worth it: to the west is the Pacific Ocean; to the north the mouth of the Columbia River, Youngs Bay, and Astoria; and to the east Cascade peaks in both Oregon and Washington.

Return the way you came.

▲ SADDLE MOUNTAIN

DIRECTIONS

From Seaside, head south on U.S. 101 for 3.8 miles. Use the right lane to take U.S. 26 and head east for 10 miles. After milepost 10, turn left onto a paved road at a sign for Saddle Mountain. Continue for 7 miles to the parking area and trailhead at the road's end.

GPS COORDINATES: 45.96288, -123.68998 / N45° 57.7728' W123° 41.3988'

BEST NEARBY BITES

Unwind with hearty fare and large portions at **Camp 18 Restaurant** (42362 U.S. 26, Elsie, 503/755-1818, www.camp18restaurant.com, 8am-8pm daily). Famous for serving massive cinnamon rolls, Camp 18 dishes out classic comfort food in a wood cabin-like interior. From the trailhead, the 15-mile drive east takes 25 minutes via U.S. 26.

Cape Falcon
OSWALD WEST STATE PARK

Head to the top of Cape Falcon for views of nearby Neahkahnie Mountain and the Pacific Ocean, and walk through coastal rain forest to the beach.

BEST: Winter Hikes, Dog-Friendly Hikes
DISTANCE: 5.8 miles round-trip
DURATION: 3 hours
ELEVATION CHANGE: 640 feet
EFFORT: Easy/moderate
TRAIL: Dirt trail, paved path, rocks, roots, stream crossings
USERS: Hikers, leashed dogs
SEASON: Year-round
PASSES/FEES: None
MAPS: USGS topographic map for Arch Cape
CONTACT: Oregon State Parks, 503/368-3575, www.oregonstateparks.org

START THE HIKE

▶ **MILE 0-2: Cape Falcon Trailhead to Upper Blumenthal Falls**
Start hiking from the **Cape Falcon Trailhead** at the western edge of the parking area, through a forest of Douglas fir and Sitka spruce. Short Sand Creek is to your left but mostly out of sight. After 0.5 mile of mostly level hiking, you'll arrive at a T-junction; to the left, a short trail takes you down to the beach and a day-use picnic area. Ignore this spur for now, and turn right, following a sign for Cape Falcon, through a dense forest of western red cedar, western hemlock, and more Sitka spruce. In 0.3 mile, cross a small stream via logs and stones, then follow the trail as it twists and turns through the forest for another 1.1 mile, when you'll cross another stream via wooden footbridge. Keep an eye out in 350 feet for a 25-foot **spur trail** to your left, and follow it for views of **Upper Blumenthal Falls.**

▶ **MILE 2-2.7: Upper Blumenthal Falls to Cape Falcon Viewpoint**
Back on the main trail, you'll gradually ascend for the next 0.4 mile, through usually muddy stretches of trail and over webs of exposed roots, before arriving at an unsigned intersection with the Oregon Coast Trail. Take a left to continue west on the Cape Falcon Trail toward the headland, hiking through a veritable hallway of salal, a native shrub that can grow six feet or taller. After 0.3 mile, you'll arrive at a grassy, exposed **viewpoint** atop a 200-foot cliff on the southern face of **Cape Falcon**. This popular spot offers panoramic views of Neahkahnie Mountain, Short Sand Beach, Smugglers Cove—an inlet bordered by Neahkahnie Mountain to the south and Cape Falcon to the north—and the Pacific Ocean. Keep an

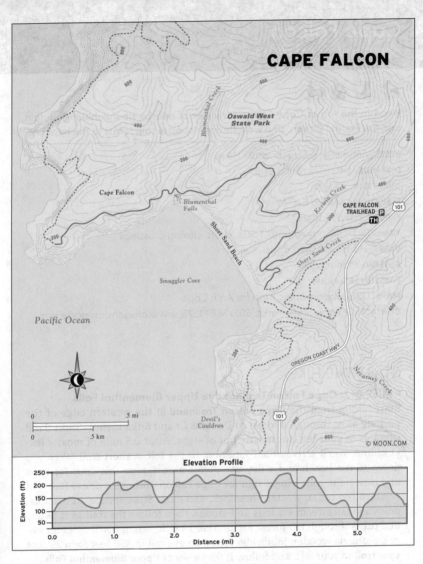

CAPE FALCON

Oswald West State Park

Blumenthal Creek

Cape Falcon

Blumenthal Falls

Short Sand Beach

Smuggler Cove

Pacific Ocean

Kerwin Creek

CAPE FALCON TRAILHEAD

101

Short Sand Creek

Devil's Cauldron

OREGON COAST HWY

Nearney Creek

101

0   .5 mi

0   .5 km

© MOON.COM

Elevation Profile

Elevation (ft)

Distance (mi)

eye out for seals and sea lions on the rocks below, and watch for migrating gray whales offshore, especially in spring and winter.

▶ **MILE 2.7–5.1: Cape Falcon Viewpoint to Short Sand Beach**
Return the way you came, but at the first (now final) junction, continue straight for an 0.2-mile **spur** down to **Short Sand Beach,** popular with picnickers, surfers, and dogs—they're allowed to be off-leash on the beach.

▶ **MILE 5.1–5.8: Short Sand Beach to Cape Falcon Trailhead**
Back at the junction, continue east on the Cape Falcon Trail to return the way you came.

▲ TAKING IN THE VIEW FROM THE TRAIL ALONG CAPE FALCON

DIRECTIONS

From Cannon Beach, head south on U.S. 101 for 9.5 miles. Turn right into the parking area at milepost 39, following a sign for the Cape Falcon Trailhead. Additional parking is available along the other side of the highway just a bit farther south along U.S. 101; take care when crossing the highway.

GPS COORDINATES: 45.76319, –123.95617 / N45° 45.7914' W123° 57.3702'

BEST NEARBY BREWS

Celebrate Oregon's public beaches with a pint at **Public Coast Brewing Co.** (264 3rd St., Cannon Beach, 503/436-0285, http://public-coastbrewing.com, noon-9pm Sun.-Thurs., noon-10pm Fri.-Sat. summer, call for hours fall-spring), where several of the brewery's craft beers are named in honor of the state's coastline. It also offers a food menu rife with fresh, seasonal ingredients. From the trailhead, the 11-mile drive north takes 20 minutes via U.S. 101.

Cape Falcon

Enjoy sweeping coastal views from atop this 1,700-foot mountain.

DISTANCE: 5.9 miles round-trip
DURATION: 3 hours
ELEVATION CHANGE: 1,110 feet
EFFORT: Easy/moderate
TRAIL: Dirt trail, roots, rocks, rock scramble
USERS: Hikers, leashed dogs
SEASON: Year-round
PASSES/FEES: None
MAPS: USGS topographic map for Nehalem
CONTACT: Oregon State Parks, 503/368-3575, www.oregonstateparks.org

Neahkahnie Mountain was formed in the wake of Columbia River basalt lava flows some 15 million years ago and has long been a spiritually important place for the Tillamook tribe of Native Americans. Roughly translated, "Neahkahnie" means "place of the creator." The mountain is also rumored to be home to buried treasure, care of two shipwrecked sailors in the 1600s. Treasure hunters have spent the last couple hundred years searching for the loot, to no avail.

START THE HIKE

▶ **MILE 0-0.3: North Neahkahnie Mountain Trailhead to Cape Falcon and Smugglers Cove Views**

Head to the southern edge of the parking area and cross U.S. 101 to find the **North Neahkahnie Mountain Trailhead.** You'll begin ascending immediately through an open field of thick salal bushes and ferns via the **Oregon Coast Trail;** this hike takes you along a short stretch of this trail, which parallels the entire Oregon Coast. Views of Cape Falcon and Smugglers Cove open up after 0.3 mile.

FOREST ON NEAHKAHNIE MOUNTAIN ▶

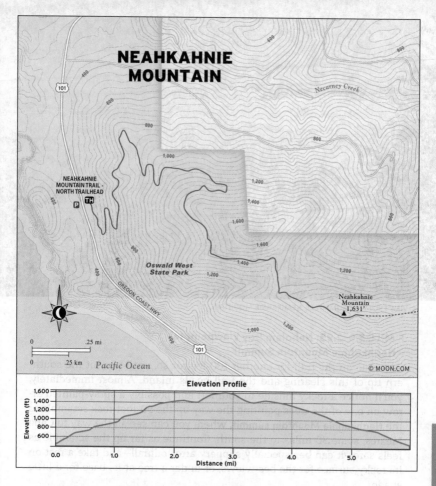

NEAHKAHNIE
MOUNTAIN

Necarney Creek

NEAHKAHNIE
MOUNTAIN TRAIL -
NORTH TRAILHEAD

Oswald West
State Park

OREGON COAST HWY

Neahkahnie
Mountain
1,631'

0   .25 mi
0   .25 km   Pacific Ocean

© MOON.COM

Elevation Profile

▶ **MILE 0.3-2.9: Cape Falcon and Smugglers
Cove Views to Nehalem Bay Viewpoint**
Continue to ascend gradually through Sitka spruce thickets, salal-heavy
stretches, tall ferns, and a western red cedar and western hemlock forest. In spring, you might also catch blooms of candy flower, Columbia
windflower, and trillium. Exposed roots, moss-covered rocks, and soft dirt
along the trail's edge can create slippery conditions, especially if it has just
rained—which it often has on the Oregon Coast—so take care. In 1.25 miles,
the trail levels out—you've gained about 1,000 feet in elevation so far—and
starts winding toward Neahkahnie Mountain's southern face through a
thick forest with little undergrowth. After another 1.3 miles, you'll arrive
at a **viewpoint** just below Saddle Mountain's southern summit. From this
vantage, you can gaze south into Nehalem Bay and the coastal town of
Manzanita.

▲ VIEW FROM THE SUMMIT OF NEAHKAHNIE MOUNTAIN

▶ **MILE 2.9–2.95: Nehalem Bay Viewpoint to Neahkahnie Mountain Summit**

Continue on the trail for another 100 feet or so, until you hit the southern tip of this clearing and the trail heads inland. Almost immediately, you'll notice a rocky hillside to your left and possibly a spray-painted arrow on one of the trees pointing the way up the 50-foot rock scramble to the **Neahkahnie Mountain summit,** where you can see all the way to Cape Meares, some 30 miles to the south. Continue as far up the scramble as feels safe—it can be especially slippery after rainfall—and take a rest on its rocky surface for the best views, or under a tree at its base for a little shade.

Return the way you came.

DIRECTIONS

From Cannon Beach, head south on U.S. 101 for 10.8 miles. Turn right into the Neahkahnie Mountain gravel parking area past milepost 40. Take care crossing the highway to the trailhead.

GPS COORDINATES: 45.74759, –123.96185 / N45° 44.8554' W123° 57.711'

BEST NEARBY BITES

Start your day right with a meal at **Yolk** (503 Laneda Ave., Manzanita, 503/368-9655, www.yolkmanzanita.com, 8am-2pm Fri.-Mon.). The charming eatery dishes up crafty takes on classic breakfast and lunch fare, including French toast made with house-baked brioche and a grilled eggplant sandwich topped with roasted red peppers, grilled onions, feta, and basil.

Kings Mountain
TILLAMOOK STATE FOREST

On this thigh-busting hike you'll start gaining elevation early and won't stop until the summit—but you'll earn views encompassing everything from the ocean to the Cascades.

DISTANCE: 5.4 miles round-trip
DURATION: 3 hours
ELEVATION CHANGE: 2,370 feet
EFFORT: Moderate
TRAIL: Dirt trail, roots, rocks
USERS: Hikers, leashed dogs
SEASON: March–November
PASSES/FEES: None
MAPS: USGS topographic map for Jordan Creek, OR
CONTACT: Oregon Department of Forestry, 503/357-2191, www.oregon.gov/odf

START THE HIKE

Trekking poles and hiking shoes with proper tread are recommended for this trail.

▶ **MILE 0–0.2: Kings Mountain Trailhead to Wilson River Trail Junction**
Start hiking from the **Kings Mountain Trailhead** at the eastern edge of the parking lot, located near an informational signboard. Stroll along this mostly flat stretch through an alder forest flanked by four- and five-foot-high sword ferns for the first 0.2 mile, at which point you'll arrive at a four-way intersection with the Wilson River Trail. Continue straight ahead on the Kings Mountain Trail, following a pointer uphill for the Kings Mountain Summit. From here you'll start ascending and, save for a few short, flat-ish stretches, continue gaining until the summit. Enjoy the lush forest, rich with alder and Douglas fir; it wasn't always this verdant. Beginning in 1933, a series of wildfires scorched 335,000 acres of old-growth forest in the Oregon Coast Range. This inspired the planting of more than 70 million seedlings and, in 1973, the creation of Tillamook State Forest.

▶ **MILE 0.2–2.1: Wilson River Trail Junction to Viewpoint**
About 0.8 mile past the trail junction, the somewhat gentle grade steepens and becomes a real thigh-burner; you'll more than double the elevation you gained in the first mile between here and the summit. In another 1.1 miles, you'll reach a T-junction; follow the 50-foot spur to your left for a **viewpoint** with sweeping vistas of the northern Oregon Coast Range.

▶ **MILE 2.1-2.3: Viewpoint to Picnic Table**

Back at the junction, continue uphill on the occasionally rocky trail. You'll pass a **picnic table**—installed by a Boy Scout troop—in about 0.2 mile. Views are limited here, but this makes a fine lunch spot, and an ideal place to catch your breath before the final push. Just past the picnic table, you'll walk through open meadows, which are covered with paintbrush, bear grass, larkspur, phlox, and other wildflowers April-June.

▶ **MILE 2.3-2.7: Picnic Table to Kings Mountain Summit**

Over the final 0.4 mile, you'll gain 625 feet, traversing steep, rocky stretches and exposed roots on narrow sections. The **Kings Mountain Summit** is denoted by a sign and trail register. From here you can see Tillamook Bay and the Pacific Ocean to the west and Mount Hood and Mount Adams to the east. The trail continues on from here, but this is your turnaround point.

Return the way you came.

VIEW FROM KINGS MOUNTAIN ▶

DIRECTIONS

From Tillamook, head east on Highway 6 for 25 miles. Just past milepost 25, turn left into the parking lot at a sign for the Kings Mountain Trailhead.

GPS COORDINATES: 45.59712, -123.50629 / N45° 35.8272' W123° 30.3774'

BEST NEARBY BITES AND BREWS

Try some of the state's best wild ales at **de Garde Brewing** (114 Ivy Ave., Tillamook, 503/815-1635, www.degardebrewing.com, 3pm-7pm Thurs.-Fri., noon-7pm Sat., 11am-5pm Sun.), which has garnered acclaim and awards for using natural, open-air yeast strains in each recipe—no two batches taste exactly alike. From the trailhead, the 25-mile drive west takes 30 minutes via Highway 6. If you're more in the mood for a scoop of house-made ice cream—and cheese samples—head 2 miles north of the brewery on U.S. 101 to find the iconic **Tillamook Creamery** (4165 U.S. 101, Tillamook, 503/815-1300, www.tillamook.com, 8am-8pm daily early June-early Nov., 8am-6pm Mon.-Fri. and 8am-8pm Sat.-Sun. early Nov.-early June).

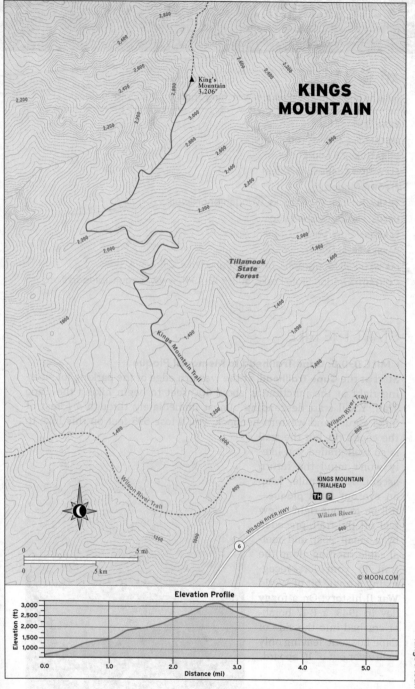

Elevation Profile

5

Cape Lookout

CAPE LOOKOUT STATE PARK

Hike to one of the best whale-watching spots on the Oregon Coast.

BEST: Spring Hikes
DISTANCE: 5.5 miles round-trip
DURATION: 2.5 hours
ELEVATION CHANGE: 1,370 feet
EFFORT: Moderate
TRAIL: Dirt trail, roots, rocks, wooden boardwalk
USERS: Hikers, leashed dogs
SEASON: Year-round
PASSES/FEES: None
MAPS: USGS topographic map for Sand Lake, OR
CONTACT: Oregon State Parks, 503/842-4981, www.oregonstateparks.org

START THE HIKE

▶ **MILE 0-0.6: Cape Trailhead to Memorial Plaque**
Start at the **Cape Trailhead,** at the western edge of the parking lot, veering right at the junction in about 100 feet to begin hiking the Cape Trail. You'll start descending almost immediately through a forest of Sitka spruce and western hemlock; you'll lose 595 feet on this hike to the cape's tip, but the trail is so well graded you likely won't mind the return ascent. At 0.6 mile, keep an eye out for a **plaque**—it'll be to your right a few feet off the trail, preceded by a small post and metal cable running along the trail to your left—recognizing a tragic bit of World War II history: On a foggy day in 1943, a B-17 bomber crashed into the side of Cape Lookout, leaving only 1 survivor out of 10 aboard.

CAPE LOOKOUT ▶

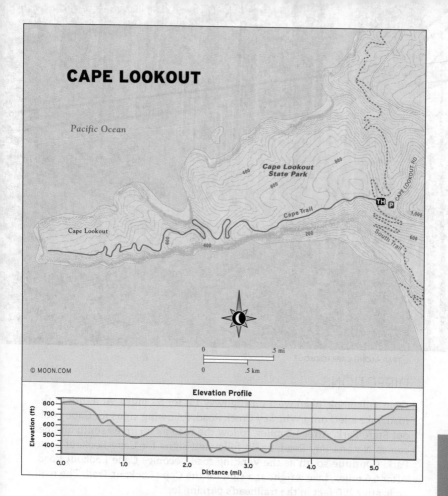

CAPE LOOKOUT

Pacific Ocean

Cape Lookout
State Park

Cape Trail

Cape Lookout

South Trail

© MOON.COM

0   .5 mi

0   .5 km

Elevation Profile

▶ MILE 0.6-1.4: Memorial Plaque to Boardwalks

In 0.4 mile, the trail switchbacks several times, offering occasional ocean views. When looking southward, keep an eye out for Cape Kiwanda and Haystack Rock near Pacific City. In another 0.4 mile, the trail becomes muddier and more slippery; short stretches of wooden boardwalk have been installed to lessen the impact, but it's tough to avoid tromping through ankle-high mud puddles here.

▶ MILE 1.4-2.75: Boardwalks to Cape Lookout

After another 1.1 miles, ocean views open up as you leave the forest for the final 0.25-mile stretch toward the **tip of Cape Lookout,** where you'll find a bench and 270-degree views. Take a seat and look for gray whales; they're most commonly spotted during their migration in winter and spring. On a clear day, you might also be able to see Tillamook Head, Cape Falcon, and Cascade Head.

Return the way you came.

▲ TRAIL ALONG CAPE LOOKOUT

DIRECTIONS

From Tillamook, head west on Highway 131 for 5.1 miles. At a fork in the road, take a left onto Whiskey Creek Road, following signs for Cape Lookout State Park. After 1.2 miles, follow the road as it curves south and becomes Netarts Bay Road, again following signs for Cape Lookout State Park. Continue south as the winding road becomes Cape Lookout Road. After 6.6 miles, take a right at a sign for the Cape Lookout Trail. The road ends after 250 feet in the trailhead's parking lot.

GPS COORDINATES: 45.34095, -123.9737/ N45° 20.457′ W123° 58.422′

BEST NEARBY BREWS

Sip a beer in the most scenic dining room in Oregon at **Pelican Brewing Company** (33180 Cape Kiwanda Dr., Pacific City, 503/965-7007, http://pelicanbrewing.com, 10:30am-10pm Sun.-Thurs., 10:30am-11pm Fri.-Sat.). It offers more than a dozen classic and seasonal styles, all served mere feet from the Pacific Ocean. From the trailhead, the 11-mile drive south takes 15 minutes via Cape Lookout Road and Sandlake Road.

OREGON COAST

Cape Lookout

6

Cascade Head
CASCADE HEAD PRESERVE

The hike to the summit of Cascade Head has it all: old-growth coastal rain forest, dazzling wildflowers, and panoramic ocean views.

DISTANCE: 5.2 miles round-trip

DURATION: 2.5 hours

ELEVATION CHANGE: 1,150 feet

EFFORT: Easy/moderate

TRAIL: Dirt trail, roots, rocks, wooden boardwalk, wooden steps, footbridges, gravel paths

USERS: Hikers

SEASON: Year-round

PASSES/FEES: None

MAPS: USGS topographic map for Neskowin; free trail map at the old trailhead 0.4 mile into the hike

CONTACT: The Nature Conservancy, 503/802-8100, www.nature.org

START THE HIKE

▶ **MILE 0-0.6: Cascade Head Trailhead to Old Cascade Head Trailhead**

Start hiking from the **Cascade Head Trailhead** next to the informational signboard at the northern edge of the parking lot. You'll immediately cross a small footbridge, the first of many, before entering a forest of ferns, salal, and Sitka spruce. After 350 feet, head straight to cross Three Rocks Road, and continue on past a sign for the Cascade Head Preserve. You'll briefly walk along wooden boardwalk. In 0.4 mile you'll emerge from the forest at a Y-shaped intersection with **Savage Road** and Ridge Road. Head left to cross Savage Road, then follow the gravel path on the road's shoulder to continue northward; several signs at this junction point the way. This stretch crosses private property, so stick to the path at all times. Follow Savage Road for 0.1 mile and, when it curves left, cross the road again, returning to the forest at a sign for the **old Cascade Head Trailhead,** where you can grab a trail map.

▶ **MILE 0.6-1.6: Old Cascade Head Trailhead to Meadow**

Cross a small footbridge and climb a set of wooden steps to begin ascending in earnest through a forest of old-growth spruce. In 0.2 mile, keep left at an unsigned, Y-shaped junction to remain on the trail. You'll gain steadily for 0.7 mile, at which point you'll arrive at a Cascade Head informational signboard and, 0.1 mile past it, a **meadow** with sweeping views of the ocean and, to the south, the mouth of the Salmon River. This is a good spot to apply sunscreen if you haven't done so already; the rest of the trail is almost entirely exposed.

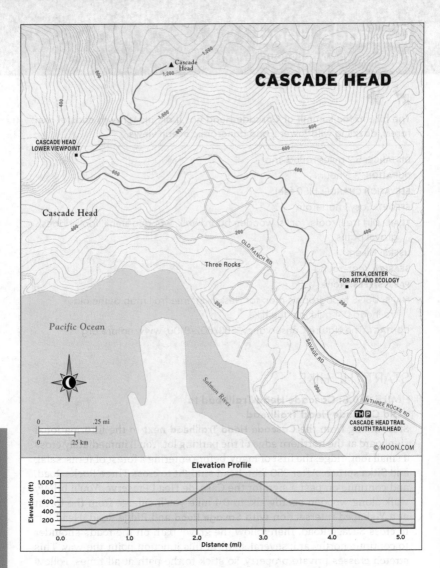

CASCADE HEAD

Cascade Head

CASCADE HEAD
LOWER VIEWPOINT

Cascade Head

Pacific Ocean

Three Rocks

OLD RANCH RD

SITKA CENTER
FOR ART AND ECOLOGY

SAVAGE RD

Salmon River

N THREE ROCKS RD

TH P
CASCADE HEAD TRAIL
SOUTH TRAILHEAD

0   .25 mi

0   .25 km

© MOON.COM

Elevation Profile

Elevation (ft): 1,000 / 800 / 600 / 400 / 200

Distance (mi): 0.0 / 1.0 / 2.0 / 3.0 / 4.0 / 5.0

▶ **MILE 1.6–2.6: Meadow to Cascade Head Viewpoint**

As you switchback up the southern face of Cascade Head, take care to keep
to the trail so as not to trample wildflowers, including foxglove, hairy check-
ermallow, Cascade Head catchfly, and the rare blue violet—a vital food source
for larvae of the Oregon silverspot butterfly, a federally threatened species
that emerges from its cocoon July-September. Continue ascending the uneven, occasionally rocky trail, gaining 670 feet over the final 1 mile, after
which you'll arrive at a **viewpoint,** indicated by an unsigned metal post. This
meadow is just below the summit of Cascade Head, but the views here are
the best on the headland. Keep an eye out for elk, deer, coyote, bald eagles,
owls, and various raptors. The trail continues on, connecting with a northern
trailhead in about a mile, but this is a fine spot to stop, relax, and have a snack.
Return the way you came.

▲ VIEW OF THE SALMON RIVER FROM CASCADE HEAD

DIRECTIONS

From Lincoln City, head north on U.S. 101 for 6.1 miles. Soon after milepost 104, take a sharp left onto North Three Rocks Road. Follow it for 2.3 miles. At the T-junction, turn left to remain on the road, following a sign for the Cascade Head Trailhead. In about 450 feet, just before a Dead End sign, turn left into the parking lot at Knight Park.

GPS COORDINATES: 45.04202, -123.99226 / N45° 2.5212' W123° 59.5356'

BEST NEARBY BREWS

Whether you're thirsting for beer, cider, mead, wine, or kombucha, you'll find it all at **Black Squid Beer House** (3001 SW U.S. 101, Lincoln City, 541/614-0733, www.blacksquidbeerhouse.com, 3pm-10pm Wed.-Thurs., 3pm-11pm Fri., 1pm-11pm Sat., 3pm-9pm Sun.). Black Squid prides itself on serving a mix of popular and hard-to-find ales and lagers from regional breweries; it offers a variety of styles, from sours and saisons to IPAs and stouts. From the trailhead, the 10-mile drive south takes 20 minutes via North Three Rocks Road and U.S. 101.

Traverse old-growth forest and a dramatic suspension bridge on your way to a waterfall.

BEST: Waterfall Hikes
DISTANCE: 4.4 miles round-trip
DURATION: 2 hours
ELEVATION CHANGE: 570 feet
EFFORT: Easy/moderate
TRAIL: Dirt trail, rocks, roots, suspension bridge
USERS: Hikers, leashed dogs
SEASON: Year-round
PASSES/FEES: Northwest Forest Pass
MAPS: USGS topographic map for Stott Mountain; U.S. Forest Service map for Drift Creek Falls, available online and at the trailhead
CONTACT: Siuslaw National Forest, 503/392-5100, www.fs.usda.gov

START THE HIKE

▶ **MILE 0-1.2: Drift Creek Falls Trailhead to Homer Creek**

Begin at the **Drift Creek Falls Trailhead,** at the eastern edge of the parking lot. You'll descend gradually through a forest of second-growth Douglas fir, vine maple, alder, ferns, and salal. Keep an eye out for white, three-petaled trillium if it's spring, and watch for nurse logs alongside the trail; you might see new shrubs, mushrooms, or trees sprouting from the decaying wood. After 0.8 mile, you'll arrive at a junction with the North Loop; head right to continue descending on the well-graded Drift Creek Falls Trail. In 0.4 mile, you'll arrive at **Homer Creek;** you wouldn't guess from this gentle trickle that most of the water cascading down Drift Creek Falls comes from this creek! Ignore another junction with the North Loop for now, crossing a bridge over the creek and continuing on the Drift Creek Falls Trail.

▶ **MILE 1.2-1.9: Homer Creek to Drift Creek Falls**

For the next 0.4 mile, the trail mostly follows Homer Creek through a forest of western red cedar and Sitka spruce, at which point you'll arrive at an impressive 240-foot **suspension bridge** spanning **Drift Creek.** From the bridge, Drift Creek Falls comes into view to your right. After crossing the bridge, descend the last 0.25 mile to the base of 75-foot-tall **Drift Creek Falls.** The falls' rock face broke away in 2010, revealing columnar basalt that formed 55 million years ago. Have a seat on one of the shaded rocks, gather energy for your return ascent, and admire the view.

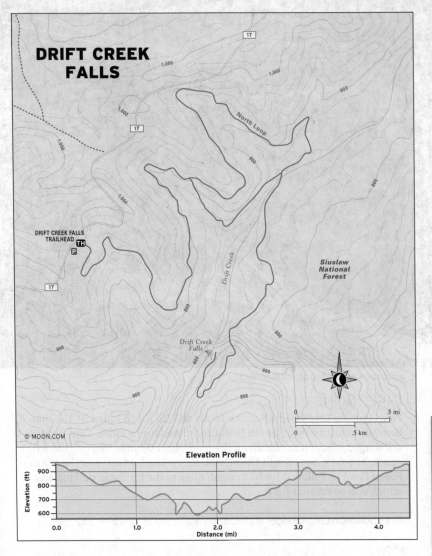

DRIFT CREEK
FALLS

DRIFT CREEK FALLS
TRAILHEAD

North Loop

Drift Creek

Siuslaw
National
Forest

Drift Creek
Falls

© MOON.COM

0   .5 mi

0   .5 km

Elevation Profile

▶ **MILE 1.9–4.4: Drift Creek Falls to Trailhead (via North Loop)**

Head back the way you came and cross Homer Creek. But instead of returning the way you came, on the Drift Creek Falls Trail, take a right onto the **North Loop.** You'll steadily ascend through a dense grove of old-growth Douglas fir, vine maple, huckleberry bushes, salmonberry, and ferns before reconnecting with the **Drift Creek Falls Trail** in 1 mile; turn right at the original junction you encountered on the trail, and head uphill to return to your vehicle.

▲ SUSPENSION BRIDGE AND DRIFT CREEK FALLS

DIRECTIONS

From Lincoln City, head 3.5 miles south on U.S. 101 to milepost 119, then turn left to head east on South Drift Creek Road for 1.6 miles. Turn right at a T-shaped junction to remain on the road. After 0.4 mile, head to the left, uphill, at a fork, onto South Drift Creek Camp Road, which soon becomes Forest Road 17. Follow it for 10.2 paved miles to the trailhead parking area, which will be on your right.

GPS COORDINATES: 44.93555, –123.85555 / N44° 56.133' W123° 51.333'

BEST NEARBY BREWS

Enjoy quality craft beer and creative pizzas along U.S. 101 at **Rusty Truck Brewing** (4649 U.S. 101, Lincoln City, 541/994-7729, http://rustytruckbrewing.com, brewpub 4pm-9:30pm Mon.-Thurs., 11am-11pm Sat.-Sun. summer; taproom 4pm-9:30pm Mon.-Thurs., 11am-11pm Fri.-Sat., and 11am-10pm Sun. summer, 4pm-9pm Fri., noon-10pm Sat., and noon-9pm Sun. fall-spring). The brewery regularly incorporates cherries, oranges, berries, and other fruits into classic recipes for flavorful twists. From the trailhead, the 13-mile drive west takes 30 minutes via Forest Road 17, South Drift Creek Camp Road, and U.S. 101.

OREGON COAST

Drift Creek Falls

Cape Perpetua
SIUSLAW NATIONAL FOREST

Link a series of scenic trails to experience some of the region's most fascinating natural features, including what the U.S. Forest Service calls "the best view on the Oregon Coast."

BEST: Brew Hikes
DISTANCE: 5.8 miles round-trip
DURATION: 2.5 hours
ELEVATION CHANGE: 1,020 feet
EFFORT: Easy/moderate
TRAIL: Dirt trail, paved path, wooden steps, roots, rocks
USERS: Hikers, leashed dogs
SEASON: Year-round
PASSES/FEES: Northwest Forest Pass
MAPS: USGS topographic map for Yachats; U.S. Forest Service map for Cape Perpetua, available online and at the Cape Perpetua Visitor Center
PARK HOURS: Sunrise-sunset daily
CONTACT: Siuslaw National Forest, 503/392-5100, www.fs.usda.gov

START THE HIKE

▶ **MILE 0-0.8: Captain Cook Trail Loop from Cape Perpetua Visitor Center**

Head south from the **Cape Perpetua Visitor Center,** following the paved **Captain Cook Trail**—named for Captain James Cook, who first observed Cape Perpetua in 1778. You'll descend gradually through a forest of salal and western hemlock. After 0.1 mile, ignore the sign to your left for the Oregon Coast Trail, and instead head right to walk through a tunnel under U.S. 101. Make a left at the junction just after the tunnel, and then head right at the next junction in another 250 feet—following signs for Tidepools and Spouting Horn at each junction—to embark on a short loop.

The 0.4-mile **loop trail** showcases some of Cape Perpetua's most popular natural features. If the tide's low enough, you can follow an old paved path off the northern end of the loop onto a rocky stretch of shore to **tide pools,** where you might spot starfish, sea anemones, and urchins. On the southern end of the loop, you'll see **Thor's Well,** a 20-foot-deep hole in the rocky shoreline that appears to drain the Pacific Ocean once the surf washes onto the shore. South of Thor's Well is **Spouting Horn,** which puts on a geyser-like show whenever waves crash into a partially buried sea cave; at high tide, some of the water shoots upward through an opening in the cave's ceiling, looking much like a whale's spout.

Complete the counterclockwise loop and, back on the main trail, return to the visitors center the way you came.

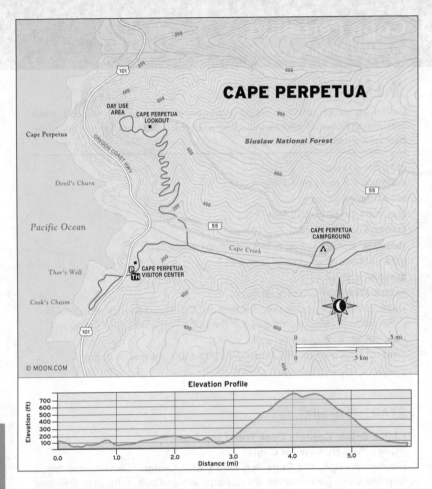

CAPE PERPETUA

Elevation Profile

▶ MILE 0.8-1.9: Cape Perpetua Visitor Center to Giant Spruce of Cape Perpetua

Head north through the visitors center's plaza to find the **Giant Spruce Trail.** The 1.1-mile paved path transitions to gravel and dirt as it curves inland along **Cape Creek.** You'll notice intersections with other trails to your left along the way (including one about 0.3 mile from the visitors center for the Saint Perpetua Trail, which you'll return to), but continue straight on the mostly flat Giant Spruce Trail through a forest of Sitka spruce and vine maple to the aptly named **Giant Spruce of Cape Perpetua.** The 550-year-old Sitka spruce is 185 feet tall and 15 feet thick, and began its life as a seedling, growing atop a nurse log.

▶ MILE 1.9-2.8: Giant Spruce of Cape Perpetua to Saint Perpetua Trailhead

Head back in the direction from which you came. In 0.2 mile, head right at a junction toward the Cape Perpetua Campground. Cross a bridge over the creek, and stroll the 0.2-mile **loop trail** through the forest on the creek's northern shore. It concludes at a **restroom;** cross the creek again to

▲ SPOUTING HORN AT CAPE PERPETUA

reconnect with the Giant Spruce Trail, turning right to head back in the direction of the visitors center for 0.5 mile. At the junction, make a hard right onto the **Saint Perpetua Trail.**

▶ **MILE 2.8–4.1: Saint Perpetua Trailhead to Cape Perpetua Lookout**
Cross Cape Creek once more and enter the **Cape Perpetua Campground.** Make a left on the road through the campground and walk about 100 feet, then pick up the trail again to your right, ascending as it steadily switchbacks up a forested hillside, with views gradually opening up as you approach the cape's highest point. After ascending 1.25 miles, you'll arrive at an unsigned junction, some 800 feet above sea level; head left 100 feet to arrive at the **Cape Perpetua lookout,** which the Forest Service calls "the best view on the Oregon Coast." From here you can see 37 miles out to sea and 70 miles up and down the coast. There are excellent whale-watching opportunities winter-spring, as well as dazzling sunsets on clear evenings.

▶ **MILE 4.1–4.3: Whispering Spruce Trail Loop**
Continue following the trail as it curves northwest. Just past the lookout, at a Y-shaped junction, follow a sign for the Stone Shelter for a quick 0.2-mile loop on the **Whispering Spruce Trail.** On the loop you'll pass the **West Shelter,** as it's officially known. It was built by the Civilian Conservation Corps in the 1930s and sits atop a clearing that overlooks the ocean; largely protected from wind and rain, it makes a fine place for lunch. A platform at the shelter's western edge offers great ocean views. Continue clockwise on the loop, keeping right at an intersection with the Amanda Trail to remain on the Whispering Spruce Trail.

Cape Perpetua

▲ CAPE PERPETUA

▶ **MILE 4.3-5.8: Cape Perpetua Lookout to Cape Perpetua Visitor Center**

After completing the loop, turn left to return to the Cape Perpetua lookout, then head downhill to return the way you came to the visitors center.

DIRECTIONS

From Yachats, head south on U.S. 101 for 3 miles. Past milepost 167 make a left, following signs for the Cape Perpetua Visitor Center. The road ends soon after in the parking area.

GPS COORDINATES: 44.280887, -124.108527 / N44° 16.8532' W124° 6.5116'

BEST NEARBY BREWS

The beers at **Yachats Brewing** (348 U.S. 101, Yachats, 541/547-3884, http://yachatsbrewing.com, 11:30am-9pm Sun.-Thurs., 11:30am-10pm Fri.-Sat.) reflect the region, with many named for nearby landmarks and several incorporating local fruits and malts. From the trailhead, the 3-mile drive north takes 5 minutes via U.S. 101.

HECETA HEAD LIGHTHOUSE STATE SCENIC VIEWPOINT

Make your way from one the Oregon Coast's most iconic lighthouses to a magical trail that winds its way to a beach.

DISTANCE: 5 miles round-trip
DURATION: 2.5 hours
ELEVATION CHANGE: 800 feet
EFFORT: Easy/moderate
TRAIL: Dirt trail, gravel, roots, rocks, sand, wooden steps
USERS: Hikers, leashed dogs
SEASON: Year-round
PASSES/FEES: $5 day-use fee per vehicle
MAPS: USGS topographic map for Heceta Head
CONTACT: Oregon State Parks, 541/547-3416, www.oregonstateparks.org

START THE HIKE

▶ **MILE 0-0.5: Lighthouse Trailhead to Heceta Head Lighthouse**
Head to the northern edge of the parking lot to find the **Lighthouse Trailhead,** and start ascending a gentle grade on a packed gravel path. You'll pass the old **assistant lighthouse keeper's house** after 0.3 mile—today a bed-and-breakfast—before arriving in another 0.2 mile at the **Heceta Head Lighthouse** and its attendant buildings. Rising 205 feet above the ocean, the lighthouse is among the most popular and photographed destinations on the Oregon Coast. It was first illuminated in 1894 and, as the strongest beam on the coast, can be seen more than 20 miles from land. Lighthouse tours (541/347-3416) are offered seasonally. Walk to the end of the bluff on which the lighthouse sits, and keep an eye out for migrating gray whales, shorebirds, seals, and sea lions frolicking below.

▶ **MILE 0.5-1.3: Heceta Head Lighthouse to Heceta Head**
To continue on the trail, head to the **oil house,** the easternmost building, and begin hiking steeply uphill at an interpretive panel via a few wooden steps that give way to a well-maintained dirt trail. Hike into the thick Sitka spruce forest for 0.1 mile to arrive at a **viewpoint** overlooking the lighthouse. These views will be swallowed up by the dense forest as you ascend 420 feet over the next 0.6 mile. Some 0.1 mile after you stop climbing, you'll arrive at a bench atop **Heceta Head,** overlooking a stretch of coastline to the north, including your eventual destination: Hobbit Beach.

▶ **MILE 1.3-2.5: Heceta Head to Hobbit Beach**
Slowly descend from here through a forest of Sitka spruce, salal, and shore pine. After 0.75 mile, the trail levels out with U.S. 101, off to your right,

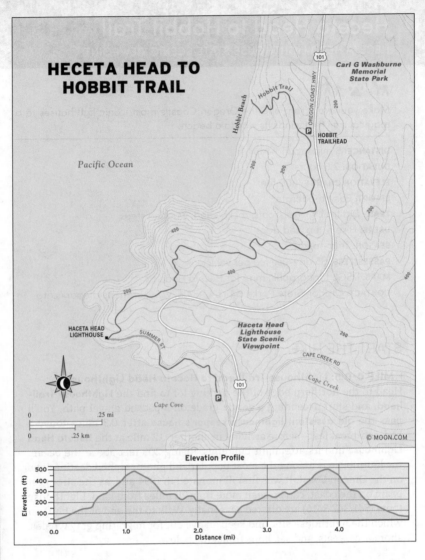

HECETA HEAD TO HOBBIT TRAIL

Elevation Profile

and you'll arrive at a junction. Continue north, straight ahead, onto the **Hobbit Beach Trail.** Twisting and turning down to the shoreline through a dense thicket of salal, rhododendron, and Sitka spruce, this enchanting trail makes you feel at times as if you're hiking through a tunnel of trees and overgrowth. After 0.3 mile, you'll pass an octopus-like tree that appears to have eight trunks stemming from one base. The trail ends 0.15 mile beyond it, at **Hobbit Beach.** You'll likely share the beach with dozens of hikers, families, and campers in high summer; otherwise, this stretch of coastline in the shadow of Heceta Head tends to be quiet.

Return the way you came.

▲ HOBBIT BEACH

DIRECTIONS

From Florence, head north on U.S. 101 for 11.4 miles. Just past a tunnel, turn right onto Cape Creek Road, following a sign for the Heceta Head Lighthouse. Continue on the road as it curves briefly to the right and then passes under U.S. 101, ending in a parking area after a few hundred feet.

GPS COORDINATES: 44.13515, –124.12296 / N44° 8.109' W124° 7.3776'

BEST NEARBY BREWS

Popular with locals, the **Beachcomber Pub** (1355 Bay St., Florence, 541/997-6357, http://beachcomberpub.com, 7am–midnight Sun.-Thurs., 7am–1am Fri.-Sat.) pours craft beer from along the Oregon Coast and throughout the Pacific Northwest, as well as serves classic pub fare. From the trailhead, the 13-mile drive south takes 20 minutes via U.S. 101.

Cape Sebastian

CAPE SEBASTIAN STATE SCENIC CORRIDOR

🦌 ❀ 🐾

Start the hike with stellar views and then descend through coastal forest to a largely inaccessible stretch of shoreline.

DISTANCE: 3.8 miles round-trip
DURATION: 2 hours
ELEVATION CHANGE: 590 feet
EFFORT: Easy/moderate
TRAIL: Dirt trail, roots, rocks
USERS: Hikers, leashed dogs
SEASON: Year-round
PASSES/FEES: None
MAPS: USGS topographic map for Cape Sebastian
CONTACT: Oregon State Parks, 541/469-2021, www.oregonstateparks.org

START THE HIKE

Long pants are recommended given some poison oak on the trail.

▶ **MILE 0-0.2: Parking Lot Viewpoint to Sitka Spruce Forest**
Before embarking on your hike, take a moment to appreciate the parking lot's vantage. This popular **viewpoint** is set more than 200 feet above the ocean, offering visibility more than 40 miles to the north—in which direction you might spy the large peak of Mount Humbug—and nearly 50 miles to the south, where Crescent City, California, is just visible. Also keep an eye out in winter and spring for migrating gray whales.

From the western edge of the parking lot, follow the paved path onto the **Oregon Coast Trail**—this is one small piece of the 382-mile trail that parallels the Oregon Coast. Views are quickly swallowed up by the hall of salal you'll enter just a few hundred feet from the trailhead. The first 0.2 mile of trail is mostly flat and heads briefly west before curving south, when you'll enter a dense forest of Sitka spruce.

▶ **MILE 0.2-1.4: Sitka Spruce Forest to Ocean View Clearings**
You'll descend gradually over next 0.7 mile, losing 275 feet of elevation along the way. Keep an eye out for purple iris, pink or purple salal, and the purple Bridges' brodiaea. The forest thins out as you make your way down a series of switchbacks, revealing ocean views. Poison oak starts to crowd the trail along this bushy stretch, so proceed cautiously. After 0.5 mile, the trail levels out, roughly 50 feet above the waterline. Several clearings along the trail here offer room to sit and enjoy ocean views.

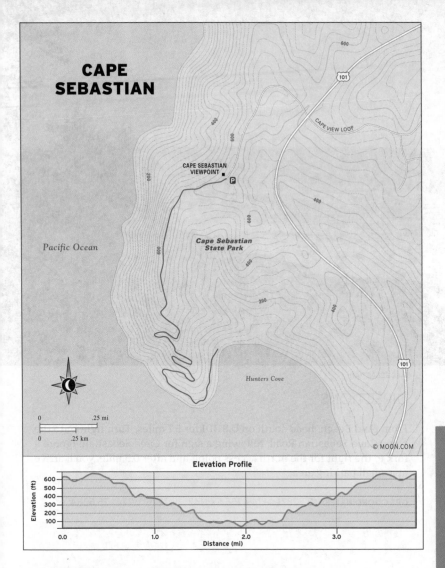

▶ MILE 1.4-1.9: Ocean View Clearings to Hunters Cove

Follow the trail another 0.4 mile to cross a small footbridge. You'll arrive at a rocky, steep slope that ends soon after at **Hunters Cove;** this last little stretch is often muddy and slick, but a series of cables provide assistance. It might be easiest to walk backward while gripping the cables on your way down. Since there's limited public access to this bit of coastline, you'll likely have it all to yourself. Enjoy a quiet stroll around the beach, assuming you're not here at high tide—when the waves leave little room to wander—and take in the ocean views, which encompass Hunters Island just offshore.

Return the way you came.

▲ CAPE SEBASTIAN

DIRECTIONS

From Gold Beach, head south on U.S. 101 for 5.7 miles. Turn right onto the steep Cape Sebastian Road, following a sign for Cape Sebastian. Ignore a fork to the right for the north access point, and after 0.5 mile, you'll arrive at a small parking area.

GPS COORDINATES: 42.32871, –124.42564 / N42° 19.7226' W124° 25.5384'

BEST NEARBY BREWS

You'll find exactly three taps at **Arch Rock Brewing Company** (28779 Hunter Creek Rd., Gold Beach, 541/247-0555, http://archrockbeer. com, 11am-6pm Tues.-Fri., 11am-5pm Sat.). But all three—a pale ale, lager, and porter—are great excuses to spend some time in the pint-sized taproom. From the trailhead, the 5-mile drive north takes 5 minutes via U.S. 101 and Hunter Creek Road.

11 River View Trail to Redwood Nature Trail

ALFRED A. LOEB STATE PARK AND ROGUE RIVER–SISKIYOU
NATIONAL FOREST

Hike along the Chetco River and into a grove of massive redwood trees.

DISTANCE: 3.3 miles round-trip
DURATION: 1.5 hours
ELEVATION CHANGE: 590 feet
EFFORT: Easy/moderate
TRAIL: Dirt trail, rocks, roots, gravel, bark dust
USERS: Hikers, leashed dogs (Redwood Nature Trail only)
SEASON: Year-round
PASSES/FEES: None
MAPS: USGS topographic map for Mount Emily; free trail maps available at the River View Trailhead and Redwood Nature Trailhead
CONTACT: Oregon State Parks, 541/469-2021, www.oregonstateparks.org; Rogue River–Siskiyou National Forest, 541/247-3600, www.fs.usda.gov

START THE HIKE

Long pants are recommended given some poison oak on the trail.

▶ **MILE 0-0.9: River View Trailhead to Redwood Nature Trailhead**
Start hiking on the **River View Trail** from the northern edge of the parking area. This narrow trail is mostly flat and winds through a grove of Oregon myrtle; native to southwestern Oregon and northwestern California, this evergreen hardwood is noted for its beautiful colors and wide variety of grain patterns. As you head deeper into the grove, watch out for poison oak. You'll also see sword ferns, western hemlock, and vine maple, which turns vibrant shades of yellow and orange in fall. To your right are views of the **Chetco River,** which begins in the Klamath Mountains before flowing into the Pacific Ocean; a few steep spur trails head down to its rocky banks. After 0.8 mile, the trail curves left and ends at North Bank Chetco River Road. Cross the road and continue straight, heading west, past a sign for the Rogue River-Siskiyou National Forest and Redwood Nature Trail. Roughly 0.1 mile beyond the road crossing, just past a small parking area, you'll find an unsigned, Y-shaped junction.

▶ **MILE 0.9-2.4: Redwood Nature Trail Loop**
Hop onto the **Redwood Nature Trail,** turning right to begin a 1.5-mile counterclockwise loop through one of the northernmost redwood groves on Earth. You'll ascend steadily on the loop trail, gaining 390 feet, before descending. The redwoods along this trail are considered "young" at 300-800

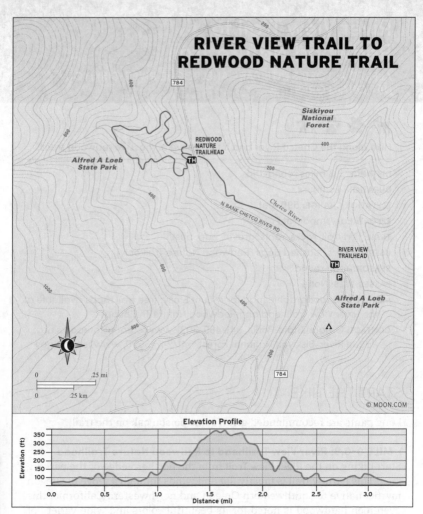

RIVER VIEW TRAIL TO REDWOOD NATURE TRAIL

Elevation Profile

years old—for context, the oldest redwood trees on record are more than 2,000 years old. Some of the redwoods here are more than 12 feet in diameter, with one of the largest being 286 feet tall; trees of this size contain enough wood to build eight two-bedroom homes. Also growing in the grove are myrtle, bigleaf maple, red alder, and Douglas fir. Keep an eye out for redwood sorrel, noted for its small pink flowers when in bloom, and the California rough-skinned newt, whose orange skin secretes a potentially deadly toxin when ingested.

▶ **MILE 2.4–3.3: Redwood Nature Trailhead to River View Trailhead**
Ignore the unsigned junction near North Bank Chetco River Road as you near the end of the trail; continue left to complete the loop. Take a right to return to the parking area, and return the way you came.

▲ REDWOOD NATURE TRAIL

DIRECTIONS

From Brookings, head east on North Bank Chetco River Road, following a sign for Loeb State Park. After 7.7 miles, turn right into Alfred A. Loeb State Park. Continue through the first intersection and, after 500 feet, turn right into a small gravel parking area with room for a half-dozen cars.

GPS COORDINATES: 42.11275, −124.18772 / N42° 6.765′ W124° 11.2632′

BEST NEARBY BREWS

With 16 vegan-friendly taps, you're sure to find a few palate-pleasers at **Chetco Brewing Company** (830 Railroad St., Brookings, 541/661-5347, http://chetcobrew.com, noon-9pm Sun.-Thurs., 11:30am-10pm Fri.-Sat. summer, call for hours fall-spring). The award-winning brewery prides itself on putting inventive spins on classic styles. From the trailhead, the 9-mile drive southwest takes 15 minutes via North Bank Chetco River Road and U.S. 101.

NEARBY CAMPGROUNDS

NAME	DESCRIPTION	FACILITIES	SEASON	FEE
Saddle Mountain State Natural Area	campground at the base of Saddle Mountain	10 tent sites, restrooms	April-October	$11
Saddle Mountain State Park Rd., Cannon Beach, 503/368-5943, www.oregonstateparks.org				
Cape Lookout State Park	campground north of Cape Lookout	52 full-hookup sites, 170 tent sites, 1 electrical site with water, 13 yurts, 6 cabins, restrooms	year-round	$21-91
Cape Lookout Road, Tillamook, 503/842-4981, www.oregonstateparks.org				
Cape Perpetua Campground	quiet campground along Camp Creek	37 nonelectric sites, restrooms	March-September	$26
U.S. 101, Yachats, 541/547-4580, www.fs.usda.gov				
South Beach State Park	popular campground just south of Newport	227 electrical sites, 59 tent sites, 27 yurts, 3 group sites, restrooms	year-round	$21-78
U.S. 101, Newport, 541/867-4715, www.oregonstateparks.org				
Jessie M. Honeyman Memorial State Park	popular campground surrounded by coastal dunes	47 full-hookup sites, 121 electrical sites, 187 tent sites, 10 yurts, restrooms	year-round	$21-56
U.S. 101, Florence, 541/997-3851, www.oregonstateparks.org				
Alfred A. Loeb State Park	pastoral campground along the Chetco River	48 electrical sites, 3 log cabins, restrooms	year-round	$24-52
North Bank Chetco River Rd., Brookings, 541/469-2021, www.oregonstateparks.org				

BEND AND THE CENTRAL OREGON CASCADES

The high desert of Central Oregon boasts a landscape unlike anywhere else in the state. Cascade peaks stretch to the sky like an erratic EKG, their bases covered in clear mountain streams and ponderosa pine forests, before giving way to wide-open vistas, broken up only by seas of sagebrush and islands of juniper as you head east. In between, you'll find lunar lava flows, spring-fed rivers, old-growth Douglas fir, and cartoonishly blue pools. You'll find no better home base for exploring the variety of landscapes in the area than Bend, the region's largest city, with more than 90,000 residents—and, happily, dozens of craft breweries, perfect for capping off a day of hiking.

▲ FLATIRON ROCK TRAIL

▲ PATH ON TUMALO MOUNTAIN

1 **McKenzie River Trail to Tamolitch (Blue Pool)**
DISTANCE: 4.6 miles round-trip
DURATION: 2.5 hours
EFFORT: Easy

2 **Little Belknap Crater**
DISTANCE: 5.3 miles round-trip
DURATION: 3 hours
EFFORT: Easy/moderate

3 **West Metolius River**
DISTANCE: 5.7 miles round-trip
DURATION: 3 hours
EFFORT: Easy/moderate

4 **Black Butte**
DISTANCE: 4.8 miles round-trip
DURATION: 2.5 hours
EFFORT: Moderate

5 **Tam-a-láu Trail**
DISTANCE: 7.1 miles round-trip
DURATION: 3.5 hours
EFFORT: Easy/moderate

6 **Misery Ridge-River Trail Loop**
DISTANCE: 4.2 miles round-trip
DURATION: 2.5 hours
EFFORT: Easy/moderate

7 **Tumalo Mountain**
DISTANCE: 4.4 miles round-trip
DURATION: 2.5 hours
EFFORT: Moderate

8 **Shevlin Park Loop**
DISTANCE: 4.8 miles round-trip
DURATION: 2 hours
EFFORT: Easy

9 **Flatiron Rock**
DISTANCE: 6.3 miles round-trip
DURATION: 2.75 hours
EFFORT: Easy/moderate

10 **Paulina Peak**
DISTANCE: 4.7 miles round-trip
DURATION: 2.5 hours
EFFORT: Moderate

▾ MCKENZIE RIVER NEAR BLUE POOL

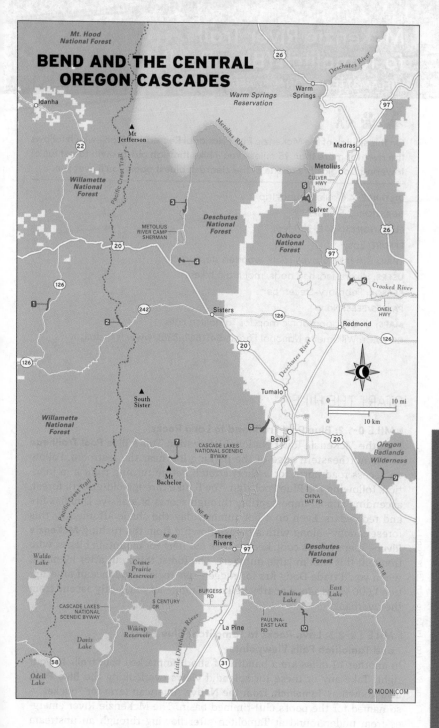

1 McKenzie River Trail to Tamolitch (Blue Pool)

WILLAMETTE NATIONAL FOREST

On this stretch of the McKenzie River National Recreation Trail—which follows the river for more than 25 miles—you'll hike through old-growth forest full of towering Douglas firs to one of the clearest, bluest pools you'll ever see.

DISTANCE: 4.6 miles round-trip
DURATION: 2.5 hours
ELEVATION CHANGE: 280 feet
EFFORT: Easy
TRAIL: Dirt trail, gravel, roots, wooden steps, rocks
USERS: Hikers, leashed dogs, mountain bikers
SEASON: February–December
PASSES/FEES: None
MAPS: USGS topographic map for Tamolitch Falls
CONTACT: Willamette National Forest, 541/822-3381, www.fs.usda.gov

START THE HIKE

▶ MILE 0-1.2: Blue Pool Trailhead to Lava Rocks

Find the McKenzie River National Recreation Trail's **Blue Pool Trailhead** at the northeastern edge of the parking lot, near the restroom. Follow an access road north for a short stretch before turning right at a junction, following the Blue Pool sign. You'll hike through old-growth forest, ascending almost imperceptibly through scores of massive Douglas firs and red cedars. Even on a hot summer day, the shade afforded by this forest canopy—along with a breeze flowing from the rushing **McKenzie River**—keeps hikers cool. Keep an eye out here for mountain bikers, who frequent this trail in large numbers. The forest thins out after 1.2 miles, when you'll trade Doug firs for rugged lava rocks—evidence of an eruption 1,600 years ago of nearby Belknap Crater—as you gently ascend from the riverbank.

▶ MILE 1.2-2.3: Lava Rocks to Tamolitch (Blue Pool) and Tamolitch Falls Viewpoints

In another 1.1 miles are a handful of short, unmarked **spur trails** to your right. Take any of these for splendid views overlooking the **Blue Pool,** also known as **Tamolitch,** from the Native American term for "bucket"— so named for the pool's cliff-rimmed basin. The McKenzie River emerges from underground at Tamolitch after flowing through an upstream

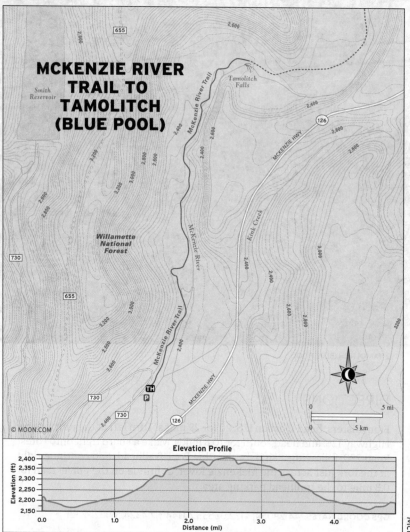

MCKENZIE RIVER TRAIL TO TAMOLITCH (BLUE POOL)

Smith Reservoir

Tamolitch Falls

Willamette National Forest

McKenzie River Trail

McKenzie River

McKenzie HWY

Kink Creek

TH
P

© MOON.COM

0   .5 mi
0   .5 km

Elevation Profile

lava tube, producing some of the clearest water you'll ever see. If you visit spring-early summer, you'll also enjoy views of **Tamolitch Falls,** the seasonal waterfall that partially feeds the pool, at the eastern edge of the basin. From these vantage points some 50 feet above the river, the topaz-colored water appears no deeper than a backyard pool, though it can easily be 50 feet deep or more—and the water is a chilly 37°F on average! Although you may see some hikers diving into the Blue Pool, this is dangerous—people have died doing so.

The McKenzie River National Recreation Trail continues north, but these viewpoints make a nice turnaround point. Return the way you came.

▲ TAMOLITCH (BLUE POOL)

DIRECTIONS

From Sisters, head west on U.S. 20 for 29 miles. Turn left at the junction for Highway 126, and head south for 10.8 miles. Make a sharp right onto Forest Road 730, following a sign for the Blue Pool Trailhead, and continue right at the fork just across the McKenzie River. Continue on the gravel road for 0.3 mile to the trailhead parking area.

GPS COORDINATES: 44.29054, -122.03535 / N44° 17.4324' W122° 2.121'

BEST NEARBY BREWS

Sisters's only brewery, **Three Creeks Brewing** (721 Desperado Ct., Sisters, 541/549-1963, www.threecreeksbrewing.com, 11:30am-9pm Sun.-Thurs., 11:30am-10pm Fri.-Sat.), produces roughly 50 beers each year, including year-round varietals, seasonal releases, and one-off brews. From the trailhead, the 41-mile drive east takes 45 minutes via Highway 126 and U.S. 20.

Hike part of the Pacific Crest Trail through centuries-old lava fields to a crater's summit boasting towering mountain views.

DISTANCE: 5.3 miles round-trip
DURATION: 3 hours
ELEVATION CHANGE: 1,020 feet
EFFORT: Easy/moderate
TRAIL: Dirt trail, sand, lava rock, rock scramble
USERS: Hikers, horseback riders, leashed dogs
SEASON: Summer-early fall
PASSES/FEES: $1 day-use permit required Friday before Memorial Day weekend–last Friday in September, available for purchase by phone or online only (877/444-6777, www.recreation.gov)
MAPS: USGS topographic map for Mount Washington, OR
CONTACT: Mount Washington Wilderness, Willamette National Forest, 541/822-3381, www.fs.usda.gov

START THE HIKE

A sturdy pair of hiking boots is recommended given some jagged lava rocks; for this reason, although leashed dogs are allowed here, you might want to think twice about bringing your pet. Much of this hike is exposed, so you'll also want to bring plenty of water and sunscreen.

▶ **MILE 0-0.8: Pacific Crest Trail to Lava Flow**
From the parking lot, head northeast toward the sign welcoming you to the Mount Washington Wilderness. Just next to it, hop onto the **Pacific Crest Trail (PCT)**. You'll soon find yourself in the first of two "islands" of forest you'll encounter on this hike, each of them surrounded by miles of lava rock. You'll emerge briefly onto lava flow at 0.4 mile, and then leave the forest behind for good in another 0.4 mile. After exiting the second forest "island," you'll see two peaks ahead: The barren slope to your left is Belknap Crater, and the smaller stump to your right is Little Belknap Crater. Most of the lava rock you're about to traverse formed after these shield volcanoes erupted more than a thousand years ago.

▶ **MILE 0.8-2.4: Lava Flow to Little Belknap Trail**
From here, you steadily ascend on the well-graded trail, gaining about 625 feet on this exposed stretch. You might notice a few gnarled whitebark pines along the way. Pause for a water break at some point, a good excuse to turn around and look back toward the trailhead, where North and

BEND AND THE CENTRAL OREGON CASCADES

Little Belknap Crater

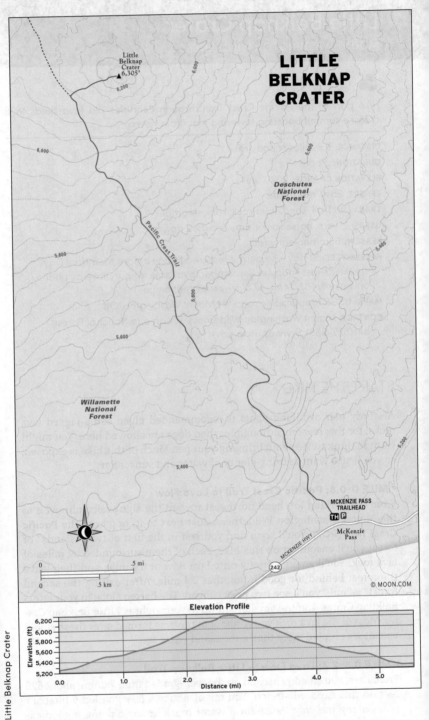

Middle Sister tower over the surrounding peaks on a clear day. In 1.6 miles, head right onto the **Little Belknap Trail**.

▶ **MILE 2.4-2.65: Little Belknap Trail to Little Belknap Crater Summit**
This 0.25-mile spur gains 100 feet along the way. You'll scramble steeply over some rocks before arriving at the **Little Belknap Crater summit.** From here, peaks seem to rise in every direction: Belknap Crater sits to the west, Mount Washington dominates views to the north, symmetrical Black Butte rises in the northeast, and Black Crater—which has a vertical notch at its summit—is visible to the southeast.

Return to the junction and take a left to head south and return the way you came.

LITTLE BELKNAP CRATER TRAIL ▶

DIRECTIONS

From Sisters, head west on Highway 242 (McKenzie Highway) for 15.1 miles, turning right into the parking area indicated by a sign sporting a hiker symbol. This highway opens every June and usually closes by October, depending on snow levels; check with the Oregon **Department of Transportation** (800/977-6368, http://tripcheck.com) for road closures before planning your hike.

GPS COORDINATES: 44.2604, -121.81 / N44° 15.624' W121° 48.6'

BEST NEARBY BITES, BREWS, AND A BONUS
Can't decide between coffee, beer, and pizza? You don't have to at **Hop & Brew** (523 U.S. 20, Sisters, 541/719-1295, http://hopandbrew. com, 7am-8pm Sun.-Thurs., 7am-9pm Fri.-Sat.). Grab breakfast burritos and bagel sandwiches before your hike, or unwind with pizza, sandwiches, beer, or cider afterward. From the trailhead, the 16-mile drive east takes 30 minutes via Highway 242. On the way, you might want to stop at **Dee Wright Observatory** (541/822-3381 or visit www. fs.usda.gov), located just 0.5 mile east of the trailhead parking area along Highway 242. The observatory was completed in 1935 by the Civilian Conservation Corps and affords 360-degree views of surrounding peaks; on a clear day, visitors can see Mount Washington, Mount Jefferson, the Three Sisters, Little Belknap Crater, and more.

Follow the banks of the vibrant Metolius River to a fish hatchery in the middle of a pine forest.

BEST: Dog-Friendly Hikes, Kid-Friendly Hikes
DISTANCE: 5.7 miles round-trip
DURATION: 3 hours
ELEVATION CHANGE: 270 feet
EFFORT: Easy/moderate
TRAIL: Dirt trail, roots
USERS: Hikers, leashed dogs
SEASON: Year-round
PASSES/FEES: None
MAPS: USGS topographic map for Candle Creek
CONTACT: Deschutes National Forest, 541/383-5300, www.fs.usda.gov

While wildflowers steal the show in spring and early summer, there's no bad time to hike along the Metolius, one of the largest spring-fed rivers in the United States. It remains remarkably clear year-round, and aspen groves alongside it put on colorful fall foliage displays.

START THE HIKE

▶ MILE 0-0.4: West Metolius Trailhead to Spring

Find the **West Metolius Trailhead** at the southeastern edge of the parking area near a bend in the **Metolius River.** Follow the single-track trail along the river through a forest of Douglas fir, aspen, and pine, with wildflowers blooming in mid-spring, including yellow balsamroot, western buttercup, red paintbrush, yellow monkeyflower, and purple lupine. If you're lucky, you may spy the pink- or purple-chuted Peck's penstemon; this rare wildflower grows in the forests near the town of Sisters—and nowhere else in the world. After 0.4 mile, look west to see a small **spring**—seemingly originating from the middle of the Metolius's steep riverbank—feeding into the river. Take time to admire the sapphire-colored, crystal-clear waters.

▶ MILE 0.4-2.3: Spring to Metolius Riverbank

You'll start swapping fir trees for a thick forest of old-growth ponderosa pine over the next 0.4 mile as the trail curves north, and begin gradually descending before the trail flattens out near the riverbank in another 1.5 miles—where you'll see several small islands in the middle of the Metolius. They're usually covered in wildflowers in spring, and are key habitats for local fish and bird populations.

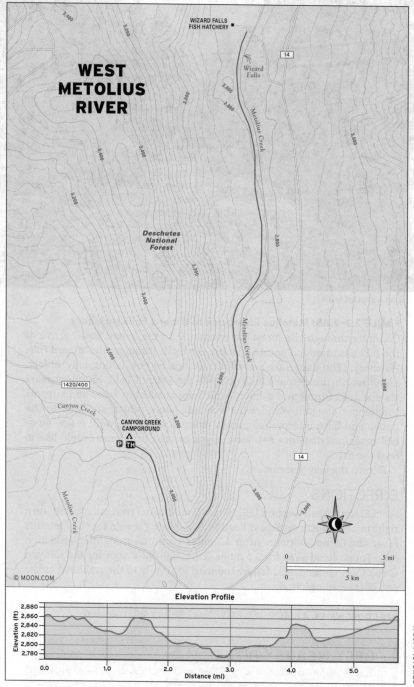

WEST
METOLIUS
RIVER

WIZARD FALLS
FISH HATCHERY

14

Wizard
Falls

Metolius Creek

Deschutes
National
Forest

3,400
3,200
3,000
2,800

1420/400

Canyon Creek

CANYON CREEK
CAMPGROUND

P
TH

Metolius Creek

14

3,000

N

0   .5 mi
0   .5 km

© MOON.COM

Elevation Profile

2,880
2,860
2,840
2,820
2,800
2,780

Elevation (ft)

0.0   1.0   2.0   3.0   4.0   5.0

Distance (mi)

▲ WEST METOLIUS RIVER

▶ **MILE 2.3-2.85: Metolius Riverbank to Wizard Falls Hatchery**
Continue through the forest for another 0.5 mile, when you'll arrive at the hike's turnaround point and a fun family destination: the **Wizard Falls Hatchery.** (The namesake waterfalls are nearby but, falling only 12 feet, aren't worth the detour.) Built in 1947, the Wizard Falls Hatchery rears six species of trout and salmon, which are stocked in lakes and streams throughout Oregon. Wander the open-air pools, which are open to the public and have interpretive panels. Bring quarters, as well: A few gumball machines dispense fish food, if you or your little ones would like to feed the fish.

Return the way you came.

DIRECTIONS

From Sisters, head west on U.S. 20 for 10 miles. Just past milepost 91, turn right to head north on Forest Road 1419, following a sign for the Metolius River and Camp Sherman. After 4.8 miles, continue straight at a junction onto Forest Road 1420 for 3.3 miles. Turn right at a sign for the Canyon Creek Campground, and follow the road for 1 mile to the trailhead at the end of the campground.

GPS COORDINATES: 44.5009, -121.6411 / N44° 30.054' W121° 38.466'

BEST NEARBY BITES
Step back in time at **Sno Cap Drive In** (380 W. Cascade Ave., Sisters, 541/549-6151, 11am-7pm daily). The classic diner serves burgers and other American fare, not to mention more than 30 flavors of homemade ice cream. From the trailhead, the 18-mile drive south takes 30 minutes via Forest Roads 1419 and 1420 and U.S. 20.

4

Black Butte

DESCHUTES NATIONAL FOREST

Panoramic views of nearby Cascade peaks from this symmetrical stratovolcano's summit make the unrelenting ascent worth it.

DISTANCE: 4.8 miles round-trip
DURATION: 2.5 hours
ELEVATION CHANGE: 1,560 feet
EFFORT: Moderate
TRAIL: Dirt trail, rocks, roots
USERS: Hikers, leashed dogs
SEASON: June-October
PASSES/FEES: Northwest Forest Pass (May-Sept.)
MAPS: USGS topographic map for Black Butte, OR, and Little Akawa Butte, OR
CONTACT: Deschutes National Forest, 541/383-5300, www.fs.usda.gov

START THE HIKE

Consider getting an early start on this trail if you're hiking in the summer—shade is rare after you pass through an old-growth forest early on. Bring plenty of water and sunscreen.

▶ MILE 0-0.8: Black Butte Trailhead to Switchback

Find the trailhead at the eastern edge of the parking area—thankfully, already about halfway up the butte—and begin ascending on the **Black Butte Trail.** On this early stretch you'll hike through an old-growth, mossy ponderosa pine forest. After 0.8 mile and 620 feet of elevation gain, you'll reach the hike's sole **switchback**—and also leave the forest behind for Black Butte's exposed southern hillside. You'll notice the Black Butte Ranch vacation resort to the south and Mount Washington to the southwest as you exit the forest.

BLACK BUTTE TRAIL ▶

Black Butte

BEND AND THE CENTRAL OREGON CASCADES

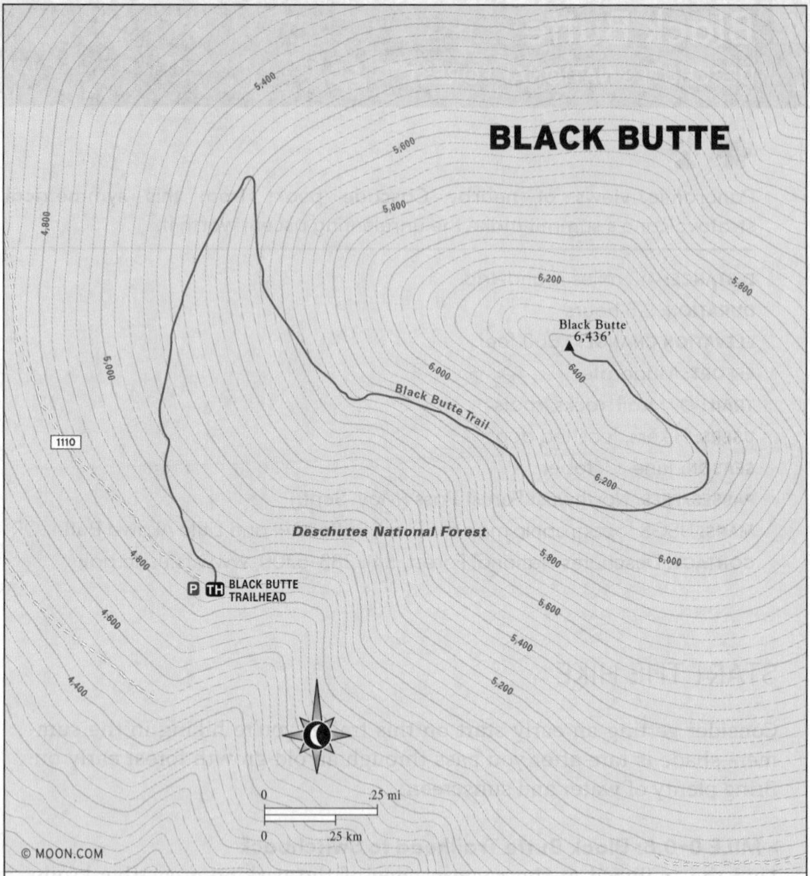
BLACK BUTTE
Black Butte
6,436'
Black Butte Trail
Deschutes National Forest
BLACK BUTTE
TRAILHEAD
1110
0
.25 mi
.25 km
© MOON.COM

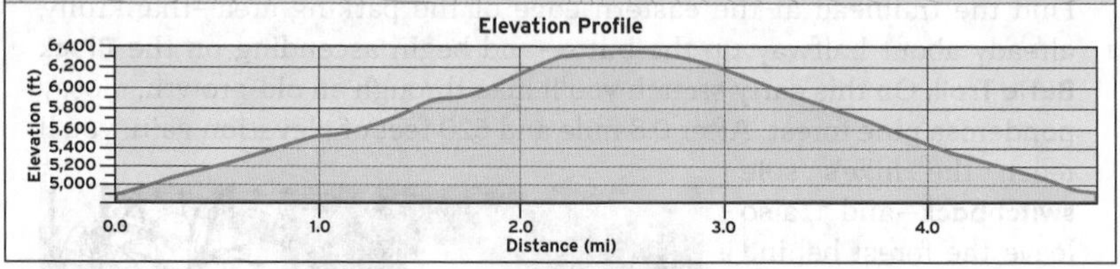
Elevation Profile
Elevation (ft)
Distance (mi)

▸ MILE 0.8–2.4: Switchback to Black Butte Summit

Continue hiking steadily up the trail's well-graded incline. In late spring and early summer, you may spot white Washington lilies, purple lupine, pinemat manzanita, and other wildflowers. In 1 mile, you'll start traversing scattered groves of lodgepole pine, whitebark pine, and subalpine fir. You'll gain another 425 feet over the next 0.6 mile before arriving at the **Black Butte summit,** indicated by a sign for the Black Butte Lookout Tower. To your left, on the butte's southern edge, is a **fire lookout,** built in 1995; not open to the public, it's still used to spot wildfires during summer. To your right is a **cupola** that was built in 1922, which was also used as a fire lookout until 1934. Interpretive signs near the cupola identify the many dramatic peaks before you: Broken Top, South and North Sister, Belknap

▲ VIEW FROM BLACK BUTTE

Crater, Mount Washington, Three Fingered Jack, Mount Jefferson, and—on a clear day—Mount Hood and Mount Adams to the far north.

Return the way you came.

DIRECTIONS

From Sisters, head west on U.S. 20 for 6 miles. Turn right onto Forest Road 11, just past milepost 95, following signs for Indian Ford Campground. After 3.8 miles, head left at the fork to drive uphill on Forest Road 1110. After another 4 miles, take a sharp right to stay on Forest Road 1110. From here, it's 1.2 rough and rutted miles to the trailhead at road's end. Low-clearance vehicles can handle the terrain but should proceed cautiously.

GPS COORDINATES: 44.39502, –121.64777 / N44° 23.7012' W121° 38.8662'

BEST NEARBY BREWS

While the town of Sisters is closer, since you just hiked Black Butte, head a bit farther to Bend for a thematic pairing: Cool off with a Black Butte Porter at **Deschutes Brewery Bend Public House** (1044 NW Bond St., Bend, 541/382-9242, www.deschutesbrewery.com, 11am-10pm Sun.-Thurs., 11am-11pm Fri.-Sat.), the region's oldest brewery. From the trailhead, the 39-mile drive southeast takes an hour via U.S. 20.

5

Tam-a-láu Trail

THE COVE PALISADES STATE PARK

🦌 ❀ 🐾

Hike to a juniper- and sage-covered plateau overlooking the Deschutes River, Crooked River, and Lake Billy Chinook, not to mention Cascade peaks and other landforms.

DISTANCE: 7.1 miles round-trip

DURATION: 3.5 hours

ELEVATION CHANGE: 790 feet

EFFORT: Easy/moderate

TRAIL: Dirt trail, paved path, wooden steps, rocks

USERS: Hikers, leashed dogs

SEASON: March-November

PASSES/FEES: $5 day-use fee per vehicle

MAPS: Oregon State Parks map for The Cove Palisades State Park, available online and at both campground registration stations in the park

PARK HOURS: Sunrise-sunset daily

CONTACT: Oregon State Parks, 541/546-3412, www.oregonstateparks.org

START THE HIKE

Save this hike for a cool or cloudy day, and get an early start if possible, because it's quite exposed. Wear sunscreen and bring plenty of water.

▸ **MILE 0-0.4: Parking Lot to Tam-a-láu Trailhead**
Start your hike at the northeastern edge of the parking lot, following the Tam-a-láu Trail sign. You'll hike through a forest of juniper and pine before crossing an unnamed road in 0.4 mile. Shortly after, cross Southwest Jordan Road and pass through a small opening in the fence line to arrive at the official **Tam-a-láu Trailhead,** at the southern end of **Deschutes Campground.** (If you're camping, you can start from here and shave this opening mileage off the hike.)

VIEW FROM THE SUMMIT OF TAM-A-LÁU ▸

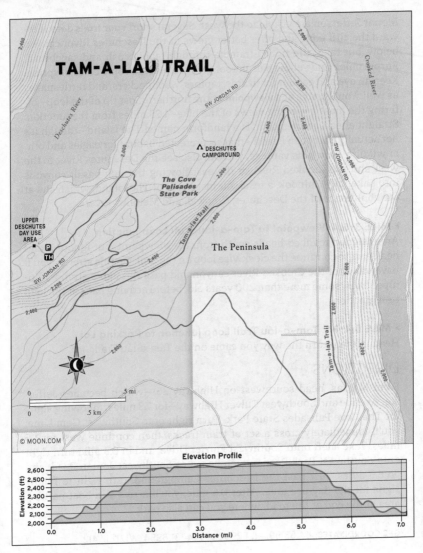

TAM-A-LÁU TRAIL

Elevation Profile

▶ **MILE 0.4-1.75: Tam-a-láu Trailhead to Tam-a-láu Trail Loop Junction**

Over the next 0.75 mile, you'll gain 450 feet as you switchback up and occasionally climb wooden stairs, with little shade. Along the way, you'll notice several boulders dotting the trail. The word "Tam-a-láu" comes from a Native American phrase that translates to "place of big rocks on the ground," and these are the namesake boulders. In 0.6 mile, you'll have gained most of the hike's elevation as you arrive at the Y-shaped junction for the **Tam-a-láu Trail Loop**.

▶ **MILE 1.75-3: Tam-a-láu Trail Loop Junction to Viewpoint**

Head left to begin a 3.6-mile clockwise loop around **The Peninsula,** as the summit of this lava plateau is known. On a clear day, the Three Sisters and

Mount Jefferson are visible to the west. Several short **spur trails** detour toward the cliff edge and offer better views of the Deschutes River canyon below, but take care not to trample through rabbitbrush and sagebrush. Purple phlox and yellow balsamroot give the plateau some color in spring. Keep an eye and ear out for lizards, raptors, woodpeckers, and rattlesnakes as well. You'll arrive at a **viewpoint** at the northernmost tip of the loop—offering the most sweeping views of the hike—1.25 miles from the junction. Straight ahead, to the north, is a landform named The Island—though it's not actually part of an island—that's a protected habitat for eagles and other wildlife. From this vantage, you can also see the Deschutes River to the west and the Crooked River to the east flowing through basalt canyons into Lake Billy Chinook, a reservoir just north of The Island, which sits at the confluence of the Deschutes, Crooked, and Metolius Rivers.

▶ **MILE 3-5.4: Viewpoint to Tam-a-láu Trail Loop Junction**
An unsigned roadbed heads south from the viewpoint, but ignore it and head east to continue the clockwise loop on the trail. On this stretch, you'll have views of the Crooked River canyon and pass through a strand of juniper trees, some more than 200 years old, before arriving back at the loop trail junction.

▶ **MILE 5.4-7.1: Tam-a-láu Trail Loop Junction to Parking Lot**
Head left to return the way you came on the Tam-a-láu Trail.

DIRECTIONS

From Madras, head southwest on Highway 361—which becomes Jefferson Avenue and Southwest Culver Highway—for 7.3 miles, following signs for The Cove Palisades State Park. Turn right onto Southwest Gem Lane; you'll immediately cross a set of train tracks, then continue west for 1.5 miles. Take a left onto Southwest Frazier Drive, and in 0.3 mile turn right onto Southwest Peck Road, which becomes Southwest Jordan Road, and go 6.5 miles. Just past the Deschutes Campground, turn right to follow signs for the day-use area. After 0.6 mile, you'll arrive at a boat parking area at the end of the road, where you can also park.

GPS COORDINATES: 44.53159, −121.2902 / N44° 31.8954′ W121° 17.412′

BEST NEARBY BITES

Enjoy fresh and healthy fare at **Great Earth Café & Market** (46 SW D St., Madras, 541/475-1500, www.greatearthcafemarket.com, 7am-6pm Mon.-Fri., 10am-3pm Sat.). It serves light breakfast items, fresh and filling sandwiches, soups, salads, and more. From the trailhead, the 15-mile drive northeast takes 30 minutes via Southwest Jordan Road and Highway 361.

Smith Rock is one of Oregon's most popular state parks for good reason, and views of its jagged formations and Cascade peaks are just some of the highlights of this hike.

BEST: Fall Hikes, Dog-Friendly Hikes
DISTANCE: 4.2 miles round-trip
DURATION: 2.5 hours
ELEVATION CHANGE: 880 feet
EFFORT: Easy/moderate
TRAIL: Dirt trail, paved path, wooden stairs, boardwalk
USERS: Hikers, leashed dogs, mountain bikers, horseback riders
SEASON: Year-round
PASSES/FEES: $5 day-use fee per vehicle
MAPS: Oregon State Parks map for Smith Rock State Park, available online and at pay stations in the park
PARK HOURS: Dawn-dusk daily
CONTACT: Oregon State Parks, 541/548-7501, www.oregonstateparks.org

Smith Rock's formations first took shape some 30 million years ago following prolonged periods of volcanic activity in the area. Basalt lava flows then poured into the region 500,000 years ago, and the Crooked River gradually eroded and sculpted the surrounding landscape—creating the rock formations you're exploring today.

START THE HIKE

▸ **MILE 0-0.5: Smith Rock Welcome Center to Crooked River Bridge**
Start hiking from the trailhead near the pay station just northeast of the **Smith Rock Welcome Center.** Follow the path, turning right at the T-shaped junction onto the **Rim Rock Trail.** In another few hundred feet, take a left at the junction to start descending on the **Canyon Trail.** You'll encounter intersections with numerous other trails on the short way down, but keep following the well-signed Canyon Trail toward the river. (You could opt to take the Chute Trail that appears to your right soon after you begin your descent, cutting 0.6 mile off the round-trip trek, but it's steeper and less scenic.) Cross over the **Crooked River bridge** at 0.5 mile.

▸ **MILE 0.5-1.8: Crooked River Bridge to Misery Ridge Summit**
At this junction, continue straight, climbing a few stone steps and beginning to ascend via the **Misery Ridge Trail,** on which you'll gain 580 feet over the next 0.6 mile, along with progressively better views of the Crooked River snaking its way through the khaki-colored canyon—and of rock

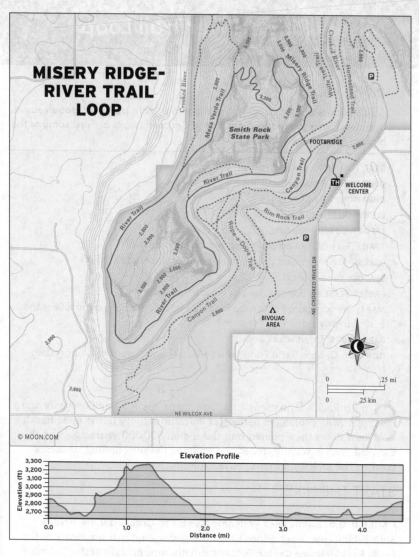

MISERY RIDGE–RIVER TRAIL LOOP

Crooked River

Wolfe Trail Canyon

Crooked River

Homestead Trail

Mesa Verde Trail

Misery Ridge Trail

Smith Rock State Park

FOOTBRIDGE

Canyon Trail

River Trail

WELCOME CENTER

Rim Rock Trail

River Trail

Rope-a-Dope Trail

NE CROOKED RIVER DR

Canyon Trail

BIVOUAC AREA

NE WILCOX AVE

© MOON.COM

0   .25 mi

0   .25 km

Elevation Profile

Elevation (ft): 3,300 / 3,200 / 3,100 / 3,000 / 2,900 / 2,800 / 2,700

Distance (mi): 0.0 / 1.0 / 2.0 / 3.0 / 4.0

climbers attempting some of the park's routes. Loose gravel dominates much of the upper Misery Ridge Trail, so watch your step. After another 0.7 mile of steady, strenuous climbing, you'll arrive at the **Misery Ridge summit.** Just left off the trail is a **viewpoint** with sweeping vistas of the surrounding rock formations and Central Oregon farmland.

▶ **MILE 1.8–2.2: Misery Ridge Summit to Monkey Face**
Head right to continue on the Misery Ridge Trail. In a few hundred feet, you'll arrive on the summit's western bluff, which has views of the Three Sisters, Broken Top, Mount Bachelor, Black Butte, and Mount Washington. On a clear day, you can see all the way north to Mount Hood. Continue on the trail for 0.3 mile, then pause to enjoy an up-close encounter with **Monkey Face,** one of Smith Rock's most iconic formations.

▶ **MILE 2.2–3.7: Monkey Face to Crooked River Bridge**

After taking a few photos, head left at the intersection onto the **Mesa Verde Trail,** following it as it drops 615 feet to the riverbank. The Mesa Verde Trail meets up with the **River Trail** after 0.4 mile. Continue straight to follow the River Trail for 1.1 miles, alongside the Crooked River and occasionally over short stretches of wooden boardwalk. Keep an eye out along this stretch for beavers, river otters, prairie falcons, and other wildlife. At the height of summer, watch out for rattlesnakes.

▶ **MILE 3.7–4.2: Crooked River Bridge to Smith Rock Trailhead**

Back at the bridge you initially crossed, head right and up the **Canyon Trail** to return the way you came.

SMITH ROCK STATE PARK ▶

DIRECTIONS

From Redmond, head north on U.S. 97 for 5.7 miles, then turn right to head east on Smith Rock Way, following signs for Smith Rock State Park. After 1.5 miles, turn left onto Northeast 17th Street. Continue for 0.5 mile before turning right at a T-shaped junction onto Northeast Wilcox Avenue. Continue for 0.5 mile, then turn left at the sign for Smith Rock State Park onto Northeast Crooked River Drive. Follow this road north for about 0.5 mile before arriving at the first of Smith Rock's numerous parking areas. The Smith Rock Welcome Center, housed in a green yurt, sits 0.1 mile past the first parking area along the western edge of Northeast Crooked River Drive, between a restroom and pay station.

GPS COORDINATES: 44.3668, –121.13617 / N44° 22.008' W121° 8.1702'

BEST NEARBY BREWS

Wild Ride Brewing (332 SW 5th St., Redmond, 541/516-8544, www.wildridebrew.com, 11am–10pm daily) pours more than a dozen beers and hosts a large outdoor seating area, several fire pits, and on-site food carts. From the trailhead, the 10-mile drive south takes 15 minutes via Northeast Smith Rock Way and U.S. 97.

If the ascent doesn't take your breath away, the views will: Mount Bachelor, Broken Top, and other peaks rise around Tumalo Mountain's open summit.

BEST: Brew Hikes
DISTANCE: 4.4 miles round-trip
DURATION: 2.5 hours
ELEVATION CHANGE: 1,340 feet
EFFORT: Moderate
TRAIL: Dirt trail, rocks, roots
USERS: Hikers, leashed dogs (May–Oct.)
SEASON: June–October
PASSES/FEES: None
MAPS: USGS topographic map for Mount Bachelor
CONTACT: Deschutes National Forest, 541/383–4000, www.fs.usda.gov

START THE HIKE

This hike is mostly shaded for the first 0.8 mile, and then not at all thereafter, so aim for a morning hike, wear sunscreen, and bring plenty of water. Note that the trail can also be quite dusty summer-early fall.

▶ MILE 0-0.9: Tumalo Mountain Trailhead to Meadows

You'll find the **Tumalo Mountain Trailhead** near a vault toilet at the northwestern edge of the Dutchman Flat Sno-Park parking lot. Almost immediately you'll come upon an unmarked intersection—the path that parallels the highway here is reserved for mountain bikers, so continue straight ahead to begin your steady ascent. The trail switchbacks five times over the first 0.6 mile, during which you'll gain 375 feet as you hike through a forest of ponderosa pine and mountain hemlock. In another 0.3 mile, you'll leave the forest for exposed meadows, dotted with lodgepole pine and whitebark pine. Keep an eye out for purple lupine, Davidson's penstemon, red paintbrush, and other wildflowers, which bloom well into July.

▶ MILE 0.9-2.1: Meadows to Tumalo Mountain Summit

In 0.25 mile, take a moment to turn around and appreciate your first views of Mount Bachelor to the west. After 0.9 mile more of steady ascent, you'll encounter a series of eight switchbacks that conclude at the **Tumalo Mountain summit.**

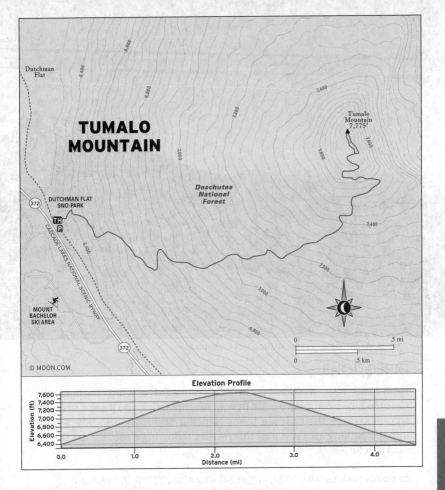

Elevation Profile

▶ MILE 2.1–2.3: Tumalo Mountain Summit Loop

Red cinder rocks denote the 0.25-mile **loop trail** around the summit that affords views in every direction. Stay within these cinder rocks, and resist the urge to follow the social trails on the northern flank; Tumalo Mountain is a protected habitat for wildflowers and wildlife, including deer and elk. Head right to start the loop and, after several hundred feet, you'll pass the concrete pilings of a long-gone **fire lookout.** From here, you can see Bend and the community of Sunriver to the east. Farther along, enjoy unimpeded views of Broken Top, as well as North and Middle Sister, at the loop's northernmost point. As you make your way back to the main trail, Mount Bachelor towers over its surroundings to the west.

▶ MILE 2.3–4.4: Tumalo Mountain Summit to Tumalo Mountain Trailhead

Back at the junction, return 2.1 miles the way you came.

▲ MOUNT BACHELOR VIEW FROM TUMALO MOUNTAIN TRAIL

DIRECTIONS

From Bend, head west on Southwest Century Drive, which becomes the Cascade Lakes National Scenic Byway. After 17 miles, you'll see a roadside sign promoting the Cascade Lakes National Scenic Byway; take a right into the parking area just past this marker, following a sign for the Dutchman Flat Sno-Park.

GPS COORDINATES: 44.00004, –121.66371 / N44° 0.0024' W121° 39.8226'

BEST NEARBY BREWS

Enjoy more views of Cascade peaks at **Crux Fermentation Project** (50 SW Division St., Bend, 541/385-3333, www.cruxfermentation.com, 11am-10pm Sun.-Thurs., 11am-11pm Fri.-Sat. summer, call for hours fall-spring), which has a large outdoor seating area and nearly 25 taps. From the trailhead, the 21-mile drive east takes 25 minutes via the Cascade Lakes National Scenic Byway.

Hike this loop trail through a ponderosa pine forest, largely along the canyon walls above Tumalo Creek, just minutes from downtown Bend.

DISTANCE: 4.8 miles round-trip
DURATION: 2 hours
ELEVATION CHANGE: 250 feet
EFFORT: Easy
TRAIL: Dirt trail, rocks, roots
USERS: Hikers, wheelchair users, leashed dogs, mountain bikers
SEASON: March–November
PASSES/FEES: None
MAPS: Bend Parks and Recreation District map for Shevlin Park
PARK HOURS: 5am-10pm daily
CONTACT: Bend Parks and Recreation District, 541/389-7275, www.bendparksandrec.org

START THE HIKE

▶ **MILE 0-0.2: Parking Area to Shevlin Loop Trail**

Walk through the entry gate at the southern edge of the parking area. Just past the gate, turn left, following a sign for Aspen Meadow and the Tumalo Creek Trail. In 0.1 mile, head left at an unsigned junction onto the **Tumalo Creek Trail.** In another few hundred feet, continue straight at the four-way junction—you'll encounter numerous junctions on this hike, but they're typically well signed—to proceed on the **Shevlin Loop Trail,** crossing a footbridge over the creek.

▶ **MILE 0.2-2.7: Shevlin Loop Trail to Tumalo Creek**

High desert plant life abounds as you gently ascend to the canyon rim, following its mostly flat edge southwest on this clockwise loop. Continue straight at a four-way intersection in 0.8 mile to remain on the Shevlin Loop Trail, which joins with an **unnamed road** in about 0.1 mile. Head right onto the roadbed and continue for 0.25 mile, then turn right at a sign for the Shevlin Loop to return to the single-track trail. Continue on this flat stretch for 0.7 mile before heading right at a junction and then, in about 0.2 mile at a map signboard, straight, to continue on the trail. You'll ascend 75 feet over the next 0.4 mile before descending toward **Tumalo Creek** and crossing it via wooden bridge. Admire its crystal-clear waters from a shaded bench to your right.

▶ **MILE 2.7-4.3: Tumalo Creek to Fremont Road Trail**

A couple hundred feet after crossing the creek, you'll arrive at a five-way junction; veer left—but not hard left—continuing on the Shevlin Loop Trail and beginning to loop back northeast. At another junction in another couple hundred feet, continue right to remain on the trail through an arid stretch of ponderosa pine. In 1.4 miles you'll arrive at a four-way intersection; here the trail crosses paths with the Historic Shevlin Railway Trail. Veer to the right just past the railway sign to remain on the loop trail. In another few hundred feet, you'll arrive at an X-shaped junction. Head right toward the **Fremont Road Trail**—which you'll reach in 0.1 mile—that bisects Shevlin Park.

▶ MILE 4.3–4.8: Fremont Road Trail to Parking Area

Closed whenever summertime fire danger is high, this paved road cuts through a forest that burned in a 2015 human-caused fire, giving hikers an up-close look at the effects of wildfire. Underbrush is rare, though stray stands of pine are flourishing. Continue north for 0.5 mile along this accessible road to return to the parking area.

DIRECTIONS

From Bend, head west on Northwest Newport Avenue, which becomes Northwest Shevlin Park Road after 1.6 miles and a handful of roundabouts. Continue on Northwest Shevlin Park Road for 2.3 miles, and turn left into the Shevlin Park parking area, just past Tumalo Creek.

GPS COORDINATES: 44.08316, –121.37791 / N44° 4.9896' W121° 22.6746'

BRIDGE OVER TUMALO CREEK ▶

BEST NEARBY BREWS

GoodLife Brewing Company (70 SW Century Dr., Bend, 541/728-0749, www.goodlifebrewing.com, noon–10pm daily) pays tribute to the "good life" in Bend with outdoors-inspired beers, locally sourced fare, and a seasonal beer garden on the lawn. From the trailhead, the 4-mile drive southeast takes 10 minutes via Northwest Shevlin Park Road and Southwest Century Drive.

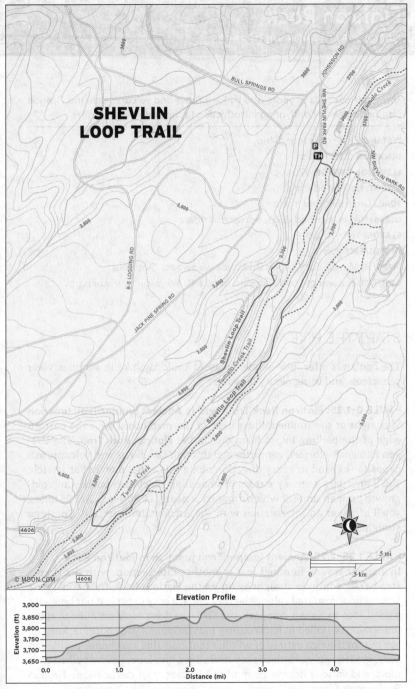

9

Flatiron Rock

OREGON BADLANDS WILDERNESS

Formed thousands of years ago by lava flows and volcanic ash, the Oregon Badlands offer a captivating introduction to the state's high desert.

DISTANCE: 6.3 miles round-trip
DURATION: 2.75 hours
ELEVATION CHANGE: 220 feet
EFFORT: Easy/moderate
TRAIL: Dirt trail, sand, rocks
USERS: Hikers, leashed dogs, horseback riders
SEASON: Year-round
PASSES/FEES: None
MAPS: BLM map for Oregon Badlands Wilderness Overview
CONTACT: Bureau of Land Management, 541/416-6700, www.blm.gov

START THE HIKE

The badlands offer little shade, so avoid a midday hike in summer, wear sunscreen, and bring plenty of water.

▶ **MILE 0-1.25: Flatiron Rock Trailhead to Ancient Juniper Trail Junction**
Veer right at the trailhead, just next to the map board near the eastern edge of the parking lot, to head out on the **Flatiron Rock Trail.** The Oregon Badlands—formed centuries ago through lava flows and volcanic ash deposits—expand in every direction along this wide, mostly flat stretch. You'll also pass a steady stream of knee-high sagebrush bushes and old-growth juniper, some of which dates back nearly 1,000 years. At 1.25 miles, you'll arrive at an intersection with the Ancient Juniper Trail. Continue straight.

▶ **MILE 1.25-2.75: Ancient Juniper Trail Junction to Flatiron Rock**
In another several hundred feet is another intersection, with the Homestead Trail; continue straight again on the Flatiron Rock Trail. You'll pass several unofficial trails along the way, and it's easy to get lost out here—it's a good idea to have a compass and GPS—so don't stray onto these spurs unless you're skilled in backcountry navigation. As you continue, keep an eye out for the rich variety of wildlife that calls this area home: prairie falcons, golden eagles, rattlesnakes, mule deer, antelope, yellow-bellied marmots, and various lizards. In another 1.5 miles, your destination—**Flatiron Rock**—comes into view, towering over the surrounding landscape.

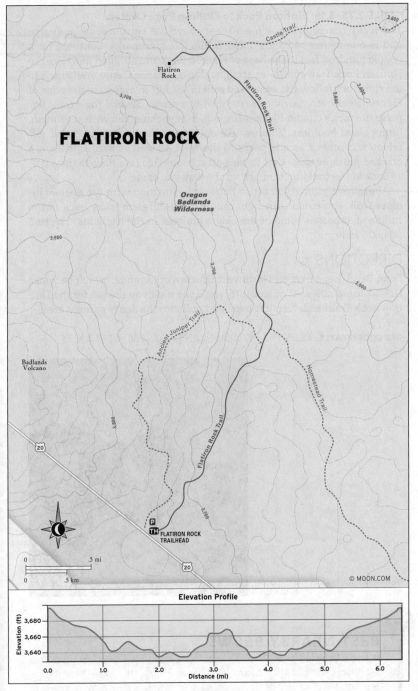

FLATIRON ROCK

Oregon
Badlands
Wilderness

Flatiron
Rock

Castle Trail

Flatiron Rock Trail

3,700

3,800

Ancient Juniper Trail

Badlands
Volcano

3,800

Flatiron Rock Trail

Homestead Trail

20

P
TH FLATIRON ROCK
TRAILHEAD

20

3,600

3,600

3,600

3,600

0   .5 mi

0   .5 km

© MOON.COM

Elevation Profile

3,680

3,660

3,640

Elevation (ft)

0.0   1.0   2.0   3.0   4.0   5.0   6.0

Distance (mi)

▶ **MILE 2.75-3.15: Flatiron Rock to Flatiron Rock Center**

The rocky outcrop rises some 50 feet above the surrounding landscape and is one of the badlands' most distinctive landmarks. Continue for a couple hundred feet to the base of Flatiron Rock and a signed junction; the Flatiron Rock Trail continues straight ahead, and the Castle Trail heads to the right, but follow the **unmarked trail** to the left to ascend to the edge of Flatiron Rock before arriving in its bowl-like center. Several short trails traverse the rock's citadel-like interior, which is pockmarked with sagebrush, juniper, and boulders. Window-like openings afford views of Mount Jefferson and other Cascade peaks to the west, as well as Badlands Rock, a cracked pressure ridge that formed after a long-ago lava flow, to the east.

Back at the trail junction, return the way you came.

Alternatively, once you arrive back at the junction with the **Ancient Juniper Trail,** you could turn right onto it for a different route back to the trailhead; it passes some of the oldest junipers in the badlands. The trail adds 0.7 mile.

DIRECTIONS

From Bend, head east on Northwest Greenwood Avenue, which becomes U.S. 20, for 16 miles. At milepost 16, you'll see a sign on the left for the Flatiron Rock Trailhead; turn left here, and pull into the dusty parking area.

GPS COORDINATES: 43.957764, -121.051824 / N43° 57.4658' W121° 3.1094'

FLATIRON ROCK TRAIL IN THE OREGON BADLANDS ▶

BEST NEARBY BREWS

Worthy Brewing (495 NE Bellevue Dr., Bend, 541/639-4776, http://worthybrewing.com, 11:30am-10pm Sun.-Thurs., 11:30am-11pm Fri.-Sat.) offers a variety of hoppy beers and locally sourced food, plenty of outdoor seating, and an observatory, complete with a telescope for post-sunset stargazing. From the trailhead, the 13-mile drive west takes 15 minutes via U.S. 20.

10

Paulina Peak

NEWBERRY NATIONAL VOLCANIC MONUMENT, DESCHUTES NATIONAL FOREST

Hike to the highest point within the Newberry National Volcanic Monument and enjoy expansive views of Central Oregon's volcanic legacy.

DISTANCE: 4.7 miles round-trip

DURATION: 2.5 hours

ELEVATION CHANGE: 1,340 feet

EFFORT: Moderate

TRAIL: Dirt trail, rocky stretches, exposed roots, sand, gravel

USERS: Hikers, leashed dogs

SEASON: June-October

PASSES/FEES: $5 day-use fee or $10 three-day pass per vehicle, or Northwest Forest Pass

MAPS: USGS topographic map for Paulina Peak

CONTACT: Deschutes National Forest, 541/383-5700, www.fs.usda.gov

This trail sits entirely within the Newberry Volcano, the largest volcano in the Cascade Range—at 1,200 square miles, the monument's geologic features cover an area the size of Rhode Island. Repeated eruptions over 400,000 years gave Newberry Volcano its shield-like shape, and a major explosion 75,000 years ago left behind a caldera.

START THE HIKE

▶ **MILE 0-1.1: Crater Rim-Paulina Peak Trailhead to Viewpoint**
Start the hike on the east side of Paulina Peak Road at the **Crater Rim and Paulina Peak Trailhead.** Two lakes sit within Newberry Volcano's caldera, and you'll catch your first glimpse of one—Paulina Lake—through the trees after 0.6 mile of steady ascent on the **Crater Rim Trail.** Over the next 0.4 mile, you'll gain 620 feet via a few switchbacks. Look west for your first views of the Three Sisters and Mount Bachelor. In 0.1 mile, as the trail curves northeast, you'll arrive at a **viewpoint,** to your left. Look north for your first glimpse of East Lake, the other lake in the caldera; northeast for the Big Obsidian Flow, a massive lava flow of gray pumice and shiny, black obsidian; and southeast for Paulina Peak, sitting atop the Newberry caldera's steep slopes.

▶ **MILE 1.1-2: Viewpoint to Paulina Peak Trail**
You'll trade mountain hemlock for whitebark pine in another 0.7 mile, leaving the shade behind but gaining spectacular views of Paulina Lake behind you. Another 0.2 mile on, a clearing to your left reveals grand views of the Three Sisters, Mount Bachelor, and Deschutes National Forest. Shortly after, head left at the junction onto the **Paulina Peak Trail.**

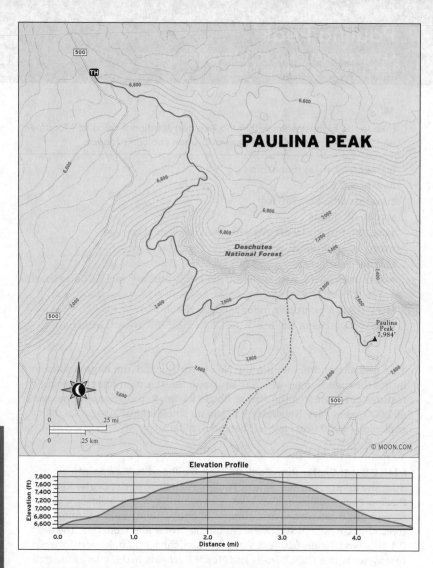

Elevation Profile

▶ **MILE 2-2.35: Paulina Peak Trail to Paulina Peak**

In 0.25 mile, you'll start walking through sand and obsidian, and arrive at an unsigned Y-shaped junction; going in either direction takes you to the summit, but the right-hand trail is well graded and spares you a nerve-racking trek alongside the cliff edges. In a couple hundred feet, you'll arrive at the parking lot atop **Paulina Peak**—yes, you could have driven to this view, but where's the fun in that? At 7,984 feet, this is the highest point on Newberry Volcano. At the western edge of the parking lot, find and hike the short trail that heads up rocky terrain for slightly better views that include Broken Top and Mount Jefferson.

Return the way you came.

▲ BIG OBSIDIAN FLOW

DIRECTIONS

From Sunriver, head south on U.S. 97 for 8.7 miles. Take a left to head east onto Paulina Lake Road, following a sign for the Newberry Caldera and Paulina and East Lakes. Continue straight on this road for 11.3 miles, at which point you'll arrive at a staffed check-in station. Continue straight, and take a right after another 1.7 miles onto Paulina Peak Road, at a sign for the Paulina Lake Campground. The road turns from pavement to gravel in 0.4 mile, and trailhead parking is on the right after another 0.3 mile.

GPS COORDINATES: 43.7009, -121.2727 / N43° 42.054' W121° 16.362'

BEST NEARBY BREWS

Sunriver Brewing Company (57100 Beaver Dr., Bldg. 4, Sunriver, 541/593-3007, www.sunriverbrewingcompany.com, 11am-10pm Sun.-Thurs., 11am-11pm Fri.-Sat.) prides itself on award-winning beer, regionally sourced fare, and a family-friendly atmosphere. From the trailhead, the 24-mile drive northwest takes 30 minutes via Paulina Lake Road and U.S. 97.

BEND AND THE CENTRAL OREGON CASCADES

Paulina Peak

NEARBY CAMPGROUNDS

NAME	DESCRIPTION	FACILITIES	SEASON	FEE
The Cove Palisades State Park	popular park with two campgrounds near Lake Billy Chinook	Crooked River Campground: 88 electrical sites, restrooms; Deschutes Campground: 82 full-hookup sites, 91 tent sites, 3 group sites, restrooms	Crooked River Campground: February-December; Deschutes Campground: May-September	$20-97

SW Jordan Road, Culver, 541/546-3412, www.oregonstateparks.org

NAME	DESCRIPTION	FACILITIES	SEASON	FEE
Creekside Campground	bustling campground near downtown Sisters	27 full-hookup sites, 33 tent sites, hiker-biker area, restrooms	April-October	$5-45

U.S. 20, Sisters, 541/323-5218, www.ci.sisters.or.us

NAME	DESCRIPTION	FACILITIES	SEASON	FEE
Tumalo State Park	campground along the Deschutes River near Bend	23 full-hookup sites, 54 tent sites, 7 yurts, 2 group camping areas, restrooms	year-round	$8-77

O. B. Riley Road, Bend, 541/388-6055, www.oregonstateparks.org

NAME	DESCRIPTION	FACILITIES	SEASON	FEE
LaPine State Park	quiet sites in a subalpine pine forest	81 full-hookup sites, 48 electrical sites, 10 log cabins, restrooms	year-round	$26-99

off U.S. 97, La Pine, 541/536-2428, www.oregonstateparks.org

NAME	DESCRIPTION	FACILITIES	SEASON	FEE
Paulina Lake Campground	popular campground along the southwest shore of Paulina Lake	68 tent and RV sites, restrooms	May-September	$18

Paulina Lake Rd., La Pine, 541/383-5300, www.fs.usda.gov

JOHN DAY RIVER BASIN

The John Day River Basin is home to some of Oregon's most diverse geologic features. At its western edge, the Ochoco National Forest hosts forested mountaintops, alpine scenery, volcanic rock formations, and high prairie expanses. Farther east along the John Day River are steep river canyons, rolling hills, and rocky terrain. But the John Day Fossil Beds National Monument, drawing more than 200,000 visitors annually, is the area's premier attraction. Volcanic eruptions and retreating glaciers scarred the landscape, which offers a glimpse into Oregon's geological past. Encompassing 14,000 acres, it holds fossils evidencing more than 40 million years of changing climates, ecosystems, and natural evolution, as well as the Painted Hills, famed for their surrealistic, colorful layers.

▲ VIEW FROM LOOKOUT MOUNTAIN

▲ WILDFLOWERS NEAR STEINS PILLAR

1 **Steins Pillar**
DISTANCE: 4.5 miles round-trip
DURATION: 2.25 hours
EFFORT: Easy/moderate

2 **Lookout Mountain**
DISTANCE: 7.7 miles round-trip
DURATION: 4 hours
EFFORT: Easy/moderate

3 **Carroll Rim Trail**
DISTANCE: 1.7 miles round-trip
DURATION: 1 hour
EFFORT: Easy

4 **Sutton Mountain**
DISTANCE: 7.5 miles round-trip
DURATION: 4 hours
EFFORT: Moderate

5 **Blue Basin Overlook**
DISTANCE: 3.4 miles round-trip
DURATION: 1.75 hours
EFFORT: Easy/moderate

▼ BLUE BASIN

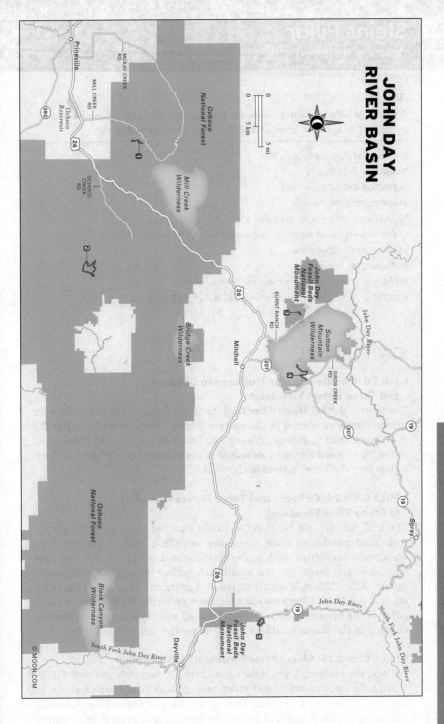

JOHN DAY
RIVER BASIN

A pleasant hike through ponderosa pine forests and springtime wildflower meadows ends at the base of a 350-foot column of rhyolite ash.

DISTANCE: 4.5 miles round-trip
DURATION: 2.25 hours
ELEVATION CHANGE: 740 feet
EFFORT: Easy/moderate
TRAIL: Dirt paths, rocks, wooden stairs
USERS: Hikers, leashed dogs, mountain bikers, horseback riders
SEASON: April-November
PASSES/FEES: None
MAPS: USGS topographic map for Steins Pillar
CONTACT: Ochoco National Forest, 541/416-6500, www.fs.usda.gov

START THE HIKE

▸ **MILE 0-0.6: Steins Pillar Trailhead to Ochocos and Three Sisters Viewpoint**

The mostly shaded **Steins Pillar Trail** starts out flat in a pine forest from an informational signboard at the eastern edge of the parking lot. After 0.3 mile, you'll start to ascend, gaining 200 feet over the next 0.3 mile—most of the hike's elevation—to a **viewpoint** of the surrounding Ochocos and, on a clear day, the Three Sisters to the west.

▸ **MILE 0.6-1.25: Ochocos and Three Sisters Viewpoint to Steins Pillar Viewpoint**

The trail flattens out here and, 0.4 mile past the viewpoint, the cinnamon-hued ponderosa pine gives way to rolling hills of juniper, lemon-scented sagebrush, and, in the spring, meadows of wildflowers. Late May-June, you might see red paintbrush, yellow balsamroot, and purple lupine. After 0.25 mile, you'll arrive at a junction; head left for a quick jaunt to the **Steins Pillar viewpoint,** a clearing offering the best views you'll enjoy of the column, which formed some 40 million years ago during the collapse of the Wildcat Caldera, rising above the surrounding forest.

▸ **MILE 1.25-2.25: Steins Pillar Viewpoint to Steins Pillar**

Back on the main trail, you'll descend about 270 feet over the next 1 mile, mostly via wooden stairs and steep switchbacks. You'll arrive at a sign that reads "End of Maintained Trail" at the base of **Steins Pillar.** The trail peters out to gravel and rock here; take care because even in dry weather it can be slippery (the ground slopes toward the pillar's base). In sunnier months, you might see rock climbers ascending the column.

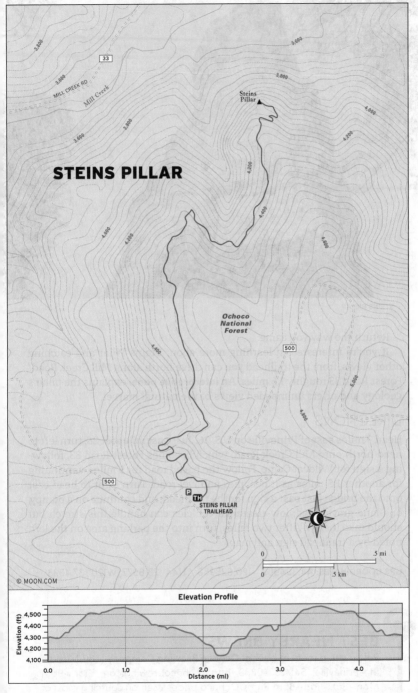

STEINS PILLAR

Steins Pillar

Mill Creek

MILL CREEK RD

Ochoco National Forest

STEINS PILLAR TRAILHEAD

© MOON.COM

0 .5 mi
0 .5 km

Elevation Profile

▲ STEINS PILLAR

Return the way you came.

If you're interested in learning more about Steins Pillar and catching other views, from the trailhead you can drive north along Mill Creek Road/Forest Road 33 roughly 1.5 miles. An **interpretive panel** explains the pillar's geology and offers unimpeded views of the natural marvel.

DIRECTIONS

Head 9 miles east of Prineville on U.S. 26. Just past milepost 28, turn left to head north onto Mill Creek Road, which becomes Forest Road 33, following a sign for Wildcat Camp. Follow the paved road for 5 miles, continuing for another 1.5 miles as it becomes a gravel road. Turn right to head east onto the bridge just past a sign for the trailhead, and continue on a bumpy, one-lane gravel road; low-clearance vehicles can handle this stretch but should take it slow. After two miles, turn into the parking area on the left, noted by a trailhead sign and map.

GPS COORDINATES: 44.394962, –120.623988 / N44° 23.6977' W120° 37.4393'

BEST NEARBY BREWS

Relax with a meal or beer at **Ochoco Brewing Company** (380 N. Main St., Prineville, 541/233-0883, http://ochocobrewing.com, 11am-9pm Mon.-Sat., 11am-8pm Sun.). Ochoco prides itself on sourcing most of the ingredients for its small-batch beers and food offerings from as close to Prineville as possible. From the trailhead, the 16-mile drive west via U.S. 26 takes just under 30 minutes.

This clockwise loop trail offers something for everyone: wildflowers, Cascade peaks, alpine forests, wildlife, meadows, and vistas.

DISTANCE: 7.7 miles round-trip
DURATION: 4 hours
ELEVATION CHANGE: 1,130 feet
EFFORT: Easy/moderate
TRAIL: Dirt paths, rocky paths, minor stream crossing
USERS: Hikers, leashed dogs, mountain bikers, horseback riders
SEASON: May-November
PASSES/FEES: None
MAPS: USGS topographic maps for Lookout Mountain and Gerow Butte
CONTACT: Ochoco National Forest, 541/416-6500, www.fs.usda.gov

START THE HIKE

▶ **MILE 0-2.6: Independent Mine Trailhead to Brush Creek**
Head to the east side of the parking area to the **Independent Mine Trailhead.** Blue diamonds indicating the route to the summit are nailed to trees every hundred or so feet, just above eye level; should you sidestep a downed tree or go off-trail to avoid an early-season snow drift, keep an eye out for these blazes. Traveling southeast on the trail, you'll quickly encounter a forest rich with ponderosa pine and grand fir trees. In spring, you may hear the high-pitched call of the hermit thrush or rapid-fire drumbeat of the pileated woodpecker. After 1.2 miles and 400 feet of elevation gain, you'll find yourself in ponderosa pine and sagebrush meadows. In the late spring and early summer, a variety of wildflowers line the way, including bigleaf lupine, arrowleaf balsamroot, yellow bells, and sand lilies. You'll lose about 100 feet of elevation over the next 1.4 miles, cutting through a mix of sagebrush-covered meadows and subalpine fir forests. Keep an eye out for hummingbirds, elk, deer, and wild horses—the U.S. Forest Service estimated in 2018 that 135 wild horses call the region home.

▶ **MILE 2.6-4.5: Brush Creek to Lookout Mountain Summit**
Hop a few rocks to cross the bubbling **Brush Creek,** and then begin steadily ascending toward the summit, cutting through large swaths of fir trees broken up by frequent meadows—covered with mountain bluebells, false hellebore, and other wildflowers in spring and summer—and offering views of the Ochocos to the south. You'll arrive at an unsigned junction in another 1.3 miles; a spur trail shoots off to the left, but ignore it and continue straight, heading west on the Independent Mine Trail. As you follow the dirt trail, gradually heading north, the fir forests give way to a

sagebrush-covered hillside. You'll gain 250 feet over the next 0.6 mile before arriving at a junction, and the **Lookout Mountain summit,** among the Ochocos' highest peaks.

▶ MILE 4.5-5: Lookout Mountain Summit to Lookout Mountain Trail

Head left on the short, unmarked trail to find the remnants of an **old stone corral,** which once formed the base of the fire lookout for which the mountain is named. On a clear day, this clearing offers the hike's best views, with the Three Sisters, Mount Bachelor, and other prominent Cascade peaks visible to the west. If the winds aren't whipping, this **viewpoint** makes a fine spot for lunch. Back at the junction, turn left to begin your descent, following the sign for the **Lookout Mountain Trail.** In another few hundred feet, you'll come to another junction—a short spur trail to the right leads to a backcountry snow shelter—but continue straight. In 0.3 mile, turn left at the junction to continue descending the Lookout Mountain Trail. (To shave a mile off the hike, you could instead continue straight here to head down the steeper, shorter, less scenic **Motherlode Trail.**)

▶ MILE 5-7.7: Lookout Mountain Trail to Parking Area

From here you'll steadily descend through aspen groves and pine forests as you loop back to the trailhead. After another 2.6 miles, you'll see abandoned **mining equipment** to your right. Several mines in the area opened in the early 1900s, but all had ceased operation by the 1950s; tempting as it may be, hikers should not leave the trail to explore these dilapidated structures. Just past the equipment, you'll arrive at an unsigned fork in the trail; head right to return to the parking area in a few hundred feet.

MINE SHAFT ▶

DIRECTIONS

Drive 15.5 miles east of Prineville on U.S. 26, and take a slight right onto Ochoco Creek Road at a sign for Walton Lake. Continue straight for 8.5 miles before taking a right onto Forest Road 42 for 6.5 miles. Turn right onto Forest Road 4205, following signs for Independent Mine. Take the gravel road for 1.5 miles (low-clearance vehicles should take it slow, especially over the last mile), continuing straight at the junction and ignoring signs for the Baneberry Trailhead. The road ends in the trailhead parking area.

GPS COORDINATES: 44.33934, -120.35832 / N44° 20.3604' W120° 21.4992'

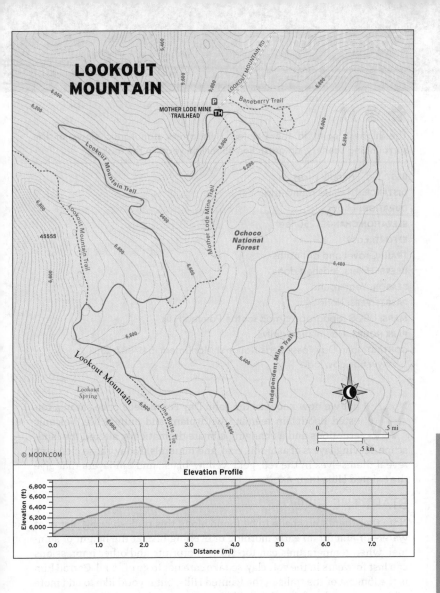

Elevation Profile

BEST NEARBY BITES

Dillon's Grill (142 NE 5th St., Prineville, 541/447-3203, www.dillons-grill.com, 11am-9pm Sun.-Thurs., 11am-10pm Fri.-Sat.) boasts a menu heavy on burgers and barbecue—with 13 regional craft beers and ciders on tap at any given time. From the trailhead, the 32-mile drive west takes one hour via Ochoco Creek Road and U.S. 26.

The highest point in the Painted Hills offers panoramic views of the surrounding scenery, an attraction 35 million years in the making.

BEST: Kid-Friendly Hikes
DISTANCE: 1.7 miles round-trip
DURATION: 1 hour
ELEVATION CHANGE: 260 feet
EFFORT: Easy
TRAIL: Gravel and dirt paths
USERS: Hikers, leashed dogs
SEASON: Year-round
PASSES/FEES: None
MAPS: USGS topographic map for the Painted Hills
PARK HOURS: Dawn-dusk daily
CONTACT: John Day Fossil Beds National Monument, 541/987-2333,
www.nps.gov/joda

What we now know as the John Day Fossil Beds once sat in a forested floodplain teeming with plant and animal life. Volcanic eruptions and a changing climate dramatically altered the landscape, leaving layers of ash, soil, coal, and minerals. Today, those elements reveal themselves in the red, gold, yellow, black, and tan layers that give the Painted Hills their name.

START THE HIKE

Note that there's no shade to be found along this trail, so bring plenty of water—or aim for an early morning or evening hike at the height of summer, when temperatures can top 110°F. Footprints and other impressions can last for years in the soft clay, so take care not to go off-trail. Carroll Rim is the longest of the trails in the Painted Hills, but if you'd like to add more hiking to your day, four other trails in the unit, ranging 0.25-0.5 mile, are accessible via Bear Creek Road.

▶ MILE 0-0.25: Carroll Rim Trailhead to Viewpoint

Find the **Carroll Rim Trailhead** on the north side of Bear Creek Road from the small pullout parking area. You'll ascend steadily, slicing through an open hillside before arriving at a wooden bench and the trail's first **viewpoint** a bit less than 0.25 mile in. From here you can see the colorful hillsides to the south.

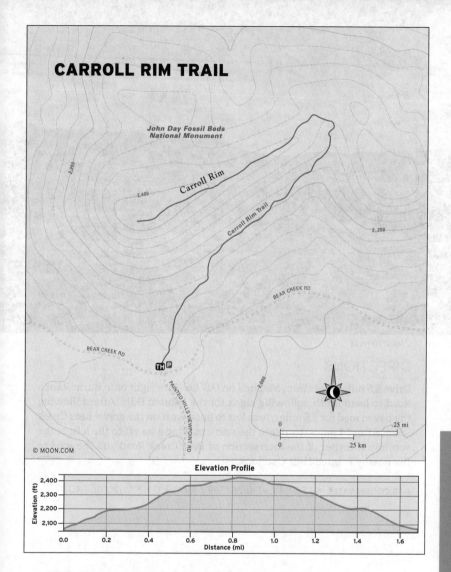

CARROLL RIM TRAIL

John Day Fossil Beds
National Monument

Carroll Rim

Carroll Rim Trail

2,200

2,400

2,200

BEAR CREEK RD

BEAR CREEK RD

TH P

PAINTED HILLS VIEWPOINT RD

2,000

© MOON.COM

0   .25 mi

0   .25 km

Elevation Profile

Distance (mi)

▶ **MILE 0.25-0.85: Viewpoint to Summit**

Continue on—views keep improving as you hike uphill—and keep an eye
out for yellow rabbitbrush, which typically blooms August-October, and
purple bitterroot, which blooms April-May along this stretch. After gaining 200 feet over 0.3 mile, you'll hit the trail's lone **switchback** as you head
west toward the summit. The trail flattens over this final 0.3-mile stretch,
with sweeping views of the Painted Hills to the south and farmland to the
north. Two wooden benches mark the **summit**—the end of the trail—and
offer great perches from which to take in the 360-degree views. The Painted Hills' colorful slopes dominate the landscape to the south and west,
lush farmlands are to the north, and Sutton Mountain rises over the hills
to the east.

When you've had your fill of the vibrant palette, return the way you came.

▲ PAINTED HILLS

DIRECTIONS

Drive 3.5 miles west from Mitchell on U.S. 26. Turn right onto Burnt Ranch Road to head north, following signs for the Painted Hills. After following the paved road for 5.5 miles, turn left to head west on the gravel Bear Creek Road. After 1.1 miles, turn into the small parking area off to the left, at the southwest corner of the intersection of Bear Creek Road and the road to the nearby Painted Hills Overlook.

GPS COORDINATES: 44.651944, −120.267339 / N44° 39.1166' W120° 16.0403'

BEST NEARBY BREWS

Tiger Town Brewing (108 Main St., Mitchell, 541/462-3663, www.tigertownbrewing.com, noon-7pm Sun.-Mon., typically noon-8pm Tues.-Thurs. and noon-9pm Fri.-Sat., though hours may vary seasonally) serves a handful of locally brewed ales and lagers alongside regional beers, ciders, and wines. The lineup changes regularly, so you'll rarely encounter the same beer twice. From the trailhead, the 10-mile drive east takes 25 minutes via Bear Creek and Burnt Ranch Roads and U.S. 26.

Sutton Mountain

SUTTON MOUNTAIN WILDERNESS STUDY AREA

Not a road, not yet a trail, this rugged path to the summit of Sutton Mountain delivers sweeping views in every direction.

DISTANCE: 7.5 miles round-trip
DURATION: 4 hours
ELEVATION CHANGE: 1,670 feet
EFFORT: Moderate
TRAIL: Washed-out dirt road, rocks, cow pies
USERS: Hikers, leashed dogs, horseback riders
SEASON: Year-round
PASSES/FEES: None
MAPS: USGS topographic map for Sutton Mountain
CONTACT: Bureau of Land Management, Prineville District, 541/415-6700, www.blm.gov

Rising more than 4,500 feet, Sutton Mountain sits at the heart of a conservation effort that would protect 58,000 acres of surrounding land for public access. That proposal sits stalled in Congress, but what's here is nevertheless a worthy trail whose views justify the relentless climb.

START THE HIKE

▶ MILE 0-1.7: Cattle Gate to Forest Departure

A closed cattle gate, just north of the grassy parking area, marks the start of the trail—"trail" being something of a misnomer, as the entirety of this hike follows an old **unnamed roadbed.** Walk around the locked gate and follow the road, at times covered in grass, rocks, mud, or, especially at the higher elevations, dry cow pies. In 0.15 mile the path switchbacks to the left, near a privately owned **barn,** and heads southwest for 0.8 mile, gaining 460 feet in elevation along the way. You'll see plenty of ponderosa pine at these lower elevations, along with a variety of wildflowers late April-mid-June, including purple lupine and red Indian paintbrush. Since the trail offers little shade, relax while you can under the trees—and keep an eye out for rattlesnakes that might sun themselves on rocks lining the trail here. You'll climb out of a juniper and sagebrush forest after another 0.7 mile, when the trail opens to views of Horse Mountain to the east and Table Mountain to the north.

▶ MILE 1.7-3.75: Forest Departure to Overlook

Watch for pronghorn, elk, mule deer, and coyotes on the surrounding hillsides. After another 0.4 mile of slow but steady climbing, you'll arrive at a cattle gate. Open it—taking care to close it behind you—and continue to a second fence line just ahead. Walk through a gap in the fence and follow

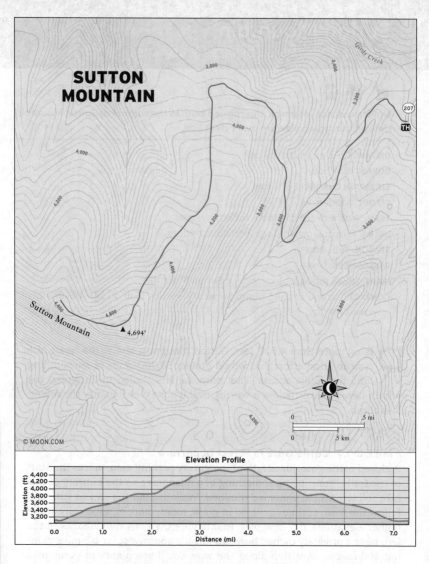

SUTTON MOUNTAIN

Elevation Profile

the roadbed uphill. The trail starts leveling out and curving around the summit in another 1.3 miles. You'll arrive at an **overlook,** just south of the summit, in 0.4 mile. The trail continues on, but this is your turnaround point. Take in the views of the Painted Hills and Ochoco Mountains.

No official trail goes to the rimrock **Sutton Mountain summit,** but if you like you can head 0.3 mile up the grassy hillside to relax in the shade of a juniper tree, look around for pink hedgehog cactus blossoms if it's spring, enjoy wide-open views of the Painted Hills and John Day River, and eye Mount Jefferson on the horizon to the west.

Return the way you came

▲ VIEW FROM SUTTON MOUNTAIN

DIRECTIONS

From Mitchell, drive 0.2 mile west on U.S. 26, and turn right to head north onto Highway 207; reset your odometer at this point, and keep an eye out at 9.5 miles. You'll see an unmarked turn to the left at a bend in the highway. (If you see a sign for Girds Creek Road, you've gone too far.) Turn left to pull into a gravel driveway; you'll immediately arrive at a barbwire gate sporting a Bureau of Land Management sign. Get out of your vehicle, open the gate—making sure to close it behind you to prevent cattle from escaping—and then turn right to head north on the washed-out road. You'll shortly arrive in a meadow with room for parking.

GPS COORDINATES: 44.664761, -120.125501 / N44° 39.8857' W120° 7.5301'

BEST NEARBY BITES

Reward yourself with a stick-to-your-ribs meal at the **Little Pine Cafe** (100 E. Main St., Mitchell, 541/462-3532, www.mitchellstagestop.com, 7:30am-7:30pm Tues.-Fri., 11:30am-7:30pm Sat.). It claims to serve the best burgers east of the Ochocos, buoyed by more than a decade of experimentation. From the trailhead, the 10-mile drive south takes 15 minutes via Highway 207 and U.S. 26.

Hike the rim of a colorful basin deep in the heart of the John Day Fossil Beds National Monument before descending to its rocky floor.

DISTANCE: 3.4 miles round-trip

DURATION: 1.75 hours

ELEVATION CHANGE: 790 feet

EFFORT: Easy/moderate

TRAIL: Dirt and gravel paths, wooden boardwalk

USERS: Hikers, leashed dogs

SEASON: Year-round

PASSES/FEES: None

MAPS: USGS topographic maps for Picture Gorge East and Picture Gorge West

PARK HOURS: Dawn-dusk daily

CONTACT: John Day Fossil Beds National Monument, 541/987-2333, www.nps.gov/joda

The Blue Basin—really more of a blue-green—was formed nearly 30 million years ago as ash settled in the wake of nearby volcanic eruptions; the resulting rock formations became home to myriad fossils, many of which are still being discovered. Note that digging for—or removing—fossils from the area is strictly prohibited.

START THE HIKE

▶ **MILE 0-1.3: Blue Basin Overlook Trailhead to Bench**

Find the trailhead at the eastern edge of the parking lot. You'll encounter a T-shaped intersection immediately. Head left to begin a clockwise loop via the **Blue Basin Overlook Trail.** Hike up the gentle incline through sagebrush meadows for the first mile, with the outer edge of the colorful basin to your right. This trail offers little cover, so catch your breath on its only shaded **bench** 1.3 miles in, from which you can see colorful fossil beds.

▶ **MILE 1.3-1.6: Bench to John Day Fossil Beds Viewpoint**

Continue on, hiking over a short section of wooden boardwalk. In 0.25 mile, you'll arrive at the **rim of the Blue Basin,** and a junction; an easy-to-miss sign is near your feet and signals you to turn right for a short **spur trail** to a **viewpoint** of the colorful rock formations and surrounding John Day Fossil Beds.

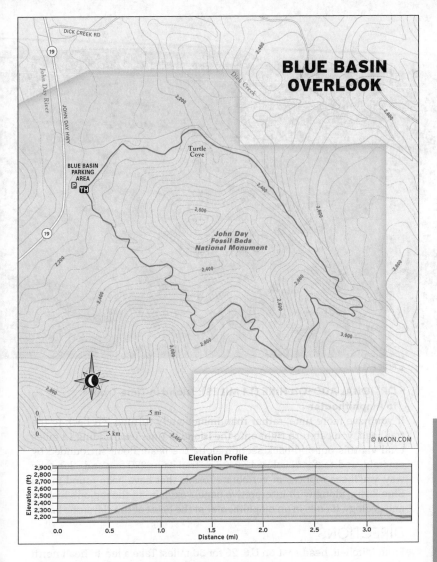

Elevation Profile

▶ MILE 1.6–3.4: John Day Fossil Beds Viewpoint to Blue Basin Overlook Trailhead

Back on the main trail, head south to continue along the basin's rim for 0.8 mile—the hike briefly enters private property, so take care not to disturb the surrounding grasslands or go off-trail here—enjoying continuous views of the colorful rocks and jagged formations. You'll descend a series of switchbacks over the next 0.8 mile to arrive at the **Blue Basin floor** and a T-shaped intersection, where the Blue Basin Overlook Trail dead-ends at the **Island in Time Trail.** Go left on the Island in Time Trail to head northwest and complete the loop back at the hike's first junction in 0.2 mile.

▲ BLUE BASIN

▶ **OPTIONAL ADD-ON HIKE (1.1 MILES): Island in Time Trail to Amphitheater**

If you have more time, rather than immediately turning left back to the trailhead, you can turn right onto the **Island in Time Trail,** adding 1.1 miles total via this out-and-back section along the basin floor, surrounded by emerald- and seafoam-colored rock. The trail gains 220 feet and, along the way, you'll see replicas of vertebrate fossils that have been found in the Blue Basin, along with interpretive panels explaining the region's history and geology. It ends in an **amphitheater** at the heart of the claystone basin.

DIRECTIONS

From Mitchell, head east on U.S. 26 for 30 miles. Take a left to head north on Highway 19 for 5.2 miles, following a sign for the Thomas Condon Visitor Center. Turn right into the parking lot for the Blue Basin trailhead.

GPS COORDINATES: 44.595616, –119.631239 / N44° 35.7370' W119° 37.8743'

BEST NEARBY BITES

Dayville Cafe (212 Franklin St., Dayville, 541/987-2122, 7am-8pm Wed.-Sat., 8am-4pm Sun.) is the kind of café where the servers' out-sized personalities—they will call you "hun" and recommend you save room for the homemade pie—are bested only by the portion sizes. From the trailhead, the 13-mile drive southeast takes 20 minutes via Highway 19 and U.S. 26.

NEARBY CAMPGROUNDS

NAME	DESCRIPTION	FACILITIES	SEASON	FEE
Ochoco Forest Campground	quaint campground near Lookout Mountain	5 tent and RV sites, restrooms	spring–early fall	$15
Forest Rd. 33, Prineville, 541/416-6500, www.fs.usda.gov				
Wildcat Campground	quiet campground along Mill Creek	17 tent and small RV sites, restrooms	spring–early fall	$15
Mill Creek Rd., Prineville, 541/416-6500, www.fs.usda.gov				
Ochoco Divide Campground	campground on the Ochocos' crest	25 first-come, first-served RV and tent sites, 3 accessible sites, restrooms	spring–early fall	$13
U.S. 26, Prineville, 541/416-6500, www.fs.usda.gov				
Walton Lake Campground	family-friendly campground on Walton Lake	27 tent and RV sites, 2 accessible sites, restrooms	spring–early fall	$15
Forest Rd. 22, Prineville, 877/444-6777, www.recreation.gov				
Mitchell City Park	sites in a small city park with a grassy field	4 RV sites, grass field for tents, restrooms	year-round except Labor Day weekend	$12–25
Mitchell, 541/462-3121, www.mitchelloregon.us				

CRATER LAKE NATIONAL PARK

Crater Lake is the centerpiece of Oregon's only national park, the deepest lake in North America, and one of the clearest lakes in the world. Roughly 7,700 years ago, the 12,000-foot Mount Mazama erupted in southern Oregon. The roof of its emptied magma chamber eventually collapsed, leaving behind this bowl-shaped caldera that filled over thousands of years with rainwater and snowmelt. Today, visitors come from around the world to admire the lake's dramatically blue hue—thanks to its depth and clarity—and explore the surrounding terrain, including old-growth forest, pumice fields, and waterfalls.

The park's primary southern entrance, the Annie Spring Entrance Station, is open year-round, while its northern entrance usually opens to vehicles between mid-May and late June and closes late October-early November, depending on snowfall. Check with the park and Oregon Department of Transportation (www.tripcheck.org) for the latest updates on access roads. The 33-mile Rim Drive circles Crater Lake; the West Rim Drive usually opens to vehicles between mid-May and late June, and the East Rim Drive generally opens between mid-June and late July. Snow may linger on trails well into July, and the first snowfall may arrive as early as mid-September.

▲ WITCHES CAULDRON ON WIZARD ISLAND

▲ VISITING CRATER LAKE

1 **Boundary Springs**
DISTANCE: 5.5 miles round-trip
DURATION: 2.5 hours
EFFORT: Easy/moderate

2 **Cleetwood Cove and Wizard Island**
DISTANCE: 4.9 miles round-trip
DURATION: 3 hours
EFFORT: Easy/moderate

3 **Garfield Peak**
DISTANCE: 3.4 miles round-trip
DURATION: 1.5 hours
EFFORT: Easy/moderate

4 **Plaikni Falls**
DISTANCE: 2.2 miles round-trip
DURATION: 1.5 hours
EFFORT: Easy

5 **Mount Scott**
DISTANCE: 4.6 miles round-trip
DURATION: 2.5 hours
EFFORT: Easy/moderate

BEST NEARBY BITES

- Oregon-grown ingredients take center stage at the **Crater Lake Lodge Dining Room** (565 Rim Dr., Crater Lake National Park, 541/594-2255, ext. 3200 or ext. 3201, www.travelcraterlake.com, 7am-10am, 11am-3pm, and 5pm-9:30pm daily May-Oct.). Situated on the southern lakeshore, the national park's fine-dining restaurant offers breakfast, lunch, and dinner with lovely views.

- Unwind with classic American fare at **Annie Creek Restaurant** (Mazama Village Road, Crater Lake National Park, 541/594-2255, www.travelcraterlake.com, hours vary daily May-Sept.). It serves breakfast, lunch, and dinner—including scrambles, omelets, burgers, sandwiches, and more—near the Annie Spring Entrance Station, the park's southern entry point.

- Save room for pie at **Beckie's Cafe** (56484 Hwy. 62, Prospect, 866/560-3565, www.unioncreekoregon.com, 8am-9pm daily summer, 8am-7pm Sun.-Thurs. and 8am-8pm Fri.-Sat. winter). Since 1926, Beckie's has served breakfast, lunch, dinner, and a selection of famous homemade pies—baked fresh daily. Beckie's is located just outside the park, 17 miles west of the Annie Spring Entrance Station via Highway 62.

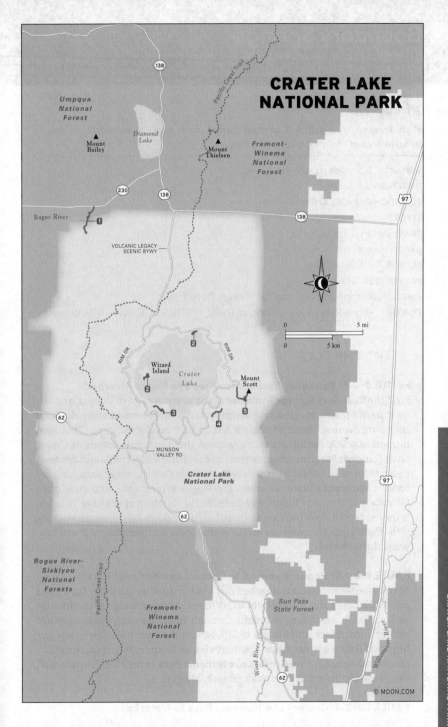

Boundary Springs

ROGUE RIVER-SISKIYOU NATIONAL FOREST,
CRATER LAKE NATIONAL PARK

Hike through a wildfire-scorched forest and past a waterfall to the headwaters of the majestic Rogue River.

DISTANCE: 5.5 miles round-trip
DURATION: 2.5 hours
ELEVATION CHANGE: 320 feet
EFFORT: Easy/moderate
TRAIL: Dirt trail, rocks, roots
USERS: Hikers
SEASON: June-November
PASSES/FEES: None
MAPS: USGS topographic map for Pumice Desert West
CONTACT: Rogue River-Siskiyou National Forest, 541/560-3400, www.fs.usda.gov

START THE HIKE

▶ **MILE 0-0.6: Boundary Springs Trailhead to Rogue Riverbed**
Find the **Boundary Springs Trailhead** at the eastern edge of the parking lot, next to the restroom. Heading south, you'll almost immediately descend into a recovering forest of Shasta red fir and ponderosa pine. This area burned in a 2015 wildfire that consumed the northwest corner of Crater Lake National Park, but even as you pass toothpick-like snags and downed trees, signs of life abound; you may hear a hairy woodpecker searching for food or see purple filaree flowers. The **Rogue River** comes into view after 0.5 mile; you'll mostly follow its banks for the duration of the hike. In a few hundred feet, follow the tree-fastened sign for Boundary Springs, veering left—the trail that continues straight has been decommissioned—and toward the riverbed.

▶ **MILE 0.6-1.9: Rogue Riverbed to Crater Lake National Park**
You'll intersect with an unmarked dirt road in another 0.5 mile. Turn right and walk down the road for about 100 feet before picking up the trail on its south side, ascending gradually through an increasingly green forest of mountain hemlock and Shasta red fir. Ignore the spur trail that heads uphill in 0.25 mile and continue south. A sign announces when you formally cross the boundary into **Crater Lake National Park** in another 0.5 mile, and the grade through this stretch is remarkably gentle.

▶ **MILE 1.9-2.4: Crater Lake National Park to Waterfall**
Another 0.5 mile past the park boundary, you'll drop to river level and enter a meadow where you may hear a Clark's nutcracker or yellow-rumped warbler, or see patches of yellow monkeyflower and blue lupine. You'll

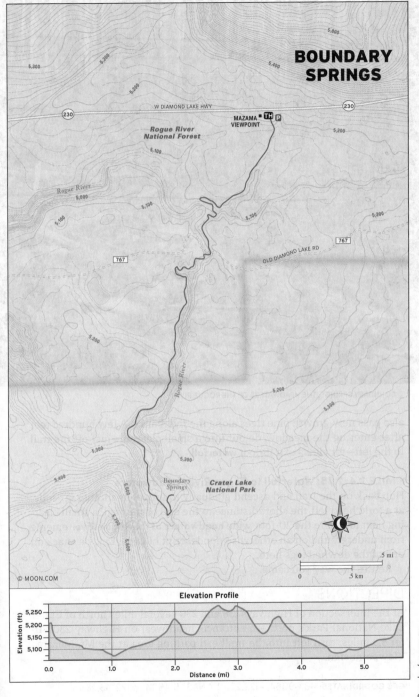

BOUNDARY SPRINGS

5,800

5,300

5,300

5,400

W DIAMOND LAKE HWY

230

230

MAZAMA
VIEWPOINT TH P

5,200

Rogue River
National Forest

5,100

5,200

Rogue River

5,000

5,100

5,100

5,200

767

5,100

OLD DIAMOND LAKE RD

767

767

5,200

5,200

Rogue River

5,200

5,300

5,300

5,300

5,400

5,600

5,700

5,600

Boundary
Springs

Crater Lake
National Park

0   .5 mi

0   .5 km

© MOON.COM

Elevation Profile

Elevation (ft)

5,250
5,200
5,150
5,100

0.0   1.0   2.0   3.0   4.0   5.0

Distance (mi)

▲ BOUNDARY SPRINGS, THE HEADWATERS OF THE ROGUE RIVER

also pass new-growth pine trees along the riverbanks. A few hundred feet after entering the meadow, detour into a small clearing—just off the trail to the left—for views of a 15-foot **waterfall.**

▶ **MILE 2.4–2.75: Waterfall to Rogue River Headwaters**
Hop back on the trail and ascend gradually to arrive, in another 0.3 mile, at a fork; head left the short distance to the end of the trail, a small clearing next to where the 20-foot-wide **headwaters of the Rogue River** emerge from underground on an otherwise nondescript hillside. Enjoy a snack on one of the downed logs here.

Return the way you came.

DIRECTIONS

At the intersection of Highways 138 and 230 several miles north of Crater Lake National Park's northern entrance, head west on Highway 230. After 5.3 miles, turn left into the trailhead parking area at the Mt. Mazama Viewpoint sign.

GPS COORDINATES: 43.09084, –122.22141 / N43° 5.4504' W122° 13.2846'

Hike the Cleetwood Cove Trail for the only safe and legal access to Crater Lake's shoreline before taking a boat out to Wizard Island to scale the mini volcano's summit.

BEST: Summer Hikes

DISTANCE: 4.9 miles round-trip (Cleetwood Cove 2.2 miles; Wizard Island 2.7 miles)

DURATION: 3 hours

ELEVATION CHANGE: Cleetwood Cove (520 feet), Wizard Island (680 feet)

EFFORT: Easy/moderate

TRAIL: Dirt trail, rocks, roots, gravel, lava rock

USERS: Hikers

SEASON: June–September

PASSES/FEES: 7-day national park pass, Crater Lake Annual Pass, America the Beautiful Passes

MAPS: USGS topographic map for Crater Lake East, free basic trail map in the Crater Lake National Park newspaper available at entry stations and at park facilities

CONTACT: Crater Lake National Park, 541/594-3000, www.nps.gov/crla

The Cleetwood Cove Trail is the most popular trail in Crater Lake National Park. At the end of the trail is a dock from which boat tours and shuttles launch for Wizard Island, a hikeable volcano within a volcano. Following Mount Mazama's eruption and collapse, subsequent eruptions formed numerous cinder cones within the caldera of Crater Lake. Today, Wizard Island is the only one that rises above Crater Lake's surface. Linking the hikes with a boat ride on Crater Lake is a wonderful way to spend a day in the park.

A ticket for a boat tour or shuttle boat is required to access Wizard Island. The **Wizard Island boat tour** ($55 adults, $37 children 3-12) includes an interpretive talk by a park ranger, lake cruising, and a three-hour stop at Wizard Island. Tours depart at 9:45am and 12:45pm daily in season. Including the stop on Wizard Island, the tour lasts approximately five hours total. You could also just take a **shuttle boat** ($28 adults, $18 children 3-12), bypassing the educational talk. It offers pick-up and drop-off and includes a three-hour stop on Wizard Island. Shuttles depart at 8:30am and 11:30am daily in season. The shuttle takes about half an hour to get to Wizard Island. Boats typically run June-September. Approximately half the tickets for every tour or shuttle are available in advance, online or by phone, and the other half are available 24 hours before each tour or shuttle at self-serve kiosks in the park's Crater Lake Lodge and Annie Creek Gift Shop. Any remaining tickets are sold at a booth in the parking area at the top of the Cleetwood Cove Trail. Give yourself 30 minutes for the descent to the

Cleetwood Cove and Wizard Island

CRATER LAKE NATIONAL PARK

shoreline and 45-60 minutes for the return ascent on the Cleetwood Cove Trail.

START THE HIKE

You must check in at the booth at the Cleetwood Cove parking area as well as at a second booth at the base of the trail for boat tours and shuttles. Be sure to bring plenty of water for this hike, and apply sunscreen; time on the boat alone will offer plenty of exposure, and the summit of Wizard Island is also exposed.

▸ MILE 0-1.1: Cleetwood Cove Trailhead to Cleetwood Cove Dock

Walk south from the Cleetwood Cove parking area after checking in, crossing Rim Drive, to arrive at the **Cleetwood Cove Trailhead.** Over the course of its 1.1 miles, you'll descend a series of nine switchbacks. The trail, wide enough for hikers to walk side-by-side, is mostly shaded, passing through a forest of lodgepole pine, Shasta red fir, and mountain hemlock, and it progressively opens up to expansive lake views. The trail ends at the **dock** and **ticket booth,** both to your left on the shore of Crater Lake. You can dive off the rocks from the lakeshore here—but note that even at the height of summer the water temperature only reaches 59°F. Check in again for your boat tour or shuttle at the ticket booth. Bathrooms are available just west of the ticket booth.

▸ MILE 1.1-2.3: Wizard Island Dock to Summit

Your boat tour or shuttle will drop you off at the **Wizard Island dock.** Follow the signage, heading left onto a dirt path to find the trailheads. (If you need a bathroom break, the trail to the right leads to a restroom in a few hundred feet.) You'll shortly arrive at a junction; turn right, following the Summit sign. You'll ascend steadily through a forest of western hemlock that gives way to whitebark pine, with a bed of ankle-high pinemat manzanita flanking the trail throughout. Along the way, you may spot golden-mantled ground squirrels and hear band-winged grasshoppers, which have wings that sound like a lawn sprinkler when in flight. After 1.2 miles you'll arrive at the **Wizard Island summit,** and a junction.

▸ MILE 2.3-2.6: Witches Cauldron Loop

Head left for an 0.3-mile clockwise loop around the crater atop Wizard Island known as the **Witches Cauldron.** The crater affords 360-degree views of Crater Lake, Mount Scott to the east, and Watchman Peak to the west. Several social trails descend to the base of the pumice-filled crater. July-August, keep an eye out for purple penstemon along the loop.

▸ MILE 2.6-4.9: Summit to Cleetwood Cove Trailhead

After completing the loop, return the 1.2 miles to the Wizard Island dock the way you came. If you have spare time and a towel, feel free to take a dip in Crater Lake's chilly waters while you wait for the boat to return. Back on the mainland, return to the parking area from the dock via the 1.1-mile Cleetwood Cove Trail. The ascent tests even those in good physical condition, thanks to the steady incline and steep grade of 11 percent.

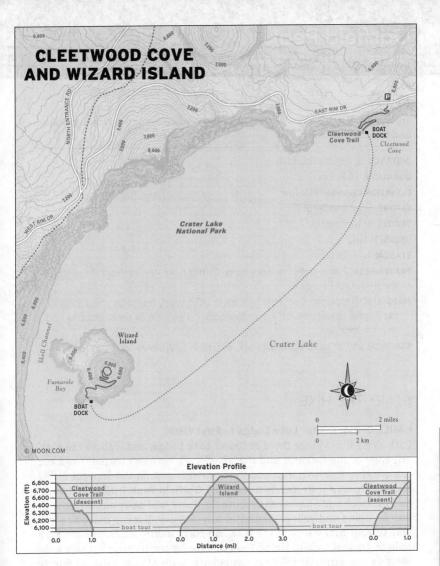

CLEETWOOD COVE AND WIZARD ISLAND

Elevation Profile

Don't be shy about taking your time; several benches line the trail for tired hikers.

DIRECTIONS

From Crater Lake National Park's northern entrance off Highway 138, drive south 8.4 miles. Turn left onto East Rim Drive, and continue 4.5 miles to the turnout for Cleetwood Cove; the parking area is north of the road. Or, from the Annie Spring Entrance Station on the park's south side, head north on Munson Valley Road for 6.5 miles. Turn left onto West Rim Drive and continue for 5.9 miles. At an intersection with the northern entry road, turn right to remain on Rim Drive for another 4.5 miles.

GPS COORDINATES: 42.97969, –122.08326 / N42° 58.7814′ W122° 4.9956′

Enjoy sweeping views of Crater Lake's massive caldera, the Klamath Valley, and Cascade peaks.

DISTANCE: 3.4 miles round-trip
DURATION: 1.5 hours
ELEVATION CHANGE: 920 feet
EFFORT: Easy/moderate
TRAIL: Dirt trail, rocks
USERS: Hikers
SEASON: July–October
PASSES/FEES: 7-day national park pass, Crater Lake Annual Pass, America the Beautiful Passes
MAPS: USGS topographic map for Crater Lake West; free basic trail map in the Crater Lake National Park newspaper available at entry stations and at park facilities
CONTACT: Crater Lake National Park, 541/594-3000, www.nps.gov/crla

START THE HIKE

▶ **MILE 0-0.4: Crater Lake Lodge to First View**
Park along Rim Village Drive at **Crater Lake Lodge,** and walk to the eastern edge of the lodge to find the paved path between its patio and the caldera rim. Follow it east counterclockwise around the lake for a few hundred feet as it descends toward the **Garfield Peak Trailhead.** Mountain hemlock and Shasta red fir flank the dusty trail early on—along with purple lupine and yellow groundsel July-August—but the tree line gives way to your first views of the lake and surrounding landscape after 0.3 mile of gradual ascent. Union Peak dominates the horizon to the southwest as you arrive at the first switchback, with Mount Ashland faintly visible to its left.

▶ **MILE 0.4-1.2: First View to Ridgeline**
After continued climbing and another switchback in just under 0.2 mile, you'll start noticing less hemlock and more whitebark pine—one of the few species of tree that can survive at this elevation and withstand the region's brutal winters. As you continue on progressively rockier stretches, keep an eye out for yellow-bellied marmots and American pikas scurrying about. Continue climbing steadily for another 0.6 mile, at which point you'll arrive on a ridgeline atop the caldera.

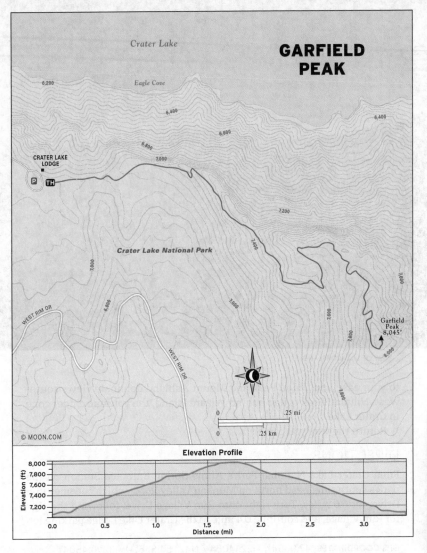

Garfield Peak

Elevation Profile

> MILE 1.2-1.4: **Ridgeline to Phantom Ship and Mount Scott Viewpoint**
At the ridgeline you'll have your first unimpeded view of Crater Lake, as
well as the 168-foot-tall rock formation poking out of the water known as
the Phantom Ship. Continue on another 0.25 mile for a **viewpoint** with a
pair of concrete benches that let you sit and take in the Phantom Ship as
well as Mount Scott, the tallest point in the park.

> MILE 1.4-1.7: **Phantom Ship and Mount Scott Viewpoint
to Garfield Peak Summit**
Continue ascending the trail 0.3 mile past the benches to arrive at the
Garfield Peak summit, where you'll be rewarded with 360-degree views,
some of the best in the park. To the north, Mount Thielsen rises over Crater Lake's caldera; the Klamath Valley sits to the south; Mount Scott rises

▲ VIEW OF WIZARD ISLAND

to your east; and Union Peak and Mount Ashland dominate views southwest. Hillman Peak is just behind Wizard Island, the volcanic cinder cone in Crater Lake.

Return the way you came.

DIRECTIONS

From Crater Lake National Park's Annie Spring Entrance Station on the park's south side, head north on Munson Valley Road, which becomes Rim Drive, for 6.6 miles. Turn right onto Rim Village Drive, following the sign for Rim Village, and continue 0.4 mile to the Crater Lake Lodge parking lot.

GPS COORDINATES: 42.90947, -122.14084 / N42° 54.5682' W122° 8.4504'

Plaikni Falls
CRATER LAKE NATIONAL PARK

This lovely forest walk features abundant wildflowers and ends at the base of a waterfall.

DISTANCE: 2.2 miles round-trip
DURATION: 1.5 hours
ELEVATION CHANGE: 140 feet
EFFORT: Easy
TRAIL: Dirt trail, gravel
USERS: Hikers, wheelchair users
SEASON: July-October
PASSES/FEES: 7-day national park pass, Crater Lake Annual Pass, America the Beautiful Passes
MAPS: USGS topographic map for Crater Lake East; free basic trail map in the Crater Lake National Park newspaper available at entry stations and at park facilities
CONTACT: Crater Lake National Park, 541/594-3000, www.nps.gov/crla

Contrary to popular belief, these falls aren't fed by Crater Lake, but by snowmelt. The name "Plaikni"—which means "from the high country"—was chosen by Klamath Native American elders.

START THE HIKE

▶ **MILE 0-0.5: Plaikni Falls Trailhead to Anderson Bluffs**
From the **Plaikni Falls Trailhead,** head north along the wide path of pumice and gravel. In a few hundred feet, you'll cross an old road and enter **Kerr Valley,** a glacier-carved canyon created in the ice ages. Numerous wooden benches can be found trailside if you wish to enjoy the scenery, including old-growth mountain hemlock, Shasta red fir, and summertime wildflowers such as purple lupine.

PLAIKNI FALLS TRAIL ▶

CRATER LAKE NATIONAL PARK

Plaikni Falls

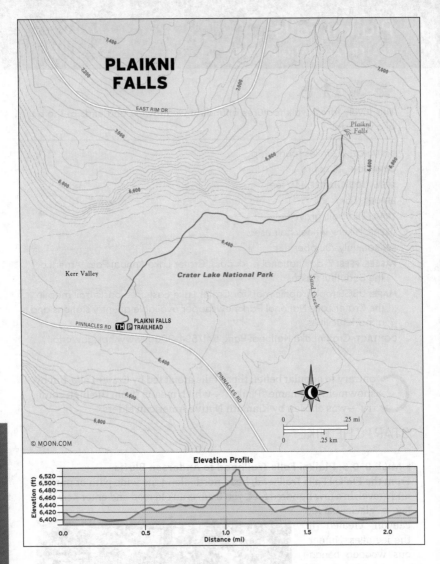

Elevation Profile

> **MILE 0.5-0.9: Anderson Bluffs to Sand Creek**

After 0.5 mile, you'll begin walking alongside the base of **Anderson Bluffs,** just behind the tree line to your left. Rock from the base of these bluffs was once extracted for use in various projects around Crater Lake National Park. In another 0.4 mile, the trail emerges from the forest into an open meadow along **Sand Creek.**

> **MILE 0.9-1.1: Sand Creek to Plaikni Falls**

From here, follow the path as it curves left, gaining 90 feet over the last 0.2 mile. (While most of the trail is accessible, this final stretch may be too steep for those in wheelchairs.) It's the longest stretch of continuous elevation gain on the trail, and it ends at a small clearing at the base of 20-foot **Plaikni Falls.** Here the spring-fed waterfall cascades over a glacier-carved

cliff and feeds Sand Creek. Heed the signs in this ecologically sensitive area and stay on-trail at all times. Several varieties of wildflowers grow at the waterfall's base, including red paintbrush and arrowleaf groundsel.

Return the way you came.

DIRECTIONS

From Crater Lake National Park's Annie Spring Entrance Station on the park's south side, follow Munson Valley Road for 3.7 miles. Turn right onto East Rim Drive and follow it for 8.2 miles, then turn right onto Pinnacles Road, following a sign for Lost Creek Campground and the Pinnacles. Continue on the road for 1.1 miles. The parking area will be on the left, just past a sign indicating the trailhead.

GPS COORDINATES: 42.90187, –122.06147 / N42° 54.1122′ W122° 3.6882′

CRATER LAKE NATIONAL PARK

Plaikni Falls

Hike to the tallest point in Crater Lake National Park—and the only place in the park where you can fit the entire lake into one photograph.

DISTANCE: 4.6 miles round-trip

DURATION: 2.5 hours

ELEVATION CHANGE: 1,150 feet

EFFORT: Easy/moderate

TRAIL: Dirt trail, sandy path, rocks, roots

USERS: Hikers

SEASON: July–October

PASSES/FEES: 7-day national park pass, Crater Lake Annual Pass, America the Beautiful Passes

MAPS: USGS topographic map for Crater Lake East; free basic trail map in the Crater Lake National Park newspaper available at entry stations and at park facilities

CONTACT: Crater Lake National Park, 541/594-3000, www.nps.gov/crla

START THE HIKE

Given its elevation, the Mount Scott Trail is among the last in the park to be completely snow-free—and the path may have some snow on it into August. Make sure to sunscreen up and bring plenty of water, as this hike is quite exposed near the summit.

▶ **MILE 0-1.1: Mount Scott Trailhead to Clearing**
Walk to the southern edge of the parking lot to find the **Mount Scott Trailhead,** and begin hiking through a mostly flat **pumice field.** Check out some of the khaki-colored, sponge-like pumice rocks along the trail—they're lighter than you think!—but be sure to put them back for others to enjoy. At 0.25 mile, you'll enter a forest of Douglas fir, lodgepole pine, and mountain hemlock—and start ascending. In another 0.5 mile, as you steadily gain elevation via a sandy, well-graded path, you'll start enjoying views of Wizard Island and Crater Lake. Keep an eye out along this stretch July-August for red paintbrush, wild onion, yellow buttercup, and other wildflowers. Also watch for black-billed magpies and blue Steller's jays, among other bird species, perched in nearby trees.

▶ **MILE 1.1-1.5: Clearing to Switchbacks**
You'll arrive in 0.35 mile at a **clearing** with views of Brown Mountain to the south and Applegate Peak—just outside the caldera—Mount Ashland, and Grizzly Peak to the southwest. The forest of hemlock starts thinning out

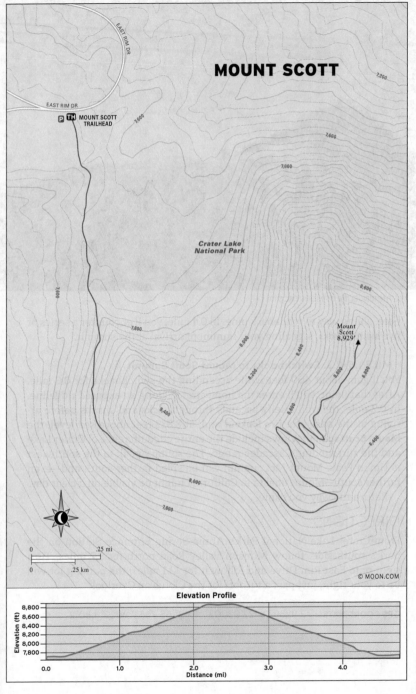

MOUNT SCOTT

EAST RIM DR

P TH MOUNT SCOTT
TRAILHEAD

7,500

7,200

7,600

7,600

7,800

Crater Lake
National Park

8,600

7,800

Mount
Scott
8,929'

8,000

8,200

8,400

8,600

8,800

8,600

8,400

8,400

8,000

7,800

0   .25 mi

0   .25 km

© MOON.COM

Elevation Profile

▲ THE RIDGELINE OF MOUNT SCOTT

here, giving way to whitebark pine. In 0.4 mile, you'll encounter a series of five **switchbacks,** signaling your imminent arrival at the summit.

▶ MILE 1.5-2.3: Switchbacks to Mount Scott Summit

You'll gain about 400 feet while ascending the switchbacks for 0.6 mile. After that point, you'll enter the homestretch along an exposed ridgeline. In 0.2 mile, the trail briefly ascends through rocks and shrubs before arriving at the base of a **fire lookout** and, at 8,832 feet above sea level, the **Mount Scott summit.** Views include the entire circumference of Crater Lake and the surrounding Cascades range. The solitary peak to the southwest is Union Peak. Mount McLoughlin can be spied farther south and—even farther south—Mount Shasta in California might be visible on a clear day.

Return the way you came.

DIRECTIONS

From Crater Lake National Park's Annie Spring Entrance Station on the park's south side, follow Munson Valley Road north for 3.7 miles. Turn right onto East Rim Drive and follow it for 12.1 miles; the parking lot will be to your right, just past a turnoff for the Cloudcap Overlook.

GPS COORDINATES: 42.92897, -122.03002 / N42° 55.7382' W122° 1.8012'

NEARBY CAMPGROUNDS

NAME	DESCRIPTION	FACILITIES	SEASON	FEE
Mazama Campground	the only developed campground within Crater Lake National Park	214 tent, RV, and group campsites, restrooms	June–September	$21–43

Mazama Village, Crater Lake National Park, 541/594-2255 ext. 3610 or 3601, www.travelcraterlake.com

NAME	DESCRIPTION	FACILITIES	SEASON	FEE
Lost Creek Campground	tent campsites inside Crater Lake National Park	16 tent sites, restrooms	July–October	$5

Pinnacles Rd., Crater Lake National Park, 541/594-3000, www.nps.gov/crla

NAME	DESCRIPTION	FACILITIES	SEASON	FEE
Diamond Lake Campground	less than 7 miles from Crater Lake National Park's northern entrance, on the shore of Diamond Lake	238 RV and tent sites, restrooms	May–October	$16–27

Hwy. 138, Chemult, 541/498-2531, www.fs.usda.gov

NAME	DESCRIPTION	FACILITIES	SEASON	FEE
Jackson F. Kimball State Recreation Site	about 15 miles south of Crater Lake's southern entrance, at the headwaters of the Wood River	10 tent sites, restrooms	April–October	$11

Sun Mountain Rd., Chiloquin, 541/783-2471, www.oregonstateparks.org

NAME	DESCRIPTION	FACILITIES	SEASON	FEE
Union Creek Campground	17 miles west of Crater Lake National Park' southern entrance station, with access to hiking and fishing	73 RV and tent sites, 3 full-hookup sites, restrooms	May–October	$22–35

Hwy. 62, Union Creek, 541/560-3900, www.roguerec.com

ASHLAND AND THE ROGUE VALLEY

Whatever natural beauty you're seeking, chances are good you'll find it in southern Oregon's Rogue Valley and Siskiyou Mountains. Choose your own adventure, whether hiking through a colorful canyon to a waterfall, traversing rolling mountain meadows, walking a stretch of the Pacific Crest Trail, taking in sweeping views of Cascade peaks, or exploring the heart of three mountain ranges in the Cascade-Siskiyou National Monument. The city of Ashland, famous for the annual Oregon Shakespeare Festival, sits at the southern edge of the Rogue Valley—and makes a fine jumping-off point for hitting many of the region's best-loved trails.

▲ VIEW OF THE SISKIYOU MOUNTAINS FROM MOUNT ELIJAH

▲ FIRE LOOKOUT ON SODA MOUNTAIN

1 Rainie Falls
DISTANCE: 4.4 miles round-trip
DURATION: 2.5 hours
EFFORT: Easy/moderate

2 Mount Elijah
DISTANCE: 5.7 miles round-trip
DURATION: 3 hours
EFFORT: Easy/moderate

3 Lower Table Rock
DISTANCE: 4.8 miles round-trip
DURATION: 2.5 hours
EFFORT: Easy/moderate

4 Grizzly Peak
DISTANCE: 5.6 miles round-trip
DURATION: 3 hours
EFFORT: Easy/moderate

5 Siskiyou Mountain Park
DISTANCE: 4.9 miles round-trip
DURATION: 2 hours
EFFORT: Easy/moderate

6 Mount Ashland (via the Pacific Crest Trail)
DISTANCE: 8.1 miles round-trip
DURATION: 4 hours
EFFORT: Moderate

7 Soda Mountain
DISTANCE: 4.5 miles round-trip
DURATION: 2.5 hours
EFFORT: Easy/moderate

▼ ROGUE RIVER NEAR RAINIE FALLS

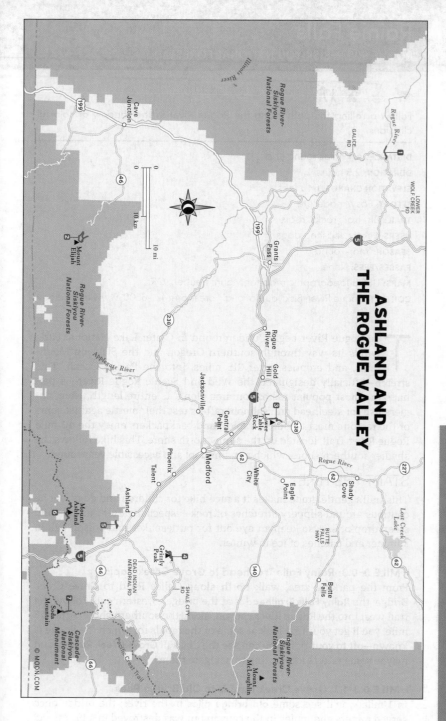

ASHLAND AND THE ROGUE VALLEY

© MOON.COM

Follow a rolling footpath along the Rogue River in the shadow of colorful cliffsides.

DISTANCE: 4.4 miles round-trip
DURATION: 2.5 hours
ELEVATION CHANGE: 640 feet
EFFORT: Easy/moderate
TRAIL: Dirt trail, rocks, roots
USERS: Hikers, leashed dogs
SEASON: Year-round
PASSES/FEES: None
MAPS: USGS topographic map for Mount Reuben, OR
CONTACT: Rogue River-Siskiyou National Forest, 541/471-6500, www.fs.usda.gov

The Rogue River begins underground in Crater Lake National Park, winds its way through southern Oregon and the Siskiyou Mountains, and empties, after 215 miles, into the Pacific Ocean. This stretch—officially designated the Wild and Scenic Rogue River—is perhaps the most popular recreation area along its entire length. Here, anglers fish for steelhead and salmon, rafters test their mettle against some of the region's most turbulent rapids, and backpackers enjoy the 40-mile Rogue River Trail, located on the sunny north shore. This hike follows the shadier southern shore, which remains cool and accessible year-round.

START THE HIKE

This trail's gentle grade makes it a nice hike for children and dogs, but be cautious around slippery stretches of rock—especially after rainfall—and steep drop-offs. Also keep an eye out for rattlesnakes and poison oak in summer and patches of ice in winter.

▸ **MILE 0-0.3: Rainy Falls Trailhead to Grave Creek Rapids**
From the parking area, walk north along Galice Road to Grave Creek Bridge; the **Rainy Falls Trailhead** is at the bridge's western end. Follow the trail west into the Rogue River canyon, along the southern shore. After 0.3 mile, you'll get your first look at some of the rapids for which the Rogue is known—off to your right you can see the Class III **Grave Creek Rapids,** and maybe some rafters attempting to navigate them.

▸ **MILE 0.3-1.3: Grave Creek Rapids to Old Bridge Piles**
In 1 mile, you'll see some **old bridge piles** in the river; the bridge once served miners and mules in the canyon but was destroyed in a 1927 flood. You'll start ascending gently but steadily here, heading into a forest of Douglas fir, oak, and madrone.

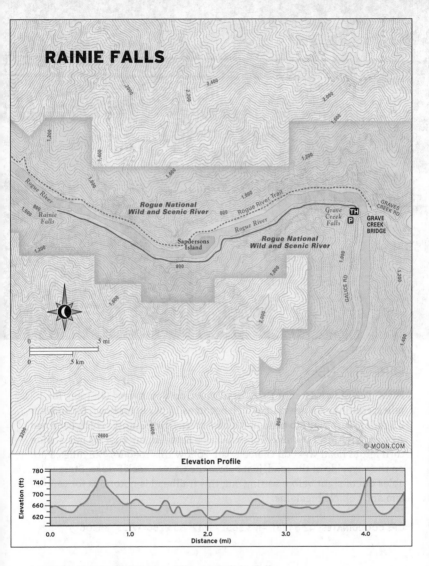

RAINIE FALLS

Elevation Profile

▶ MILE 1.3–2.2: Old Bridge Piles to Rainie Falls

In 0.4 mile you'll encounter some especially rocky terrain; it may be difficult to follow the trail through this stretch, especially as rainfall pools on the path—but simply continue straight ahead, looking for rocks that are a lighter shade of gray than the surrounding rubble. The path becomes clear again after a couple hundred feet. In another 0.4 mile, the trail ends in a mess of rocks at **Rainie Falls,** which, at 20 feet tall, looks less like a conventional waterfall than a series of Class V rapids—which it is. A sandy shoreline here offers a nice place to enjoy a snack. Watch for salmon and steelhead migrating upstream here; their leaps can propel the fish five feet in the air and six feet forward. Similarly, keep an eye out for great blue herons, kingfishers, ospreys, black bears, and otters, all of which feed on the fish.

Return the way you came.

▲ RAINIE FALLS

DIRECTIONS

From downtown Grants Pass, head west on Southwest G Street for 1.2 miles; continue on the road, which becomes Upper River Road, for another 2.5 miles. Turn right to head north on Azalea Drive Cutoff, which becomes Azalea Drive after 0.4 mile. Follow Azalea Drive for another 5.8 miles, then turn left to head west on Galice Road. Follow this road for 17.8 miles. Park on the east side of the road, just before the Grave Creek Bridge. Store valuables out of sight before setting out; this trailhead is notorious for vandalism and vehicle break-ins.

GPS COORDINATES: 42.64881, –123.5851 / N42° 38.9286′ W123° 35.106′

BEST NEARBY BREWS

Enjoy easy-drinking house brews and upscale pub fare on a creek-side patio at **Climate City Brewing Company** (509 SW G St., Grants Pass, 541/479-3725, http://climatecitybrewing.com, 11:30am-8pm Tues.-Thurs., 11:30am-9pm Fri.-Sun.). From the trailhead, the 28-mile drive southeast takes 40 minutes via Galice Road.

ROGUE RIVER-SISKIYOU NATIONAL FOREST,
OREGON CAVES NATIONAL MONUMENT & PRESERVE

Ascend through forest and meadows before basking in 360-degree views
from the summit of Mount Elijah.

DISTANCE: 5.7 miles round-trip

DURATION: 3 hours

ELEVATION CHANGE: 1,020 feet

EFFORT: Easy/moderate

TRAIL: Dirt trail, roots, rocks, old roadbed

USERS: Hikers, leashed dogs

SEASON: June-November

PASSES/FEES: None

MAPS: USGS topographic map for Oregon Caves; National Park Service trail
   map available at the Oregon Caves National Monument & Preserve

CONTACT: Rogue River-Siskiyou National Forest, 541/592-4000, www.fs.usda.gov

START THE HIKE

▶ **MILE 0-0.7: Mount Elijah-Bigelow Lakes Trailhead
to Lake Mountain and Bigelow Lakes Trail**

Start from the **Mt. Elijah-Bigelow Lakes Trailhead** at the southeastern edge
of the parking area, hiking on what was once part of **Forest Road 070,**
flanked by maple and alder. After 0.7 mile of gently but steadily ascending—with precious little shade in the summer—you'll arrive at a junction
with a map; turn left here onto the **Lake Mountain and Bigelow Lakes Trail,**
heading east and uphill into a fir forest to begin a clockwise loop.

▶ **MILE 0.7-2.2: Lake Mountain and Bigelow Lakes Trail to Clearing**

About 0.3 mile past the junction, you'll begin darting in and out of meadows, ringed by fir trees and host to a variety of wildflowers in the late
spring and early summer. Watch for purple fireweed, red and yellow western columbine, and red paintbrush. After another 0.3 mile, you'll notice a
spur trail to your right—it goes to Bigelow Lakes—but head uphill to your
left to continue on the Lake Mountain and Bigelow Lakes Trail. Continue
ascending for 0.9 mile, at which point you'll emerge from the forest into a
clearing boasting views of Bigelow Lakes, the Illinois River valley, and the
Siskiyou Mountains to the northwest. The summit of Mount Elijah rises to
your left, and the symmetrical, rounded peak straight ahead is Eight Dollar Mountain.

▶ **MILE 2.2-2.7: Clearing to Mount Elijah Summit**

You'll soon reenter the forest. At an intersection with the Elk Creek Trail in
0.1 mile, continue straight ahead on the Lake Mountain and Bigelow Lakes

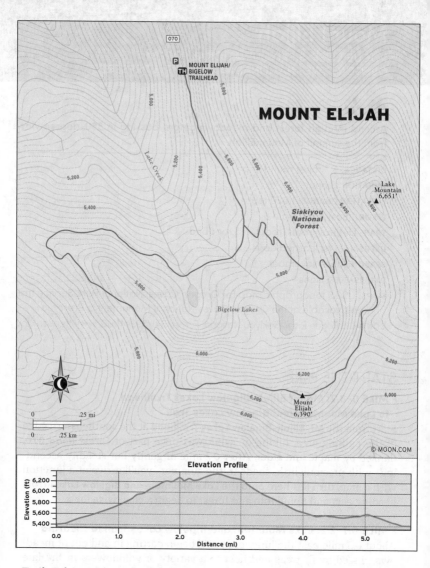

Trail. Take a right to head west at the next junction, in another 0.1 mile, following an Oregon Caves signpost. In 0.3 mile, you'll arrive at the **Mount Elijah summit,** marked by a sign and offering panoramic views. From here, you can spy Mount Shasta to the southeast and the Kalmiopsis Wilderness to the west.

▶ MILE 2.7–5.7: Mount Elijah Summit to Mount Elijah–Bigelow Lakes Trailhead

Once you've had your fill of views, continue west on the trail to start your descent. You'll return to the forest in another 0.4 mile and, after 0.9 mile in the woods, arrive at a Y-shaped junction. Turn right to reconnect with the old Forest Road 070 roadbed, following it 1 mile to complete the loop at the hike's original junction, and keeping left to continue on the road 0.7 mile to return the way you came.

DIRECTIONS

From the town of Cave Junction, located on U.S. 199, head east on Highway 46, following a sign for the Oregon Caves National Monument. Follow the road for 11.8 miles, at which point you'll pass Grayback Campground. RVs and trailers are not recommended on the winding roads past this point. Continue on Highway 46 another 7.9 miles to dead-end in the Oregon Caves parking lot; make a U-turn and backtrack 0.1 mile to make the tight right turn onto the paved fire access road uphill (it becomes gravel in another couple hundred feet) and continue for 3 miles. At the intersection, turn right onto Forest Road 070 to continue uphill. You'll arrive at a fork in 0.6 mile; stay right to remain on Forest Road 070, which ends in 0.8 mile at a small gravel parking area.

GPS COORDINATES: 42.101740, -123.378952 / N42° 6.1044' W123° 22.7371'

MOUNT ELIJAH SUMMIT ▶

BEST NEARBY BITES AND A BONUS

Once back in the parking lot, you might consider visiting the nearby **Oregon Caves National Monument & Preserve** (541/592-2100, www. nps.gov/orca, seasonal hours late Mar.-early Nov.), where you can take guided cave tours (standard tour $7-10, off-trail tour $45). Or go for some eats; the whole family will find something to love at **Wild River Pizza** (249 N. Redwood Hwy., Cave Junction, 541/592-3556, http:// wildriverbrewing.com, 11am-9pm Mon.-Thurs., 11am-10pm Fri.-Sat., noon-9pm Sun.). This popular restaurant serves filling pizzas, sandwiches, and broasted chicken, along with eight or more house beers at any time. From the trailhead, the 22-mile drive west takes 45 minutes via Highway 46.

Enjoy vernal pools and wildflowers in season, and 360-degree views of Mount McLoughlin and the Rogue Valley from atop Lower Table Rock's pancake-flat summit year-round.

BEST: Spring Hikes, Wildflower Hikes
DISTANCE: 4.8 miles round-trip
DURATION: 2.5 hours
ELEVATION CHANGE: 910 feet
EFFORT: Easy/moderate
TRAIL: Dirt trail, gravel path, rocks, wooden boardwalk
USERS: Hikers
SEASON: Year-round
PASSES/FEES: None
MAPS: USGS topographic map for Sams Valley
CONTACT: Bureau of Land Management, 541/618-2200, www.blm.gov

The Table Rocks—comprising Lower Table Rock and Upper Table Rock to its east—have existed in some form since a nearby shield volcano erupted 7.5 million years ago, sending lava into the present-day Rogue Valley. As millions of years passed, the Rogue River eroded much of that lava rock, leaving behind what you see today. Late winter and spring is the best time to see the vernal pools at their most impressive, and if you come in the latter season you'll also be treated to scads of wildflowers.

START THE HIKE

Watch for poison oak, ticks, and rattlesnakes along this trail in summertime.

▸ **MILE 0-1.1: Lower Table Rock Trailhead to Clearing**
Find the **Lower Table Rock Trailhead**—a signed wooden arch—next to the restroom at the southern edge of the parking lot. Head south on the trail to a junction; continue straight on the wide, gravel path to remain on the Lower Table Rock Trail as you enter an oak grove. After steadily ascending through madrone and oak trees, you'll arrive in 1.1 miles at a small **clearing** that offers the hike's first real views; to the east are Upper Table Rock and Mount McLoughlin.

▸ **MILE 1.1-1.6: Clearing to Vernal Pools**
The trail mostly levels out in 0.3 mile as you arrive at the exposed northern edge of **Lower Table Rock**. Follow the short, 0.2-mile round-trip **spur trail** to your left here, and enjoy panoramic views of Mount McLoughlin and Upper Table Rock. To the northeast, you'll see what appears to be a flat peak; that's the rim of Crater Lake. Back on the main trail, continue south,

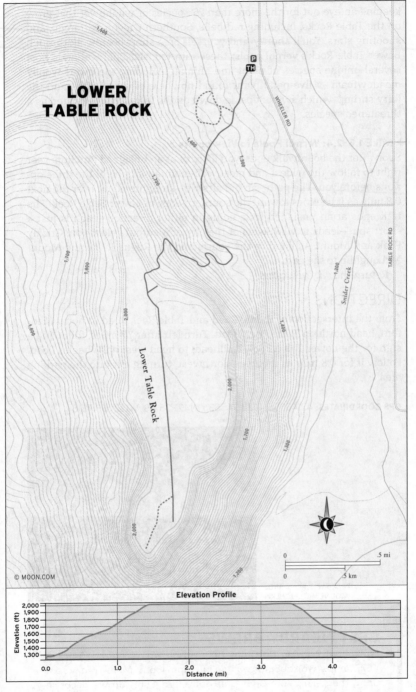

LOWER TABLE ROCK

WHEELER RD

TABLE ROCK RD

Snider Creek

Lower Table Rock

© MOON.COM

0   .5 mi

0   .5 km

Elevation Profile

Elevation (ft)

2,000
1,900
1,800
1,700
1,600
1,500
1,400
1,300

0.0   1.0   2.0   3.0   4.0

Distance (mi)

Lower Table Rock

keeping an eye out for the more than 75 species of wildflower that grow on the Table Rocks, including red bells, Southern Oregon buttercup, and shooting stars. You'll shortly find yourself on a short boardwalk through Lower Table Rock's **vernal pools;** these rain-fed, seasonal wetlands host several unique species of plant and animal, including the dwarf woolly meadowfoam—a five-petal plant found nowhere else on Earth—and the fairy shrimp, which swims upside down and is federally designated as a threatened species.

▶ MILE 1.6-2.4: Vernal Pools to Viewpoints

Soon after the boardwalk ends, you'll arrive at an unsigned junction; veer right to follow the widest and most well-maintained trail of the three options before you. The path—an old airstrip—straightens out over the next 0.8 mile as it beelines toward the southern edge of Lower Table Rock. The trail ends at an unsigned fork; going in either direction—each is just a short spur—leads to **viewpoints** of the city of Medford below you, Grizzly Peak and Mount Ashland to the south, and the Rogue River and Mount McLoughlin to the east.

Return the way you came.

DIRECTIONS

From the intersection of Biddle Road and Table Rock Road in north Medford, head north on Table Rock Road. Turn left after 7.7 miles, following a sign for the Lower Table Rock Trailhead, to head west on Wheeler Road. Follow it for 0.8 mile as it curves northwest, turning left into the parking area.

GPS COORDINATES: 42.46865, –122.94553 / N42° 28.119' W122° 56.7318'

UPPER TABLE ROCK AND
MOUNT MCLOUGHLIN ▶

BEST NEARBY BREWS

Walkabout Brewing Company (921 Mason Way, Medford, 541/734-4677, http://walkaboutbrewing.com, 3pm-8pm Mon.-Wed., 3pm-9pm Thurs.-Fri., 2pm-9pm Sat., 1pm-7pm Sun.) draws decor inspiration from the Australian Outback and serves up a variety of easy-drinking ales. From the trailhead, the 12-mile drive south takes 20 minutes via Table Rock Road.

Enjoy summertime wildflower displays and panoramic views of the Rogue Valley, Ashland, and Cascade peaks.

BEST: Brew Hikes
DISTANCE: 5.6 miles round-trip
DURATION: 3 hours
ELEVATION CHANGE: 860 feet
EFFORT: Easy/moderate
TRAIL: Dirt trail, roots, rocks
USERS: Hikers, leashed dogs, mountain bikers, horseback riders
SEASON: June-November
PASSES/FEES: None
MAPS: USGS topographic map for Grizzly Peak, OR
CONTACT: Bureau of Land Management, 541/618-2200, www.blm.gov

START THE HIKE

▶ MILE 0-0.8: Grizzly Peak Trailhead to First Meadow

At the southeast edge of the parking lot, next to the restroom, you'll find the trailhead, simply marked "Trail." Start heading steadily uphill on the **Grizzly Peak Trail** (despite the name, there are no grizzlies here—or anywhere in Oregon) through a forest of grand fir and Douglas fir. After 0.8 mile, you'll arrive at the hike's first meadow. Visit June-August, and you'll likely catch blooming wildflowers, including the purple Siskiyou onion and yellow Baker's violet. In the fall, you might encounter locals hunting for morel and chanterelle mushrooms.

▶ MILE 0.8-1.5: First Meadow to Grizzly Peak Summit

After 0.5 mile of darting in and out of meadows, you'll come to a Y-shaped junction; head right to follow the **Grizzly Peak Loop Trail** counterclockwise, west and then south. In 0.2 mile, you'll arrive at **Grizzly Peak's summit,** noted simply by a large rockpile in a shady meadow; it's underwhelming but, fortunately, better views await.

▶ MILE 1.5-3: Grizzly Peak Summit to Viewpoint

After another 0.2 mile, you'll come to an unsigned Y-shaped junction; to the right is a short **spur trail** to a meadow with views of Medford to the northwest. Head left to continue the loop. You'll pass through an area still bearing the scars of a 2002 wildfire that burned nearly 2,000 acres on the western slopes of Grizzly Peak. Listen for woodpeckers as you hike the scorched hillside. Roughly 1.3 miles farther on, you'll arrive at what might be the hike's best **viewpoint.** Just after reaching the top of the rocky

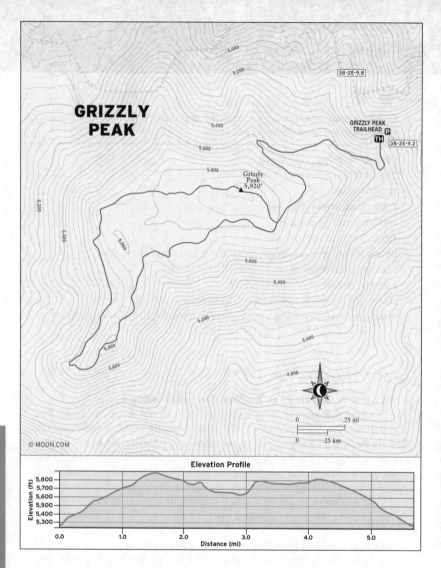

outcrop, make a hard right to its western edge, which offers views of Ashland, Emigrant Lake, and the Rogue Valley to the west; Mount Shasta and Pilot Rock to the south; and Mount McLoughlin and Diamond Peak to the north.

▶ **MILE 3-5.6: Viewpoint to Grizzly Peak Trailhead**

The trail begins to loop back northward from here; in 0.6 mile, you'll arrive at a Y-shaped junction. Head left, following the sign for the **Grizzly Peak Trail,** walking another 0.7 to complete the loop and reconnect with the original trail. Continue straight to head 1.3 miles downhill the way you came.

▲ VIEW FROM GRIZZLY PEAK

DIRECTIONS

From Ashland, head east on East Main Street for 2.9 miles. At road's end, turn right and then quickly left at the intersection to merge onto Highway 66. After 0.2 mile, turn left onto Dead Indian Memorial Road. Continue for 6.7 miles, and take a left at a sign for the Grizzly Peak Trail—the route is well-signed along the way—onto Shale City Road. After 3 miles, turn left onto the gravel Forest Road 38-2E-9.2. You'll come to a four-way junction after 0.8 mile; continue straight to head uphill, remaining on Forest Road 38-2E-9.2. The road ends, in another 0.9 mile, at the trailhead.

GPS COORDINATES: 42.272, –122.6063 / N42° 16.32′ W122° 36.378′

BEST NEARBY BREWS

Good luck deciding among the 40 house beers at **Caldera Brewing Company** (590 Clover Ln., Ashland, 541/482-4677, http://calderabrewing.com, 11am-9pm daily). Its offerings run the gamut of styles, and the brewery displays thousands of beer bottles from around the world. From the trailhead, the 12-mile drive west takes 25 minutes via Dead Indian Memorial Road.

Explore a network of trails boasting Rogue Valley views, just minutes from downtown Ashland.

DISTANCE: 4.9 miles round-trip
DURATION: 2 hours
ELEVATION CHANGE: 1,060 feet
EFFORT: Easy/moderate
TRAIL: Dirt trail, roots, rocks, old roadbed
USERS: Hikers, leashed dogs, mountain bikers (White Rabbit Trail only), horseback riders (White Rabbit Trail only)
SEASON: Year-round
PASSES/FEES: None
MAPS: USGS topographic map for Ashland, OR
CONTACT: Ashland Parks and Recreation, 541/488-5340, www.ashland.or.us

START THE HIKE

▶ **MILE 0-0.6: Parking Area to Trailhead**
From the Park Street parking area, walk uphill 0.2 mile. You'll soon trade pavement for gravel and pass a locked gate via a pedestrian pathway on either side. After another 0.4 mile of ascent, you'll arrive at a trail junction with paths veering off in seemingly every direction. Locate the map board and find the unsigned trail immediately behind it; this is the **Mike Uhtoff Trail.**

▶ **MILE 0.6-1.1: Trailhead to Clearing**
Start hiking west on the Mike Uhtoff Trail, heading uphill via switchbacks through a ponderosa pine forest for 0.5 mile to arrive at an unsigned Y-shaped junction. Continue uphill, to the left, to remain on the Mike Uhtoff Trail, and then pause in a **clearing** shortly after to enjoy your first views of the Rogue Valley.

▶ **MILE 1.1-2.3: Clearing to Queen of Hearts Loop**
Continue uphill and to the left again at a T-shaped junction in 0.2 mile to remain on the Mike Uhtoff Trail. Steadily ascend for another 0.5 mile to arrive at another junction. Head straight, remaining on the Mike Uhtoff Trail, but take a moment to rest on a bench, to your right, overlooking the city of Ashland. At this point you've ascended 715 feet, and the trail mostly flattens out from here as it traverses a fir forest. You'll arrive at an odd junction in another 0.5 mile; a sign for the Uhtoff Trail points back the way you just came, but turn left here for a partial jaunt on the (unsigned) **Queen of Hearts Loop.**

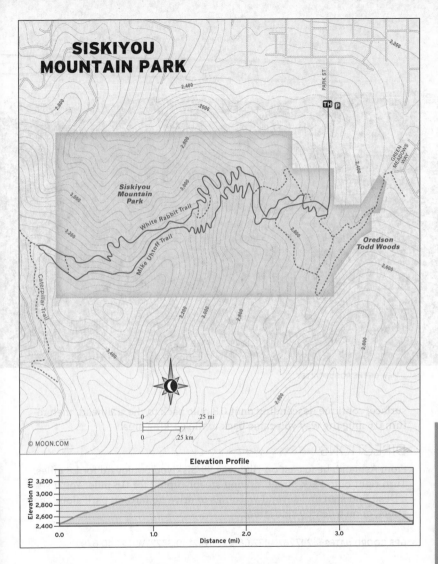

Elevation Profile

▶ **MILE 2.3-2.5: Queen of Hearts Loop to White Rabbit Trail**

Meander through ponderosa pine just below an impressive boulder field. You'll pass between two minivan-sized boulders before arriving, after 0.2 mile, at a sprawling trail junction. Make a hard right to start looping back east on the **White Rabbit Trail;** this is a multiuse path, so watch out for mountain bikers along its rolling slopes.

▶ **MILE 2.5-4.9: White Rabbit Trail to Parking Area**

In just over 0.1 mile, you'll come to a signed Y-shaped junction with the Queen of Hearts Loop and Uhtoff Trail; turn left to continue downhill and remain on the forested White Rabbit Trail. You'll intersect with other trails along the way, but just keep following signs for the White Rabbit Trail. In about 1.4 miles, the trail widens and becomes an old roadbed with a gravel

▲ VIEW OF THE ROGUE VALLEY

surface; continue descending on it 0.3 mile back to the trailhead, then return 0.6 mile the way you came back to the parking area.

DIRECTIONS

From Ashland, head east on Highway 99/Siskiyou Boulevard for 1.8 miles. Turn right onto Park Street, driving steeply uphill for 0.5 mile. You'll see a Dead End sign and several warnings to drive no farther; park along the street, or on a nearby side street.

GPS COORDINATES: 42.17287, –122.68132 / N42° 10.3722' W122° 40.8792'

BEST NEARBY BITES

Fuel up for your hike with a breakfast burrito at **Ruby's** (163 N. Pioneer St., Ashland, 541/488-7717, http://rubysofashland.com, 7am-7pm daily). The cozy café serves a variety of hefty breakfast burritos, as well as lunch sandwiches, coffee, espresso, and more. From the trailhead, the 2.5-mile drive northwest takes 10 minutes via Siskiyou Boulevard.

Mount Ashland (via the Pacific Crest Trail)

KLAMATH NATIONAL FOREST

Mount Ashland—the highest peak in the Siskiyou Mountains—is known for its popular ski resort, but just below its summit are some of the region's most breathtaking wildflower displays and views of other nearby mountain peaks.

BEST: Wildflower Hikes
DISTANCE: 8.1 miles round-trip
DURATION: 4 hours
ELEVATION CHANGE: 1,050 feet
EFFORT: Moderate
TRAIL: Dirt trail, roots, rocks, roadbed, stream crossings
USERS: Hikers, leashed dogs, horseback riders
SEASON: June–November
PASSES/FEES: None
MAPS: USGS topographic map for Mount Ashland, OR-CA
CONTACT: Klamath National Forest, 530/842-6131, www.fs.usda.gov

START THE HIKE

Don't let this hike's stats dissuade you from hiking with kids; the mostly flat, well-graded trail's elevation gain rarely feels steep and, even if young ones aren't up for the whole trek, any of the mountain's many meadows make a fine turnaround point.

▸ **MILE 0-0.6: Pacific Crest Trailhead to First Meadow**
From the parking area, cross Mount Ashland Ski Road to find the trailhead—indicated by a **Pacific Crest Trail (PCT)** marker fastened to a tree—and begin to hike through the forest of grand and red fir. After 0.6 mile, you'll arrive at the first of several meadows that dot Mount Ashland's southern slopes. In addition to views of Black Butte, Mount Eddy, and—on a clear day—Mount Shasta, you'll find wildflowers blooming here in the summer, including yellow Bigelow's sneezeweed, purple and white Henderson's horkelia, and purple larkspur.

▸ **MILE 0.6-1.5: First Meadow to Fourth and Fifth Meadows**
The next meadow comes in another 0.2 mile, and a third meadow 0.3 mile past that one. As you pass through the meadows, you'll cross several foot-wide rivulets that drain water off the mountain; the overgrowth can hide wooden planks set up for crossing, so watch your feet to keep from tripping. You'll arrive at another pair of meadows over the next 0.4 mile; look out for orange agoseris and Mount Ashland lupine—found nowhere else

Mount Ashland (via the Pacific Crest Trail)

ASHLAND AND THE ROGUE VALLEY

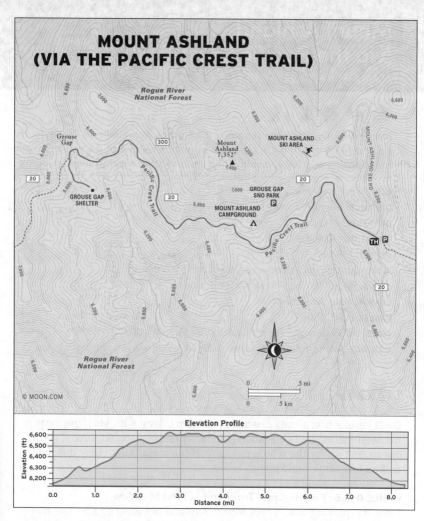

MOUNT ASHLAND
(VIA THE PACIFIC CREST TRAIL)

Elevation Profile

in the world—between June and September. Black bears and elk also roam the meadows below you, especially in the early morning and evening.

▶ MILE 1.5-1.8: Fourth and Fifth Meadows to Grouse Gap

In another 0.3 mile, continue straight across the unmarked Forest Road 40S15, and look to your right to spot the summit of Mount Ashland (along with a weather radar system). Soon after, the trail opens up in a grassy bowl known as **Grouse Gap;** here, the forest gives way almost entirely to meadows full of yellow buckwheat and several species of penstemon.

▶ MILE 1.8-4.05: Grouse Gap to Grouse Gap Shelter

In 1 mile you'll come upon a small grove of aspen trees that puts on a colorful foliage display every fall. After another 1 mile, the trail crosses Forest Road 40S30; turn left to follow the road gently downhill for 0.25 mile, then turn left into the parking area for the **Grouse Gap shelter.** The two-sided

▲ GROUSE GAP SHELTER

structure offers views of Klamath National Forest, Mount Ashland, and Mount Shasta.

Return the way you came.

DIRECTIONS

From Ashland, head south on I-5, and take exit 6, following a Mount Ashland sign. Continue on as it becomes Old Highway 99. In 1 mile, turn right at a sign for the Mount Ashland Ski Area onto Mount Ashland Ski Road. Continue for 7.2 miles, passing the milepost 7 marker before arriving at an unsigned parking area off to the right.

GPS COORDINATES: 42.07349, -122.69715 / N42° 4.4094' W122° 41.829'

BEST NEARBY BREWS

Come for the British pub experience, including a good beer selection, at **The Black Sheep Pub & Restaurant** (51 N. Main St., Ashland, 541/482-6414, http://theblacksheep.com, 11:30am-midnight Sun.-Wed., 11:30am-1am Thurs.-Sat.). The airy pub serves up British classics, along with dramatic views of nearby peaks from its 2nd-story perch. From the trailhead, the 20-mile drive north takes about 30 minutes via Mount Ashland Ski Road and I-5.

Mount Ashland (via the Pacific Crest Trail)

ASHLAND AND THE ROGUE VALLEY

SODA MOUNTAIN WILDERNESS,
CASCADE-SISKIYOU NATIONAL MONUMENT

Hike through the Cascade-Siskiyou National Monument, which sits at the
nexus of three distinct ecological regions: the Cascade, Klamath, and Siskiyou
mountain ranges, which give this region the kind of biological diversity you
won't find anywhere else in Oregon.

DISTANCE: 4.5 miles round-trip
DURATION: 2.5 hours
ELEVATION CHANGE: 710 feet
EFFORT: Easy/moderate
TRAIL: Dirt trail, rocks, roots, old roadbed
USERS: Hikers, leashed dogs, horseback riders
SEASON: June-October
PASSES/FEES: None
MAPS: USGS topographic map for Soda Mountain
CONTACT: Soda Mountain Wilderness, 541/618-2200, www.blm.gov

START THE HIKE

▶ **MILE 0-0.4: Pacific Crest Trailhead to Mount Ashland
and Pilot Rock View**

At the southern edge of the parking lot, next to the restroom, you'll find
the trailhead, indicated by a **Pacific Crest Trail (PCT)** marker. Begin hiking
under a set of power lines through a high desert meadow that teems with
summer wildflowers. Keep an eye out for western fence lizards, jackrab-
bits, and black-tailed deer. After 0.4 mile, views of Mount Ashland and Pilot Rock—the thumb-shaped crag rising above the tree line to the southwest—begin opening up to your right. Wildflowers dot the meadow along
this stretch as well.

▶ **MILE 0.4-1.6: Mount Ashland and Pilot Rock View
to Soda Mountain Lookout Road**

In 0.2 mile, you'll leave the desert to begin steadily ascending through a
forest of Douglas fir, ponderosa pine, and grand fir. In 0.8 mile, you'll see a
PCT signpost, to your left, and several feet past it an unsigned **connector
trail** that switchbacks uphill; turn left onto the connector trail and walk
0.2 mile to the unsigned **Soda Mountain Lookout Road.**

▶ **MILE 1.6-2.25: Soda Mountain Lookout Road to
Soda Mountain Summit and Fire Lookout**

Turn right onto the road and continue ascending, sometimes steeply.
There's little shade along this stretch, and you'll gain 360 feet in elevation

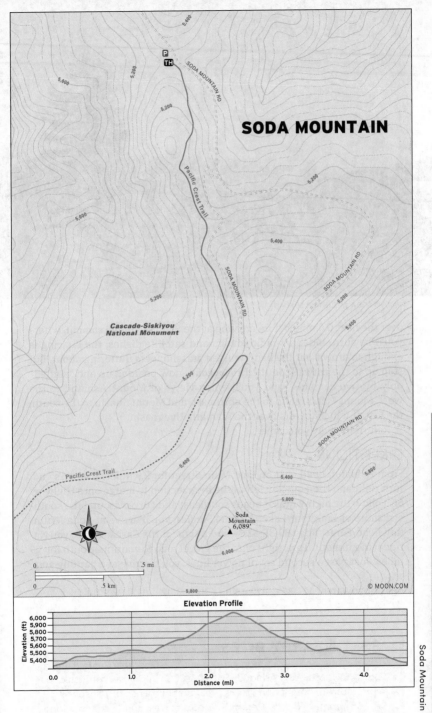

SODA MOUNTAIN

Cascade-Siskiyou
National Monument

Pacific Crest Trail

SODA MOUNTAIN RD

SODA MOUNTAIN RD

SODA MOUNTAIN RD

Soda
Mountain
6,089'

Elevation Profile

0   .5 mi

0   .5 km

© MOON.COM

▲ TRAIL TO SODA MOUNTAIN SUMMIT

over the next 0.6 mile before arriving at the **Soda Mountain summit,** where you'll be surrounded by radio towers and satellite dishes; the buzzing is enough to drown out the band-winged grasshoppers fluttering about. But step up to the catwalk on the **fire lookout**—now boarded up and "staffed" only by two cameras—and you'll enjoy views of Mount Ashland to the west, Mount McLoughlin to the northeast, and Mount Shasta to the south, the last of which towers over the Klamath River basin.

Return the way you came.

DIRECTIONS

From Ashland, head east on East Main Street for 2.9 miles. At road's end, turn right and then quickly left at the intersection to merge onto Highway 66. Follow the highway as it heads southeast and curves around the southern shore of Emigrant Lake. After 14.5 miles, you'll arrive at Soda Mountain Road/Forest Road 39-3E-32.3—and a sign for the Cascade-Siskiyou National Monument. Turn right onto the gravel road to continue south for 3.9 miles. Just past a second set of power lines, you'll arrive at a parking area.

GPS COORDINATES: 42.0852, –122.48169 / N42° 5.112′, W122° 28.9014′

BEST NEARBY BITES

Revel in the Shakespearean atmosphere of **Oberon's Restaurant & Bar** (45 N. Main St., Ashland, 541/708-6652, http://oberonsashland. com, 4pm-midnight Sun.-Thurs., 11:30am-1am Fri.-Sat.). Inspired by *A Midsummer Night's Dream,* the pub serves British comfort food amid enchanting forested decor. From the trailhead, the 22-mile drive northwest takes 45 minutes via Highway 66.

NEARBY CAMPGROUNDS

NAME	DESCRIPTION	FACILITIES	SEASON	FEE
Valley of the Rogue State Park	busy campground along the Rogue River	95 full-hookup sites, 62 tent and electrical sites, 8 yurts, restrooms	year-round	$19–53
Twin Bridges Rd., Gold Hill, 541/582-3128, www.oregonstateparks.org				
Emigrant Lake County Park	campground on the north shore of Emigrant Lake	39 tent sites, 31 RV sites, restrooms	RV sites: year-round; tent sites: March–October	$20–30
Hwy. 66, Ashland, 541/774-8183, www.jacksoncountyor.org				
Mount Ashland Campground	first-come, first-served campsites on Mount Ashland	9 tent sites, restrooms	June–October, depending on snow levels	free
Forest Rd. 20, Ashland, 530/842-6131, www.fs.usda.gov				
Schroeder Park	campground along the Rogue River	22 full-hookup sites, 22 tent sites, 2 yurts, restrooms	year-round	$20–55
Schroeder Lane, Grants Pass, 541/474-5285, www.co.josephine.or.us				
Cave Creek Campground	near Oregon Caves National Monument	17 tent sites, compostable toilets	May–September	$10
Hwy. 46, Cave Junction, 541/592-2100, www.nps.gov				

SKY LAKES WILDERNESS AND KLAMATH BASIN

Spend a few minutes on almost any trail in the Sky Lakes Wilderness, and it's easy to see how the region earned it name. It comprises three lake basins along the crest of the Cascade Range and is known for its almost unmatched water quality: Environmental Protection Agency studies in the 1980s and 1990s found that the Sky Lakes Wilderness was home to some of the most chemically pure water in the world. Just south of the Sky Lakes Wilderness, Brown Mountain straddles two worlds: Cascade forests collide with fields of lava rock, draped across the hillside like a bedsheet. Farther east, the longest linear park in Oregon hosts more than 100 miles of trails through forests, marshes, and farmland in the heart of the Klamath Basin.

▲ THE PATH TO PUCK LAKE

▲ OC&E WOODS LINE STATE TRAIL

◄ MOUNT MCLOUGHLIN AND THE BROWN MOUNTAIN LAVA FLOW TRAIL

1 Horseshoe Lake
DISTANCE: 6.1 miles round-trip
DURATION: 3 hours
EFFORT: Easy/moderate

2 Brown Mountain Lava Flow
DISTANCE: 6.1 miles round-trip
DURATION: 3 hours
EFFORT: Easy/moderate

3 Sky Lakes Basin via Cold Springs Trail
DISTANCE: 7.2 miles round-trip
DURATION: 3.5 hours
EFFORT: Easy/moderate

4 Puck Lakes via Nannie Creek Trail
DISTANCE: 5.4 miles round-trip
DURATION: 2.5 hours
EFFORT: Easy/moderate

5 OC&E Woods Line State Trail
DISTANCE: 4.7 miles round-trip
DURATION: 2.5 hours
EFFORT: Easy

BEST NEARBY BITES AND BREWS

Klamath Falls is the most likely staging point for hikes in the area as well as where the best nearby bites and brews are located. Most trails covered in this chapter are about an hour's drive from town, except for Brown Mountain Lava Flow, which is about a 1.75-hour drive.

- Fuel up before hitting the trail at **Green Blade Bakery** (1400 Esplanade St., 541/273-8999, http://green-blade.com, 6am-2pm Tues.-Sat.). This family-run artisan bakery sells a variety of breads and pastries, all made from scratch, and with as many locally sourced ingredients as possible.

- Morning, noon, or night, you'll always feel right at home at **The Grocery Pub** (1201 Division St., 541/851-9441, http://thegrocerypub.com, 8am-9pm Mon.-Sat., 9am-9pm Sun.). The Grocery pulls double duty as an inviting neighborhood restaurant-pub, and as a convenience store for grab-and-go snacks.

- Enjoy a slice and a pint at Klamath Falls' first brewery, **Mia & Pia's Pizzeria & Brewhouse** (3545 Summers Lane, 541/884-4880, http://miaandpiasklamathfalls.com, 11am-9:30pm Sun.-Thurs., 10:30am-10:30pm Fri.-Sat.). The family-friendly restaurant serves pizza, sandwiches, and brews both classic and eclectic.

- Housed in an old creamery, **Klamath Basin Brewing** (1320 Main St., 541/273-5222, http://kbbrewing.com, 11am-9pm Sun.-Thurs., 11am-10pm Fri.-Sat.) boasts a solid selection of classic styles. It brews its beers using geothermal energy, and each beer is named for an element of local culture.

- Bask in panoramic views of Mount McLoughlin at **Lake of the Woods Resort** (950 Harriman Rte., 541/949-8300, http://lakeofthewoodsresort.com, 8am-9pm daily May-Sept.), west of town. Its on-site restaurant serves classic American fare: omelets, sandwiches, burgers, and more. The Brown Mountain Lava Flow hike is particularly convenient to the Lake of the Woods Resort; from the trailhead, the 5-mile drive east takes less than 10 minutes via Highway 140.

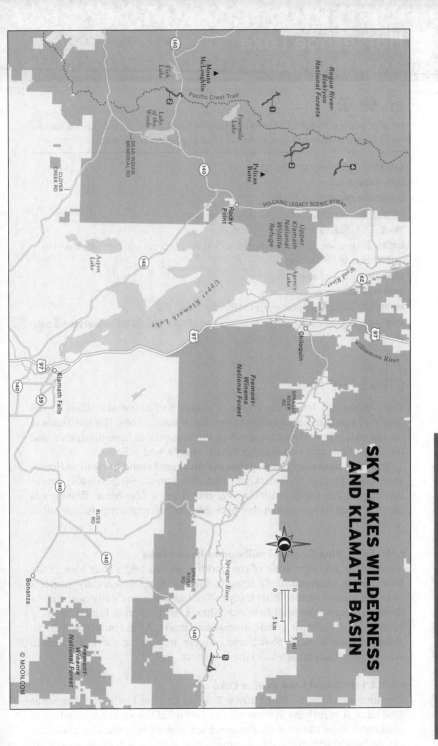

SKY LAKES WILDERNESS AND KLAMATH BASIN

© MOON.COM

Hike through a forest of Shasta red fir and hemlock to several scenic lakes—don't forget a swimsuit in summer—in the Sky Lakes Wilderness.

DISTANCE: 6.1 miles round-trip
DURATION: 3 hours
ELEVATION CHANGE: 660 feet
EFFORT: Easy/moderate
TRAIL: Dirt trail, rocks, roots
USERS: Hikers, leashed dogs, horseback riders (horses not permitted within 200 feet of lakeshores)
SEASON: June–October
PASSES/FEES: None
MAPS: USGS topographic map for Rustler Peak, OR
CONTACT: Rogue River–Siskiyou National Forest, 541/560-3400, www.fs.usda.gov

START THE HIKE

You'll share this trail with scores of hikers and horseback riders at the height of summer, not to mention swarms of mosquitoes. The ideal time to hit the trail is in early autumn, when the mosquitoes have dissipated and the forest floor turns all manner of red, orange, and yellow.

Primitive **backcountry campsites** are dispersed along the trail to Horseshoe Lake (Rogue River-Siskiyou National Forest, 541/560-3400, www.fs.usda.gov, free) and available year-round on a first-come, first-served basis, if you'd like to turn a day hike into an overnight trip. No permit is necessary.

▶ **MILE 0-1: Blue Canyon Trailhead to Round Lake**
Head to the northern edge of the parking area to begin your hike at the **Blue Canyon Trailhead.** You'll come to a fork almost immediately; turn left onto the mostly shaded Blue Canyon Trail to begin gradually descending through a dense forest of hemlock, Shasta red fir, purple lupine (in early summer), huckleberries, and pinemat manzanita. After 1 mile, you'll arrive at **Round Lake.** If you're so inclined, you can hop on the short **spur trail** to your right, which takes you to the lakeshore.

▶ **MILE 1-2: Round Lake to Blue Lake**
Continue south on the Blue Canyon Trail. In another 1 mile, you'll arrive at **Blue Lake.** A surprising view awaits at the end of the short **spur trail** off to your right: From the shoreline you can see meadows, a thick hemlock forest, and a 300-foot cliff—and accompanying rockslide—butting up against the lake. This is also an especially popular swimming spot in summer.

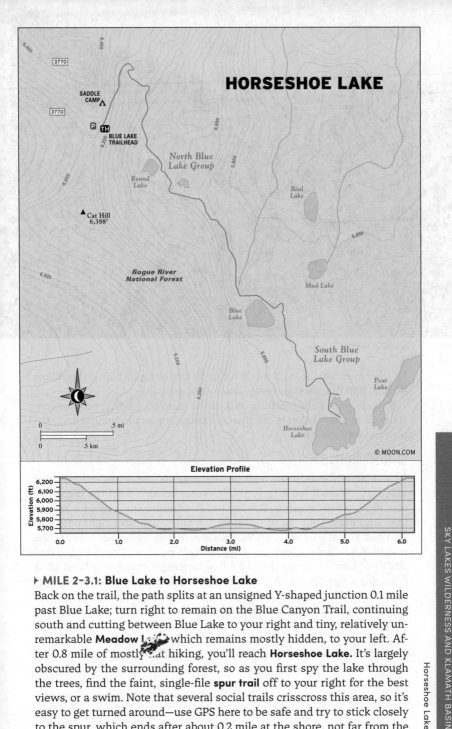

Elevation Profile

(chart: Elevation (ft) vs Distance (mi); y-axis 5,700–6,200; x-axis 0.0–6.0)

© MOON.COM

▸ MILE 2-3.1: Blue Lake to Horseshoe Lake

Back on the trail, the path splits at an unsigned Y-shaped junction 0.1 mile past Blue Lake; turn right to remain on the Blue Canyon Trail, continuing south and cutting between Blue Lake to your right and tiny, relatively unremarkable **Meadow Lake**, which remains mostly hidden, to your left. After 0.8 mile of mostly flat hiking, you'll reach **Horseshoe Lake.** It's largely obscured by the surrounding forest, so as you first spy the lake through the trees, find the faint, single-file **spur trail** off to your right for the best views, or a swim. Note that several social trails crisscross this area, so it's easy to get turned around—use GPS here to be safe and try to stick closely to the spur, which ends after about 0.2 mile at the shore, not far from the center of the horseshoe shape from which the lake gets its name. Find a log on which to sit and relax, and maybe enjoy a snack—gathering energy

▲ ROUND LAKE

for the return ascent—and watch for migrating birds, including the yellow warbler and the black-and-gray Townsend's solitaire.

Retrace your steps carefully back to the main trail; while you can continue on to a few other lakes, this one makes a fine turnaround spot. Return the way you came.

DIRECTIONS

From Klamath Falls, head west on Highway 140 for 40 miles. Just past milepost 29 (you'll see it to your left, on the south side of the highway), turn right to head north on Rye Springs Road, following a sign for Willow Lake and Butte Falls. Head north for 8.8 miles, and turn right onto Forest Road 37 just past milepost 26. Continue on the well-maintained gravel road for 6.9 miles; at a four-way junction, turn right to follow a sign to stay on Forest Road 37. In another 4.2 miles, turn right onto Forest Road 3770, following a sign for the Blue Canyon Trail. You'll come to a Y-shaped junction in 4.1 miles; head left and continue uphill, following a sign for Forest Road 3770. You'll arrive at the trailhead parking area, off to the right, in another 1.1 miles.

GPS COORDINATES: 42.53037, –122.2974 / N42° 31.8222′ W122° 17.844′

Horseshoe Lake

2

Brown Mountain Lava Flow

FREMONT-WINEMA NATIONAL FOREST

Dart between thick forests and lava fields while enjoying photo-worthy views of Mount McLoughlin, southern Oregon's tallest peak at 9,493 feet.

DISTANCE: 6.1 miles round-trip

DURATION: 3 hours

ELEVATION CHANGE: 670 feet

EFFORT: Easy/moderate

TRAIL: Dirt trail, lava fields, rocks, roots, highway crossing

USERS: Hikers, leashed dogs, horseback riders

SEASON: June-November

PASSES/FEES: Free May-October, $4 Oregon State Sno-Park day-use permit per vehicle November-April

MAPS: USGS topographic map for Mount McLoughlin

CONTACT: Fremont-Winema National Forest, 541/560-3400, www.fs.usda.gov

Although this trail lies in the shadow of 7,311-foot Brown Mountain, the summit is almost never visible along this stretch. Nevertheless, you'll feel its presence: Some 2,000 years ago, the cinder cone erupted, forming the lava fields through which you'll hike.

START THE HIKE

▶ **MILE 0-0.6: Pacific Crest Access Trailhead to Highway 140**

Find the **Pacific Crest Access Trailhead** at the western edge of the parking lot near the informational signboard. Walk through lush fir forest for just over 0.2 mile before crossing a footbridge, where you'll arrive at a T-shaped junction; turn left onto the **Pacific Crest Trail,** heading south. After 0.4 mile, the mostly flat trail hits Highway 140; look both ways, cross the highway, and follow the PCT blaze, fastened to a tree. (To shorten the hike by 1.2 miles round-trip, use an unmarked turnout and parking area at the eastern edge of the metal guardrails here.)

▶ **MILE 0.6-1: Highway 140 to Lava Field**

You'll head into a forest of fir and maple before arriving, in another 0.2 mile, at an X-shaped junction. Ignore the side trails here, and continue straight ahead on the well-maintained path to arrive soon after at an intersection with the High Lakes Trail; continue straight ahead to remain on the PCT. Some 0.15 mile past this junction, you'll head into your first full-blown **lava field,** walking on crushed red cinder, lined on either side by black lava rocks. From here you'll encounter a steady diet of old lava flows, broken up by scattered forests of hemlock, Douglas fir, and Shasta red fir.

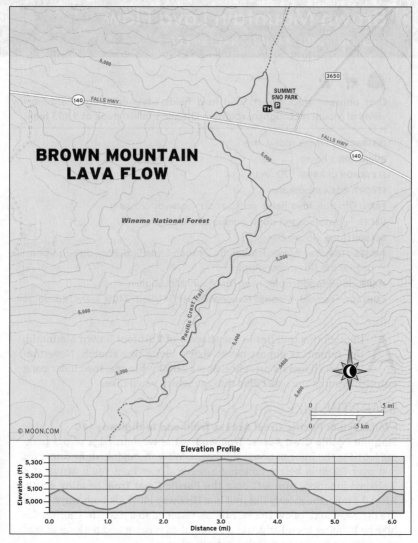

Brown Mountain Lava Flow

Elevation Profile

▶ MILE 1-3.05: Lava Field to Viewpoint Clearing

In 0.5 mile, as the gently ascending trail curves west, take a moment to turn around for your first view of Mount McLoughlin to the north. After 1.5 miles, soon after emerging from forested terrain, you'll descend slightly before arriving at a 50-foot stretch of lava rock sandwiched between two stands of Douglas fir; here, a small, mostly shaded **clearing** offers plenty of rocks on which to sit and enjoy a snack, with views of Mount McLoughlin. Listen for the plush toy-like squeaks of the pika, a rabbit-like mammal that lives in the alpine rocks.

While the trail continues on, this makes an ideal turnaround point. Return the way you came.

▲ BROWN MOUNTAIN LAVA FLOW WITH MOUNT MCLOUGHLIN

DIRECTIONS

From Klamath Falls, head west on Highway 140 for 36.3 miles. Roughly 0.5 mile past milepost 33 (to your left, on the south side of the highway), turn right at a sign for the Summit trailhead. Almost immediately after, turn left and drive 0.2 mile into a large parking area.

GPS COORDINATES: 42.3964, –122.285 / N42° 23.784′ W122° 17.1′

3

Sky Lakes Basin via Cold Springs Trail

SKY LAKES WILDERNESS

There may be no finer introduction to the Sky Lakes Wilderness than this loop trail to the shores of several mountain lakes, some of which are popular swimming holes in summer.

BEST: Summer Hikes
DISTANCE: 7.2 miles round-trip
DURATION: 3.5 hours
ELEVATION CHANGE: 490 feet
EFFORT: Easy/moderate
TRAIL: Dirt trail, rocks, roots
USERS: Hikers, leashed dogs, horseback riders (horses not permitted within 200 feet of lakeshores)
SEASON: July–October
PASSES/FEES: None
MAPS: USGS topographic maps for Pelican Butte
CONTACT: Fremont-Winema National Forest, 541/883-6714, www.fs.usda.gov

START THE HIKE

Primitive **backcountry campsites** are dispersed along this trail (Fremont-Winema National Forest, 541/883-6714, www.fs.usda.gov, free) and available year-round on a first-come, first-served basis, if you'd like to turn a day hike into an overnight trip. No permit is necessary.

▶ **MILE 0-0.6: Cold Springs Trailhead to South Rock Creek Trail**

Start this loop hike from the **Cold Springs Trailhead** at the northern edge of the parking area. Almost immediately, you'll find yourself in a forest scarred by wildfire; in 2017, lightning struck this area, igniting a blaze that burned nearly 5,000 acres and left scores of burned snags, downed trees, and almost no undergrowth. After 0.6 mile of mostly level hiking through the

ISHERWOOD LAKE ▶

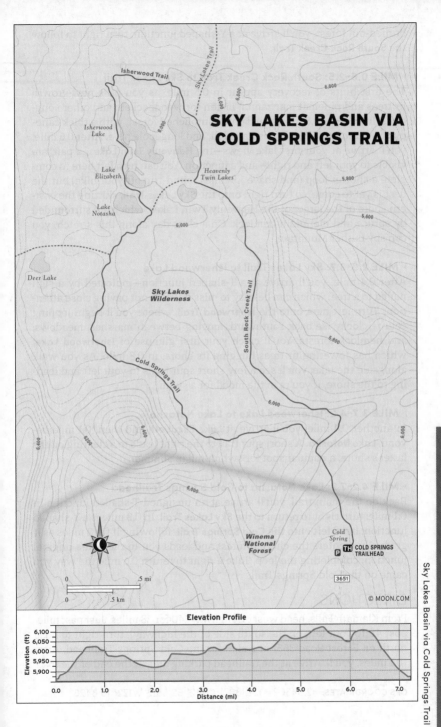

SKY LAKES BASIN VIA COLD SPRINGS TRAIL

Isherwood Trail

Sky Lakes Trail

6,000

6,000

Isherwood Lake

Lake Elizabeth

Heavenly Twin Lakes

5,800

Lake Notasha

6,000

5,600

Deer Lake

Sky Lakes Wilderness

South Rock Creek Trail

5,800

Cold Springs Trail

6,000

6,400

5,200

6,400

6,000

6,000

0   .5 mi

0   .5 km

Winema National Forest

Cold Spring

COLD SPRINGS TRAILHEAD

3651

© MOON.COM

Elevation Profile

Elevation (ft)

6,100
6,050
6,000
5,950
5,900

0.0   1.0   2.0   3.0   4.0   5.0   6.0   7.0

Distance (mi)

burned-out forest, you'll arrive at a Y-shaped junction; turn right to follow the **South Rock Creek Trail.**

▸ **MILE 0.6–2.5: South Rock Creek Trail to Sky Lakes Trail**
The first hints of recovery appear in 0.5 mile, as you pass new-growth fir trees and pinemat manzanita. Listen for woodpeckers and other songbirds. In another 0.8 mile, you'll enter untouched forest, with a thick canopy of mountain hemlock, Shasta red fir, and lodgepole pine. After 0.6 mile, you'll arrive at your first lake views—the **Heavenly Twin Lakes,** a pair, are visible to your left and right—and a junction. You can turn left here to complete a shorter loop (and shave 1.5 miles round-trip off your hike) but the best is yet to come, so turn right onto the **Sky Lakes Trail,** skirting the eastern shore of the larger of the Heavenly Twin Lakes, which are surrounded by spruce and mountain hemlock. On a clear day along this stretch, you can spy Luther Mountain.

▸ **MILE 2.5–3.7: Sky Lakes Trail to Isherwood Lake**
After 0.4 mile, you'll arrive at a T-shaped junction—indicated by a sign nailed to a tree, which can be easy to miss if you're not paying close attention. Turn left here onto the **Isherwood Trail,** where you'll begin looping counterclockwise back southward, moving between marshes, meadows, and hemlock forests. You'll catch your first glimpse of **Isherwood Lake,** which has towering fir trees hugging its shore, in 0.8 mile. As you walk alongside the lake, you'll see a few short spur trails to your left and leading to the shore, if you're in the mood for a swim.

▸ **MILE 3.7–4.2: Isherwood Lake to Lake Notasha**
In another 0.4 mile, you'll arrive at **Lake Elizabeth** and then, 0.1 mile beyond, **Lake Notasha.** A short spur trail to the right leads to a clearing on the latter's shore, a popular spot for swimming in summer.

▸ **MILE 4.2–7.2: Lake Notasha to Cold Springs Trailhead**
Back on the main trail, you'll arrive at an unsigned T-shaped junction in 0.1 mile; turn right to return to the **Sky Lakes Trail.** In 0.3 mile is a Y-shaped junction; head left onto the **Cold Springs Trail,** following it for 2 miles as it gradually reenters the charred forest and leads you to the hike's original junction, completing the loop. Take a right to return 0.6 mile the way you came on the Cold Springs Trail.

DIRECTIONS

From Klamath Falls, head west on Highway 140 for 28 miles. Just past milepost 41 (to your left, on the south side of the highway), turn right to head north on Forest Road 3651 at a sign for the Cold Springs Trailhead. After 10.1 miles, you'll arrive at the trailhead parking area at the end of the road.

GPS COORDINATES: 42.54302, –122.18071 / N42° 32.5812' W122° 10.8426'

Hike through a pleasant hemlock forest before arriving at Puck Lakes, a fine place to rest, snack, and—at the height of summer—go for a swim.

DISTANCE: 5.4 miles round-trip

DURATION: 2.5 hours

ELEVATION CHANGE: 680 feet

EFFORT: Easy/moderate

TRAIL: Dirt trail, rocks, roots

USERS: Hikers, leashed dogs, horseback riders (horses not permitted within 200 feet of lakeshores)

SEASON: July-October

PASSES/FEES: None

MAPS: USGS topographic maps for Pelican Butte and Devils Peak, OR

CONTACT: Fremont-Winema National Forest, 541/883-6714, www.fs.usda.gov

START THE HIKE

Primitive **backcountry campsites** are dispersed along the trail to Puck Lakes (Fremont-Winema National Forest, 541/883-6714, www.fs.usda.gov, free) and available year-round on a first-come, first-served basis, if you'd like to turn a day hike into an overnight trip. No permit is necessary.

▶ **MILE 0-1.6: Nannie Creek Trailhead to Trail High Point**

Begin hiking on the **Nannie Creek Trail** from the information signboard on the northwest edge of the parking lot. Ascend gradually via a handful of switchbacks through a forest of mountain hemlock and lodgepole pine and, after 0.6 mile, look to your left to catch views of the flat, expansive Klamath Basin to the east before you head into thick forest. Continue gently ascending for 1 mile; at this point, you've gained about 525 feet.

NANNIE CREEK TRAIL ▶

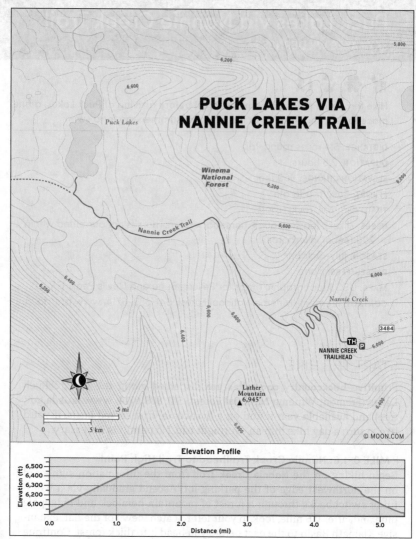

PUCK LAKES VIA NANNIE CREEK TRAIL

Puck Lakes

Winema National Forest

Nannie Creek Trail

Nannie Creek

3484

🅃🄷 🅿 NANNIE CREEK TRAILHEAD

Lather Mountain ▲ 6,945'

0 | .5 mi
0 | .5 km

© MOON.COM

Elevation Profile

▶ **MILE 1.6-2.6: Trail High Point to Unsigned Junction**

The trail levels out and then you'll start to slowly descend toward the Puck Lakes through a forest of western hemlock, new-growth fir trees, towering Shasta red fir, and huckleberry. Stay attentive or keep an eye on your GPS as you descend into the Sky Lakes Basin; with no clear signage, it's easy to miss your turnoff toward Puck Lakes, which comes after roughly 1 mile of gradual descent, when you first catch sight of the lakes through the trees to your right and arrive shortly thereafter at an unsigned junction.

▶ **MILE 2.6-2.7: Unsigned Junction to Puck Lake**

Take a right here to head north along a narrow path, which cuts through a marsh and ends, after a flat 0.1 mile, on the southern shore of 24-acre **Puck Lake,** surrounded by lodgepole pine. While you can continue meandering

▲ PUCK LAKE

along the trail to your left, heading clockwise around the larger of the two Puck Lakes, the path gets progressively fainter as it cuts between it and **Little Puck Lake** just north. And at any rate, Puck Lake is the star, famed for its clarity, and this is an ideal spot to relax, swim, and enjoy lunch. Expect to share the scene with swarms of mosquitoes in late spring and early summer—and migrating ospreys, fishing for dinner, in fall. Keep an eye out for the pink heather dotting the banks of the lake at the height of summer, as well.

Return the way you came.

DIRECTIONS

From Klamath Falls, head west on Highway 140 for 25.1 miles. Just past milepost 44, as the highway curves away from Upper Klamath Lake, turn right to head north on West Side Road, following a sign for Rocky Point, Fort Klamath, and Crater Lake National Park. After 12.2 miles, turn left onto Forest Road 3484, following a sign for the Nannie Creek Trailhead. Follow the gravel road for 4 miles; at the intersection, take a hard left to head uphill and remain on Forest Road 3484. Continue 1.5 miles to the parking lot at the end of the road.

GPS COORDINATES: 42.61382, –122.14719 / N42° 36.8292′ W122° 8.8314′

SKY LAKES WILDERNESS AND KLAMATH BASIN

Puck Lakes via Nannie Creek Trail

OC&E Woods Line State Trail

OREGON STATE PARKS

Hike along a stretch of converted railbed—part of the longest linear park in Oregon—to an abandoned rail yard along the Sprague River.

DISTANCE: 4.7 miles round-trip
DURATION: 2.5 hours
ELEVATION CHANGE: 160 feet
EFFORT: Easy
TRAIL: Dirt trail, rocks, gravel, wooden bridges, road
USERS: Hikers, leashed dogs, mountain bikers, horseback riders
SEASON: Year-round
PASSES/FEES: None
MAPS: USGS topographic maps for Beatty, OR, and Ferguson Mountain, OR
CONTACT: Oregon State Parks, 541/783-2471, www.oregonstateparks.org

On this wholly exposed hike, you'll walk along part of the OC&E Woods Line State Trail, stretching 109 miles throughout the Klamath Basin. It follows the path of an old logging railroad that served the region through much of the 20th century. Named for the Oregon, California, and Eastern Railroad, the rail lines carried as much as one million board feet of lumber per day in the early 1900s. The last of the cars ran in 1990, and it's now a rail-to-trail path.

START THE HIKE

▶ **MILE 0-1.5: OC&E Woods Line State Trailhead to Sprague River Bridge**

Find the trailhead for this section of the **OC&E Woods Line State Trail** on the east side of Godowa Springs Road. Walk through the smaller of two green gates here to begin your hike. Keep an eye out along this early stretch for sandhill cranes, bald eagles, and other birds; this region is along the Pacific Flyway, a migratory bird route that stretches from Alaska to Argentina and sees more than 350 bird species. You might also see garter snakes, antelope, badgers, and other animals. About 1.2 miles from the trailhead, the gravel path will fork; head right to continue east onto the fainter of the two paths. You'll walk through overgrowth, with expansive views of nearby sagebrush fields and marshland, before arriving in 0.25 mile at a 250-foot wooden bridge spanning the **Sprague River.**

▶ **MILE 1.5-2.2: Sprague River Bridge to Brown Cemetery**

Cross the bridge, and walk through a green gate in 0.2 mile to arrive at a T-shaped junction; turn left to head north and slightly uphill onto the **unnamed dirt road.** You'll gain roughly 100 feet over the next 0.3 mile, with views of the winding Sprague River and two-humped Saddle Mountain to the west. Turn right onto another unnamed roadbed for an 0.2-mile **spur**

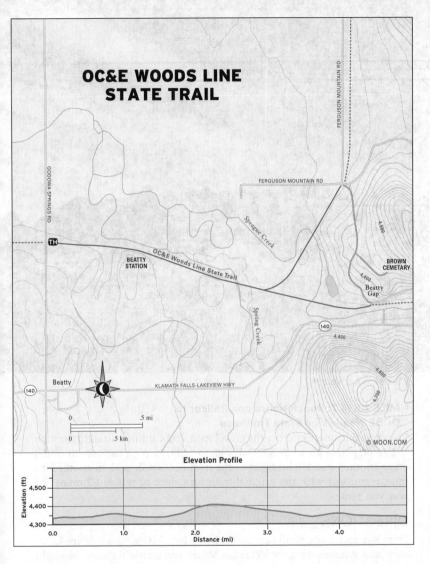

OC&E WOODS LINE STATE TRAIL

FERGUSON MOUNTAIN RD

GODOWA SPRINGS RD

FERGUSON MOUNTAIN RD

Sprague Creek

OC&E Woods Line State Trail

BEATTY STATION

BROWN CEMETARY

4,400

Beatty Gap

Spring Creek

140

4,400

TH

Beatty

140

KLAMATH FALLS-LAKEVIEW HWY

0   .5 mi

0   .5 km

© MOON.COM

Elevation Profile

Elevation (ft)

4,500
4,400
4,300

0.0   1.0   2.0   3.0   4.0

Distance (mi)

to **Brown Cemetery,** the resting place of the Modoc people who once called this area home.

▸ MILE 2.2–2.8: Brown Cemetery to Ranch House and Railcar
Walk the 0.2 mile back to the main trail, and continue north for 0.3 mile as it flattens out and then descends toward an old **ranch house.** Note that this stretch of trail borders private property, so please respect the various fences and No Trespassing signs along the way. You'll encounter a sprawling unsigned junction of trails and old roads at the house; turn right onto the red cinder rock trail—it's bounded on both sides by fences—and walk several hundred feet to check out the **abandoned railcar** off to your left; this was the site of an old rail yard.

▲ THE BROWN CEMETERY

▶ MILE 2.8–4.7: Ranch House and Railcar to OC&E Woods Line State Trailhead

Return to the junction, cross the gravel road, and continue straight through the green gate with an OC&E Trail sign to begin looping back south. You'll cross another wooden bridge over the river in 0.3 mile and, in another 0.3 mile, reconnect with the original trail; turn right to return 1.2 miles the way you came.

DIRECTIONS

From Klamath Falls, head east on Highway 140, following a sign for Lakeview and Winnemucca, for 35.1 miles. When you arrive in the no-stoplight hamlet of Beatty, turn left to head north on Godowa Springs Road, following a sign for Spodue Mountain. Continue for 0.7 mile until you reach the trailhead, noted by green gates on either side of the road. There is room for 1-3 cars to park directly in front of the gates; if there's no space available when you arrive, consider parking on the shoulder back in Beatty and walking to the trailhead.

GPS COORDINATES: 42.45223, –121.27124 / N42° 27.1338' W121° 16.2744'

SKY LAKES WILDERNESS AND KLAMATH BASIN

OC&E Woods Line State Trail

NEARBY CAMPGROUNDS

NAME	DESCRIPTION	FACILITIES	SEASON	FEE
Fourmile Lake Campground	popular campground on the shore of Fourmile Lake	29 RV and tent sites, restrooms	May–October	$15–30
Fourmile Lake Rd., Klamath Falls, 866/201-4194, www.fs.usda.gov				
Aspen Point Campground at Lake of the Woods	popular campground on the shore of Lake of the Woods	50 RV sites, 8 double campsites, 7 tent sites, restrooms	May–October	$18–36
Forest Rd. 3704, Klamath Falls, 541/883-6714, www.fs.usda.gov				
Sunset Campground	popular campground on the shore of Lake of the Woods	64 RV and tent sites, restrooms	May–October	$18–36
Dead Indian Memorial Rd., Klamath Falls, 866/201-4194, www.fs.usda.gov				
Topsy Campground	quiet campground with views of Mount McLoughlin	13 tent sites, restrooms	May–October	$7
Topsy Grade Rd., Keno, 541/883-6916, www.blm.gov				
Odessa Campground	quiet campground offering easy boat access near the western shore of Upper Klamath Lake	6 tent sites, restrooms	year-round, with reduced services October–May	free
Forest Rd. 3639, Klamath Falls, 541/885-3400, www.fs.usda.gov				

STEENS MOUNTAIN AND ALVORD DESERT

Steens Mountain is the eighth-tallest peak in Oregon, a 50-mile-long fault-block mountain rising 9,733 feet above sea level. It formed millions of years ago when several basalt flows piled atop each other like a layer cake; over time, the basalt flows expanded and contracted, and glaciers carved Steens's most distinctive geologic feature—a series of gorges. The mountain looms over the Alvord Desert, a dry lakebed of cracked alkali beneath its eastern face; receiving only six inches of rain per year, it's the driest place in the state. With sagebrush and juniper giving way to aspen and cottonwood, wildlife from rattlesnakes to pronghorn, and canyons and gorges to explore, hikers who make it to this remote playground in southeastern Oregon will be rewarded. Prepare for the weather, as snow can fall year-round at Steens's higher elevations.

▲ ON THE BORAX LAKE HOT SPRINGS TRAIL

▲ VIEW FROM PIKE CREEK CANYON TRAIL

◄ WILDHORSE LAKE

1 **Riddle Brothers Ranch and Little Blitzen River**
DISTANCE: 5.8 miles round-trip
DURATION: 2.5 hours
EFFORT: Easy/moderate

2 **Big Indian Gorge**
DISTANCE: 8.1 miles round-trip
DURATION: 4 hours
EFFORT: Moderate

3 **Wildhorse Lake**
DISTANCE: 2.8 miles round-trip
DURATION: 2 hours
EFFORT: Easy/moderate

4 **Pike Creek Canyon**
DISTANCE: 6.5 miles round-trip
DURATION: 3 hours
EFFORT: Moderate

5 **Borax Lake Hot Springs**
DISTANCE: 2 miles round-trip
DURATION: 1 hour
EFFORT: Easy

BEST NEARBY BITES, BREWS, AND A BONUS

Services around Steens Mountain are few and far between—make sure you have maps downloaded for offline use, on your phone or otherwise, as cell reception is limited. The towns of **Burns** to the north of Steens Mountain, **Frenchglen** to the west, and **Fields** to the south are your best bets for services including food and drink, as well as gas.

- Whether you're heading out from or returning to civilization, stop for a pint at **Steens Mountain Brewing Company** (353 W. Monroe St., Burns, 541/589-1159, www.steensmountainbrewingco.com, 5pm-8pm Thurs.-Fri., 3pm-8pm Sat., 2pm-6pm Sun.). The family-owned brewery uses eight varieties of heirloom hops, and each beer is inspired by a regional landmark or historical event.

- Enjoy a filling breakfast or lunch, or make reservations for a stick-to-your-ribs dinner, at **Frenchglen Hotel State Heritage Site** (39184 Hwy. 205, Frenchglen, 541/493-2825, www.frenchglenhotel.com, 7:30am-9:30am, 11:30am-2:30pm, and dinner seating 6:30pm daily mid-Mar.-Oct.). The historic hotel was built in the 1920s to host stagecoach travelers and is popular for its western-inspired decor and large porch, which affords views of Steens Mountain.

- Enjoy homecooked diner fare at **Fields Station** (22276 Fields Dr., Fields, 541/495-2275, 8am-6pm Mon.-Sat., 9am-5pm Sun.). The café serves breakfast, burgers, and sandwiches—but save room for its self-proclaimed "world famous" milk shakes. It's just 20 minutes from the Borax Lake Hot Springs trailhead.

- What better way to unwind from a hike than with a soak in hot springs? **Alvord Hot Springs** (East Steens Rd./Fields-Denio Rd., Fields, 541/589-2282, www.alvordhotsprings.com, 8am-10pm daily, $8 soaking fee pp) sit a mile below the summit of Steens Mountain, hugging the western flank of the Alvord Desert. The water comes out of the ground at 170 degrees and cools when filling the soaking pools. An on-site general store sells ice, drinks, towels, and other items. Pairing a soak here with a hike to Pike Creek Canyon is particularly convenient—it's just a few miles down the road from the trailhead.

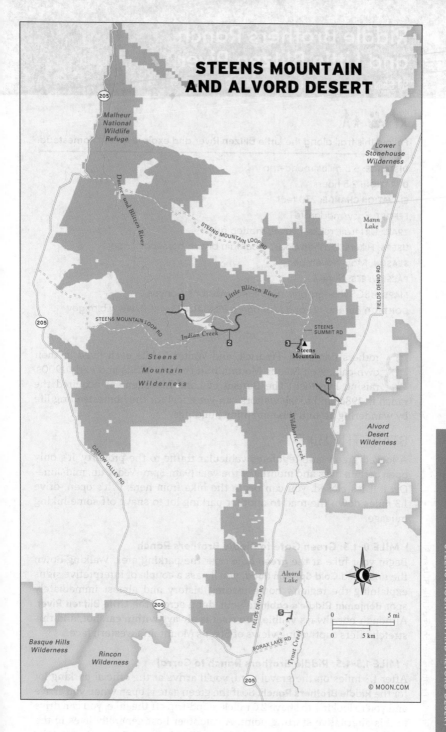

STEENS MOUNTAIN
AND ALVORD DESERT

© MOON.COM

Riddle Brothers Ranch and Little Blitzen River

STEENS MOUNTAIN WILDERNESS

Follow this trail along the Little Blitzen River and explore an old homestead.

DISTANCE: 5.8 miles round-trip
DURATION: 2.5 hours
ELEVATION CHANGE: 270 feet
EFFORT: Easy/moderate
TRAIL: Dirt trail, rocks, gravel, matted grass
USERS: Hikers, leashed dogs, mountain bikers, horseback riders
SEASON: May-November
PASSES/FEES: None
MAPS: USGS topographic map for Tombstone Canyon
CONTACT: Bureau of Land Management, 541/573-4400, www.blm.gov

Brothers Benjamin, Fredrick, and Walter Riddle each lived in their own cabins on Steens Mountain in the late 1800s and early 1900s, raising livestock. The Bureau of Land Management acquired the ranch in 1986, and today visitors can get a feel for the homesteading life by wandering around the remaining buildings.

START THE HIKE

A locked green gate regulates vehicular traffic to the property. It's only open certain days and months of the year (9am-5pm Wed.-Sun. mid-June-Oct.). If it's closed, you can begin the hike from here; if it's open, drive 1.3 miles down the road to another parking lot to shave off some hiking mileage.

▶ **MILE 0-1.3: Green Gate to Riddle Brothers Ranch**
Begin your hike at the **green gate** near the parking area. Walking down the unsigned **Cold Springs Road,** you'll pass a couple of interpretive signs explaining the region's homesteading history and almost immediately spot **Benjamin Riddle's cabin** to your right, across the **Little Blitzen River.** Although not always visible, the river is always within earshot, and this stretch offers captivating views of Steens Mountain's western face.

▶ **MILE 1.3-1.5: Riddle Brothers Ranch to Corral**
After 1.3 miles on the gravel road, you'll arrive at the official parking lot for the **Riddle Brothers Ranch.** So if the green gate is open when you arrive and you're looking to shave 2.6 miles round-trip off the hike, you can drive to this alternative starting point. A volunteer host generally lives in the **caretaker's cabin** on-site next to the parking lot June-September to take care of the property and assist hikers passing through. Just past the cabin,

RIDDLE BROTHERS RANCH AND LITTLE BLITZEN RIVER

Elevation Profile

cross a small footbridge over the river to wander the main ranch complex, which includes Fredrick Riddle's cabin, a barn, storage building, and chicken coop, as well as farm machinery and blacksmith tools.

After wandering the property, cross the footbridge to return to the parking area and follow the signpost for the **Levi Brinkley Trail** to head west. In 0.2 mile, you'll arrive at a decades-old **corral,** constructed by the Riddle brothers, made from intertwined willow.

▶ **MILE 1.5–2.9: Corral to Donner und Blitzen and Little Blitzen Rivers**
Continue west down the narrow trail, following the Little Blitzen River. You'll pass in and out of meadows flanked by juniper and aspen trees; the latter puts on dazzling foliage displays every fall. After 0.5 mile, you'll arrive at an unsigned fork; take a right, toward the river and onto a

▲ OLD CORRAL ALONG THE TRAIL

well-maintained **dirt trail.** You'll arrive at the **confluence of the Donner und Blitzen and Little Blitzen Rivers** in another 0.9 mile. Remarkably, the former river wasn't named after the reindeer but for the German words for "thunder" and "lightning" by members of the 1st Oregon Cavalry, who passed through here in 1864 and faced a massive storm. A large juniper tree here offers plenty of shade where you can enjoy a snack. See if you can spy the native redband trout in the shallow waters, and keep an eye out for mule deer.

Return the way you came.

DIRECTIONS

From the town of Frenchglen, head south on Highway 205 for 10 miles. Just past milepost 68, turn left onto the gravel Steens Mountain Loop Road, which becomes Steens Mountain Road, following a sign for the South Steens Campground and Upper Blitzen River. Continue for 18 miles, and turn left onto a gravel road, following a sign for the Riddle Brothers Ranch National Historic District. In 1.2 miles you'll arrive at a green gate. If the gate isn't open, you can park in the area just right of it, and walk 1.3 miles one-way to the official parking area. If the gate is open (9am-5pm Wed.-Sun. mid-June-Oct.) and you'd like to shave some hiking mileage, continue driving down the road to the Riddle Brothers Ranch parking lot.

GPS COORDINATES: 42.66194, –118.75342 / N42° 39.7164' W118° 45.2052'

Big Indian Gorge
STEENS MOUNTAIN WILDERNESS

Explore one of the most accessible of the glacially carved gorges for which Steens Mountain is known.

DISTANCE: 8.1 miles round-trip

DURATION: 4 hours

ELEVATION CHANGE: 920 feet

EFFORT: Moderate

TRAIL: Dirt trail, rocks, roots, stream crossings

USERS: Hikers, leashed dogs, horseback riders

SEASON: June–November

PASSES/FEES: None

MAPS: USGS topographic map for Fish Lake

CONTACT: Bureau of Land Management, 541/573-4400, www.blm.gov

Roughly 10,000 years ago, several glaciers slid 10 miles down Steens's western slopes, carving several 2,000-foot gorges and leaving U-shaped valleys in their wake—including Big Indian Gorge.

START THE HIKE

This hike involves three stream crossings, each spanning 10-15 feet. Late spring-early summer, these streams may be impassable—the water can get up to calf-deep—unless you happen upon hiker-created log crossings. In late summer-early fall, however, the water flow mellows to ankle-high levels, and the crossings are easily manageable.

The first two miles of this trail are almost entirely exposed, so bring plenty of water, and load up on sunscreen, particularly if you're hiking during the height of summer. Also, keep an eye out for rattlesnakes.

▶ MILE 0-2: Big Indian Gorge Trailhead to Big Indian Creek
From the parking lot, follow a wide gravel path east for several hundred feet to the **Big Indian Gorge Trailhead.** You'll follow an old Jeep road, once used to shuttle supplies to ranch workers on Steens Mountain, lined by occasional boulders and juniper trees. After ascending an easy 325 feet over the first 1.9 miles, you'll arrive at **Big Indian Creek,** your first stream crossing.

▶ MILE 2-2.7: Big Indian Creek to Log Cabin
You'll gradually trade juniper for cottonwood and aspen over the next 0.2 mile, when you arrive at **Little Indian Creek.** After crossing the creek, head uphill and, in 0.5 mile, find a **spur trail** to your left; walk the short, scenic stretch to see the remnants of an old **log cabin.** Also keep an eye out along this spur for wild onion, buckwheat, purple lupine, and other wildflowers.

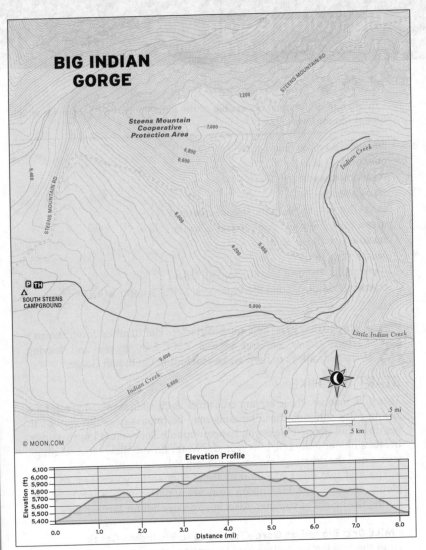

BIG INDIAN GORGE

Steens Mountain Cooperative Protection Area

7,200

7,000

6,800

6,600

6,000

6,200

6,400

STEENS MOUNTAIN RD

6,400

Indian Creek

P TH
SOUTH STEENS
CAMPGROUND

5,800

Little Indian Creek

5,000

Indian Creek

5,600

0   .5 mi

0   .5 km

© MOON.COM

Elevation Profile

Elevation (ft): 6,100 6,000 5,900 5,800 5,700 5,600 5,500 5,400

Distance (mi): 0.0 1.0 2.0 3.0 4.0 5.0 6.0 7.0 8.0

▶ MILE 2.7-3.2: Log Cabin to Big Indian Gorge

Back on the trail, continue through the forest of mountain mahogany, cottonwood, and aspen. You'll arrive after 0.5 mile at your final stream crossing, **Big Indian Creek** again. From here, sagebrush and aspen flank the trail as you gradually ascend to the foot of **Big Indian Gorge.**

▶ MILE 3.2-4.05: Big Indian Gorge to Headwall View

About 0.8 mile after the last creek crossing, you'll pass a solitary, ottoman-sized boulder—to the right of the trail—shaded by aspen trees. Enjoy a snack in the shade and continue a few hundred feet farther down the trail for a clear view of the Big Indian Gorge's headwall. Backpackers continue on another 4 miles to reach the headwall, but this is your turnaround point. Return the way you came.

▲ THE TRAIL TO BIG INDIAN GORGE

DIRECTIONS

From the town of Frenchglen, head south on Highway 205 for 10 miles. Just past milepost 68, turn left onto the gravel Steens Mountain Loop Road for 19.3 miles, following a sign for South Steens Campground and the Upper Blitzen River. Turn right at the sign for the South Steens family camping area, and continue for 0.4 mile to the parking area at the end of the loop.

GPS COORDINATES: 42.65619, –118.72406 / N42° 39.3714′ W118° 43.4436′

Descend into a glacially carved cirque and to the shore of an alpine lake near the summit of Steens Mountain.

DISTANCE: 2.8 miles round-trip
DURATION: 2 hours
ELEVATION CHANGE: 1,010 feet
EFFORT: Easy/moderate
TRAIL: Dirt trail, gravel, rocks, minor stream crossings
USERS: Hikers, leashed dogs
SEASON: July-October
PASSES/FEES: None
MAPS: USGS topographic map for Wildhorse Lake
CONTACT: Bureau of Land Management, 541/573-4400, www.blm.gov

START THE HIKE

A steady descent with scree means it's advisable to wear hiking boots with sufficient tread, bring a walking stick, and watch your step on this trail. While leashed dogs are allowed, given the rockiness it may be best to leave Fido at home.

▼ WILDHORSE LAKE

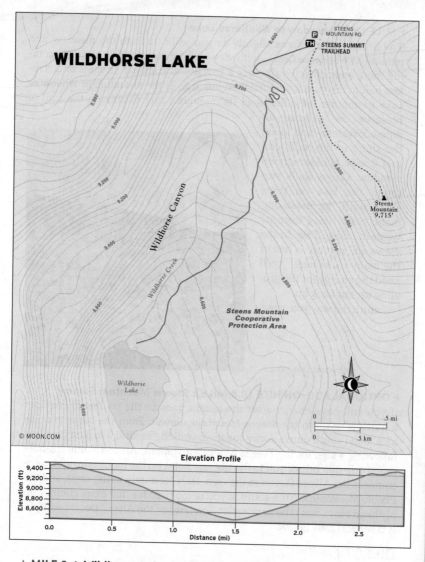

WILDHORSE LAKE

STEENS MOUNTAIN RD

P — STEENS
TH — STEENS SUMMIT TRAILHEAD

Wildhorse Canyon

Wildhorse Creek

Steens Mountain
Cooperative
Protection Area

Wildhorse
Lake

Steens
Mountain
9,715'

© MOON.COM

0 — .5 mi
0 — .5 km

Elevation Profile

Elevation (ft)

9,400
9,200
9,000
8,800
8,600

0.0   0.5   1.0   1.5   2.0   2.5

Distance (mi)

▶ **MILE 0-1: Wildhorse Lake Trailhead to Meadow**

Find the trailhead—marked by an unsigned metal post—on the west side of the gravel parking area to begin descending the rocky **Wildhorse Lake Trail.** In 0.2 mile, you'll arrive at an unsigned fork where you'll find a **trail register**—and your first view of Wildhorse Lake. Take a left to continue descending into the cirque—a bowl-like depression—and toward the lakeshore. You'll start traversing a series of switchbacks down a narrow, steep trail covered in loose rock. After 0.8 mile of careful descent, you'll enter a **meadow** just above Wildhorse Lake. In late spring and early summer, you may spy pink monkeyflower, purple lupine, yellow buckwheat, and other wildflowers. Keep an eye out on the surrounding cirque for mule deer and bighorn sheep.

▶ **MILE 1–1.4: Meadow to Wildhorse Lake**

The brutal grade softens slightly as you walk through the meadow and parallel to **Wildhorse Creek,** with views of the surrounding cirque becoming more expansive. You'll cross a handful of trickling streams and rivulets before arriving at an unsigned junction at the shoreline of **Wildhorse Lake** in another 0.4 mile. Head right—taking care to stay on the trail to preserve the delicate alpine ecosystem—and along the shore to the trail's end in a grassy, boulder-strewn meadow. Gorge walls surround the lake on three sides, with the most dramatic cliffs rising from its western shore. Take in the views and rest up on one of the many rocks here; you'll need the energy for the grueling ascent back up.

Return the way you came.

WILDHORSE LAKE TRAIL ▶

▶ **OPTIONAL ADD-ON HIKE (0.8 MILE): Steens Mountain Summit**

If you still have energy after the ascent back to the trailhead, consider a quick hike up to the **Steens Mountain summit.** From the same parking area, head south onto a rocky roadbed, walking around a locked gate and following a sign for the Steens Mountain summit. An additional 0.8-mile round-trip trek brings you to the highest point on the mountain; views encompass the Alvord Desert to the east, Hart Mountain to the west, and the Pueblo Mountains to the south. If you're too tired for that extra climb, simply head east across the parking lot for views of the Alvord Desert—roughly a vertical mile below.

DIRECTIONS

From the town of Frenchglen, head east onto the gravel Steens Mountain Loop Road for 3.1 miles. When you arrive at a T-shaped junction, turn left to continue on Steens Mountain Loop Road for another 22.4 miles. At the four-way intersection, follow signs for Wildhorse Lake and the Steens Mountain summit, driving an additional 2 miles. The road ends at the trailheads for Wildhorse Lake and the Steens Mountain summit.

GPS COORDINATES: 42.64146, –118.57976 / N42° 38.4876′ W118° 34.7856′

STEENS MOUNTAIN WILDERNESS

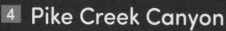

Hike into a canyon along one of the few accessible trails on Steens Mountain's sheer eastern face.

DISTANCE: 6.5 miles round-trip

DURATION: 3 hours

ELEVATION CHANGE: 1,430 feet

EFFORT: Moderate

TRAIL: Dirt trail, gravel road, rocks, stream crossings

USERS: Hikers, leashed dogs, horses

SEASON: April–November

PASSES/FEES: None, if parking along East Steens Road/Fields–Denio Road; $5 day-use fee per vehicle (payable at Alvord Hot Springs) if parking at the trailhead

MAPS: USGS topographic map for Alvord Hot Springs

CONTACT: Bureau of Land Management, 541/573-4400, www.blm.gov

START THE HIKE

▶ **MILE 0-0.7: East Steens Road/Fields–Denio Road to Pike Creek Trailhead**

If you're in a low-clearance vehicle, park at the sign for the Pike Creek Canyon trail along East Steens Road/Fields–Denio Road. On the west side of the road, you'll see a yellow cattle guard; walk across it and down the bumpy **unnamed road** through a sea of sagebrush. This section of the hike is on private property, so remain on the trail at all times. After 0.5 mile, turn left at the unsigned Y-shaped junction, and in another several hundred feet keep right, ignoring signs for Camping and Parking. In 0.15 mile you'll arrive at the end of the road, and a parking area for high-clearance vehicles noted by a juniper tree that appears to grow out of a large red boulder (those with high-clearance vehicles can drive down this road to shave 1.4 miles round-trip off the hike). Follow the unmarked trail at the northwest edge of the parking area and cross the trickling **Pike Creek** to arrive at the **Pike Creek Trailhead**.

▶ **MILE 0.7-1.75: Pike Creek Trailhead to Wooden Shed**

Roughly 0.3 mile past the creek, you'll arrive at a **trail register** at the base of the **Pike Creek Canyon**. As you enter the canyon, you'll walk across large, loose rocks, one of many such stretches from here on in, so stay mindful. As you ascend, gaining roughly 420 feet over this stretch, keep an eye out for golden eagles, bighorn sheep, pronghorn, lizards, and other wildlife. Views—both of the canyon and the Alvord Desert behind you—improve with every step. In another 0.75 mile, you'll pass a boundary sign as you officially enter the **Steens Mountain Wilderness**. This trail follows

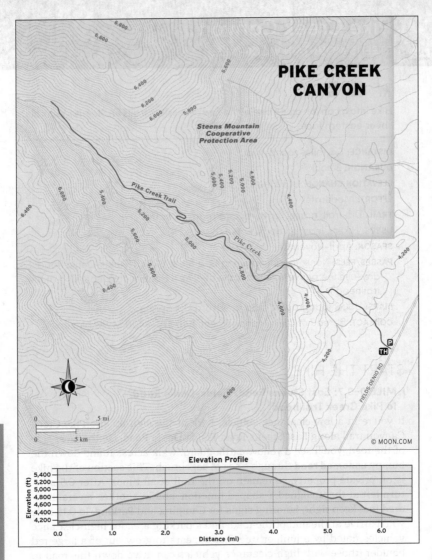

PIKE CREEK CANYON

Steens Mountain Cooperative Protection Area

Pike Creek Trail

Pike Creek

© MOON.COM

Elevation Profile

an old mining track, and just past the sign you'll see some evidence of the region's history: Behind some sagebrush to your left is a small **wooden shed**, used by miners searching for uranium in the early 1900s. Stay on the trail, and do not enter the shed.

▶ MILE 1.75–3.25: Wooden Shed to Juniper Tree Viewpoint

Past the shed, rock-hop across the trickling Pike Creek again before hiking up a few switchbacks into an open, rocky clearing. This is a nice spot to relax and enjoy a snack. Head to the clearing's northwestern edge to continue on the trail, which ascends steadily from here. You'll head up a series of switchbacks in 0.25 mile. Take time to turn around for views of Pike Creek Canyon framing the Alvord Desert below. As you gain 500 feet over the next 1.25 miles, you'll start to notice Steens's eastern face rising above

▲ VIEW ON THE PIKE CREEK CANYON TRAIL

you, its colorful canyon walls a riot of reds and oranges. Complementary yellow balsamroot and purple penstemon are just some of the wildflowers you may spy around here well into summer. After ascending a few short switchbacks, you'll arrive at a large juniper tree with several boulders beneath it—a good resting spot with views opening out to the canyon below.

The trail continues on, becoming steeper and fainter, so this is your turnaround point. Return the way you came.

If you have time, return to **Alvord Hot Springs**—where you might've bought a parking pass—for a post-hike soak. From the trailhead, the 2-mile drive southwest takes three minutes via East Steens Road/Fields-Denio Road.

DIRECTIONS

From the town of Fields, head north on East Steens Road/Fields-Denio Road. The pavement ends after 12.6 miles. Continue on the well-maintained gravel road for another 10.7 miles to the Alvord Hot Springs office and general store, where you can buy your day-use pass to park at the Pike Creek Trailhead. From here, continue north on East Steens Road/Fields-Denio Road for 2 miles until you see a yellow cattle guard on the left side of the road. If you have a low-clearance vehicle, park in the gravel parking area on the west side of the road just past the guard, near a sign for the trail. If you're in a high-clearance vehicle, you can turn left onto the rutted road and continue another 0.7 mile to reach the trailhead.

GPS COORDINATES: 42.57116, -118.52216 / N42° 34.2696' W118° 31.3296'

STEENS MOUNTAIN AND ALVORD DESERT

Pike Creek Canyon

Hike to the shores of Borax Lake—and past a series of hot springs—near the Alvord Desert.

DISTANCE: 2 miles round-trip
DURATION: 1 hour
ELEVATION CHANGE: 40 feet
EFFORT: Easy
TRAIL: Dirt trail, sandy path
USERS: Hikers
SEASON: Year-round
PASSES/FEES: None
MAPS: USGS topographic map for Borax Lake
CONTACT: The Nature Conservancy, 503/802-8100, www.nature.org

n the ice age, this valley sat buried under a lake 200 feet deep. The changing climate led to its evaporation, leaving behind only a few watery vestiges—including Borax Lake—and a bed of alkali and sodium borate. The latter is still visible on patches of trail; look for a white, snow-like substance. Tempting though it may be, forget about a soak here or even dipping a toe: The hot pools lining the trail can reach 180°F, too hot for safe contact. Borax Lake's surface temperature can reach 105°F, and arsenic levels in the lake are 25 times the critical limit for drinking water.

START THE HIKE

▶ MILE 0-0.5: Trailhead to Borax Lake

At the eastern edge of the parking area, walk through a pedestrian pass-through next to a locked gate and onto a wide, sandy trail. Almost immediately, you'll pass **Lower Borax Lake Reservoir** on your right; this shallow

⌄ BORAX LAKE

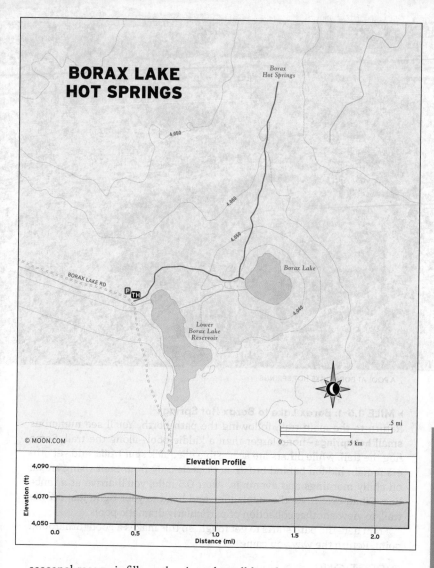

BORAX LAKE HOT SPRINGS

Borax
Hot Springs

4,050

4,060

4,050

Borax Lake

BORAX LAKE RD

P TH

Lower
Borax Lake
Reservoir

4,040

© MOON.COM

0   .5 mi

0   .5 km

Elevation Profile

4,090				
4,070				
4,050				

0.0   0.5   1.0   1.5   2.0

Distance (mi)

Elevation (ft)

seasonal reservoir fills each winter but all but dries out by midsummer. In 0.4 mile, a short spur trail to your left leads to a pair of **vats** that laborers used in the late 1800s to dissolve sodium borate crusts and produce borax. A few hundred feet later, another short spur trail, this one to your right, leads you to the shore of **Borax Lake.** The 10-acre lake is fed by hot springs and sits on a bed of sodium borate deposits. It doesn't freeze in winter, so the surrounding marshland makes an ideal habitat for Canada geese, hawks, snowy plovers, herons, and other waterfowl. The most curious wildlife here is no larger than your index finger: the Borax Lake chub. The endangered minnow lives here in Borax Lake and nowhere else on Earth; it evolved with the changing climate to thrive in the increasingly warm, alkaline water.

▲ A POOL AT BORAX LAKE HOT SPRINGS

▶ MILE 0.5-1: Borax Lake to Borax Hot Springs

Return to the main trail, following the path north. You'll see numerous small **hot springs**—none larger than a kiddie pool—along the trail. Some hug the trail, while others are accessible via quick **spur trails,** and yet others remain hidden behind brush, noticeable only from their rising steam on chilly mornings and evenings. After 0.5 mile, you'll arrive at a fence line. Climb over it via the stepladder, and head to your right, just off the trail, to view another collection of particularly dramatic pools.

From here the path starts to get rough, so this makes a good turnaround point. Return the way you came.

DIRECTIONS

From the town of Fields, head north on East Steens Road/Fields-Denio Road. Continue straight when the road forks after 1.2 miles. In 0.5 mile, turn right onto the unmarked gravel road on the north side of the power substation. Continue on this road for 2.2 miles, and turn left onto another unmarked road, and continue for 1.8 miles to pass through an unlocked wire gate. Continue past the gate for another 0.5 mile to a parking area at a turnaround that marks the end of the road.

GPS COORDINATES: 42.32641, –118.61099 / N42° 19.5846′ W118° 36.6594′

NEARBY CAMPGROUNDS

NAME	DESCRIPTION	FACILITIES	SEASON	FEE
Page Springs Campground	at the base of Steens Mountain	36 tent and RV sites, restrooms	year-round	$8
Steens Mountain Loop Rd., Frenchglen, 541/573-4400, www.blm.gov				
Jackman Park Campground	basic campground with excellent fall colors	6 tent and camper sites, restrooms	June-October	$6
Steens Mountain Loop Rd., Frenchglen, 541/573-4400, www.blm.gov				
South Steens Campground	in the heart of Steens Mountain	36 family campsites, 15 equestrian sites, restrooms	May-November	$6
Steens Mountain Loop Rd., Frenchglen, 541/573-4400, www.blm.gov				
Mann Lake Campground	no-frills campground near the Alvord Desert	5 tent sites, restrooms	year-round	free
East Steens Rd./Fields-Denio Rd., Fields, 541/573-4400, www.blm.gov				
Alvord Hot Springs	campground at the hot springs affords 24-hour access	11 tent sites, restrooms	year-round	$30
East Steens Rd./Fields-Denio Rd., Fields, 541/589-2282, www.alvordhotsprings.com				

WALLOWA MOUNTAINS AND BLUE MOUNTAINS

Northeastern Oregon is almost as rugged as the cowboys and ranchers who've called the region home for more than a century. At 9,000 feet, the Wallowa Mountains lord over the surrounding valley, dwarfing the ranches and homesteads with seemingly vertical peaks. Farther south, the arid, dusty Baker Valley still sports wagon ruts, visible some 175 years after pioneers made their way west here along the Oregon Trail. And the Elkhorn Mountains, part of the larger Blue Mountains range, host alpine lakes and forests in the shadow of granite peaks east of Baker City. Trails here offer hikers glimpses of the region's diverse natural beauty, from crystal-clear waters and summertime wildflowers to open expanses and snowcapped peaks.

▲ ANTHONY LAKE AND GUNSIGHT MOUNTAIN

▲ COVERED WAGON AT THE NATIONAL HISTORIC OREGON TRAIL INTERPRETIVE CENTER

◀ SACAJAWEA PEAK ABOVE HURRICANE CREEK

1   Hurricane Creek to Slick Rock Gorge

DISTANCE: 7.5 miles round-trip
DURATION: 3.5 hours
EFFORT: Easy/moderate

2   Iwetemlaykin State Heritage Site

DISTANCE: 2 miles round-trip
DURATION: 1 hour
EFFORT: Easy

3   Imnaha River to Blue Hole

DISTANCE: 4.6 miles round-trip
DURATION: 2.25 hours
EFFORT: Easy

4   Anthony Lake to Hoffer Lakes

DISTANCE: 3.2 miles round-trip
DURATION: 1.5 hours
EFFORT: Easy

5   National Historic Oregon Trail Interpretive Center

DISTANCE: 4.3 miles round-trip
DURATION: 2 hours
EFFORT: Easy

▼ IMNAHA RIVER

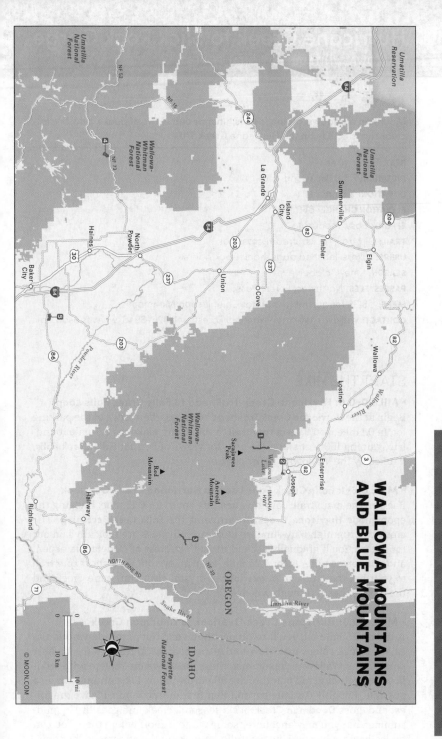

WALLOWA MOUNTAINS
AND BLUE MOUNTAINS

Hurricane Creek to Slick Rock Gorge

WALLOWA-WHITMAN NATIONAL FOREST

Mountain meadows, alpine forests, unimpeded views of peaks, and crystal-clear rivers collide on the Hurricane Creek Trail.

BEST: Brew Hikes
DISTANCE: 7.5 miles round-trip
DURATION: 3.5 hours
ELEVATION CHANGE: 860 feet
EFFORT: Easy/moderate
TRAIL: Dirt trail, rocks, stream crossings
USERS: Hikers, leashed dogs, horseback riders
SEASON: June-October
PASSES/FEES: Northwest Forest Pass
MAPS: USGS topographic map for Chief Joseph Mountain
CONTACT: Wallowa-Whitman National Forest, 541/426-5546, www.fs.usda.gov

START THE HIKE

▶ **MILE 0-0.6: Hurricane Creek Trailhead to Falls Creek Falls Loop**
Begin at the **Hurricane Creek Trailhead** at the southern edge of the parking lot. In 0.1 mile, you'll see a **spur trail** to your right; make the 0.5-mile round-trip, gaining 150 feet along the way, for views of 50-foot **Falls Creek Falls,** flanked by the Wallowas' rocky peaks.

▶ **MILE 0.6-1: Falls Creek Falls Loop to Hurricane Creek Overlook**
Back on the main trail, continue heading south for 0.15 mile, hugging the eponymous **Hurricane Creek,** to arrive at the **Falls Creek crossing.** The creek can run high May-June, so step carefully; logs are typically laid out for hikers. You'll gradually ascend through a forest of Douglas fir, aspen, and ponderosa pine. After 0.25 mile, keep an eye out for a short **spur trail** to your left that ends at an **overlook** of crystal-clear Hurricane Creek and the broader basin through which it flows.

▶ **MILE 1-2.3: Hurricane Creek Overlook to Deadman Creek**
Another 0.5 mile on, you'll begin darting in and out of meadows, and Sacajawea Peak comes into view to the south; at 9,800 feet, it's the highest point in the Wallowas. In summer, these meadows are replete with wildflowers, including red paintbrush and purple phlox. Elk sightings are also possible. Roughly 0.8 mile beyond that first meadow, you'll leave the forest and cross **Deadman Creek;** it's a seasonal creek and goes dry by midsummer, but you may encounter some winter runoff before then. You can typically cross by stepping carefully on rocks in the streambed, but don't attempt the crossing if the flow is high.

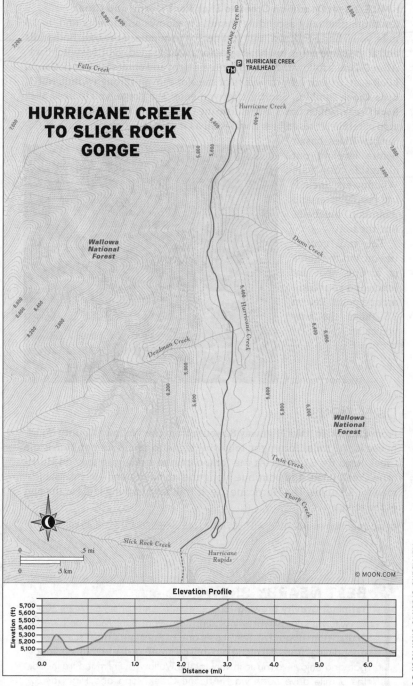

HURRICANE CREEK TO SLICK ROCK GORGE

Wallowa National Forest

Wallowa National Forest

HURRICANE CREEK RD

P HURRICANE CREEK TRAILHEAD
TH

Hurricane Creek

Falls Creek

Dunn Creek

Deadman Creek

Hurricane Creek

Twin Creek

Thorp Creek

Slick Rock Creek

Hurricane Rapids

0   .5 mi
0   .5 km

© MOON.COM

Elevation Profile

Elevation (ft)

5,700
5,600
5,500
5,400
5,300
5,200
5,100

0.0   1.0   2.0   3.0   4.0   5.0   6.0

Distance (mi)

▶ **MILE 2.3-4: Deadman Creek to Slick Rock Gorge and Creek**

Continue gradually ascending through meadows and forests and, in 1.3 mile, you'll find a **fork** at a large boulder in the middle of the trail. Both trails end at the same point, but head right for a well-graded, gentler switchback. After 0.4 mile, follow the trail as it curves right and enters **Slick Rock Gorge.** Look east, to your left, for views of the slot canyon through which **Hurricane Creek** rumbles. Shortly after you enter the gorge, you'll cross **Slick Rock Creek,** which flows into Hurricane Creek. It can run high in spring, so step carefully. It resembles a waterfall as it cascades down a chute of Co-

lumbia River basalt before leveling out alongside the trail. Wildflowers, including purple aster and mountain bluebells, line the trail.

SLICK ROCK GORGE ▶

The trail continues on, but the gorge is a fine spot for lunch and your turnaround point. Return 3.5 miles the way you came.

DIRECTIONS

From Enterprise, take Highway 82 south from the Wallowa County Courthouse for 0.3 mile. Turn right, following signs, to head south on Hurricane Creek Road for 5.1 miles. At the fork, continue straight to stay on Hurricane Creek Road, and continue along the unmaintained—but passable—road for 3.8 miles. The Hurricane Creek Trailhead parking lot is at the end of the road.

GPS COORDINATES: 45.31156, -117.30708 / N45° 18.6936' W117° 18.4248'

BEST NEARBY BREWS

Terminal Gravity Brewing (803 E. 4th St., Enterprise, 541/426-3000, www.terminalgravitybrewing.com, 11am-9pm Sun.-Mon. and Wed.-Thurs., 11am-10pm Fri.-Sat.) hosts one of the state's most scenic outdoor dining areas. Sit along a bubbling creek, order from the outdoor bar, and enjoy live music in view of the Wallowas. From the trailhead, the 9-mile drive north via Hurricane Creek Road and Highway 82 takes 20 minutes.

This short stroll in the Wallowas is just minutes from downtown Joseph and offers dramatic views of the mountains.

DISTANCE: 2 miles round-trip
DURATION: 1 hour
ELEVATION CHANGE: 100 feet
EFFORT: Easy
TRAIL: Dirt trail, gravel paths
USERS: Hikers, leashed dogs
SEASON: Year-round
PASSES/FEES: None
MAPS: Oregon State Parks map for Iwetemlaykin State Heritage Site
CONTACT: Oregon State Parks, 541/432-4185, www.oregonstateparks.org

This area is the ancestral home of the Nez Perce people, and the park's name—Iwetemlaykin (ee-weh-TEMM-lye-kinn)—is Nez Perce for "at the edge of the lake." Their leader, Old Chief Joseph, led treaty negotiations that created a reservation for the Nez Perce people around Wallowa Lake in 1855—only to be slashed in size by 90 percent just eight years later by the U.S. government, paving the path to the Nez Perce War of 1877. The tribe surrendered, and the land was earmarked for white resettlement. Today, ranches and vacation homes dot the valley.

START THE HIKE

▶ **MILE 0-0.1: Northern Parking Area Trailhead to Ridgeline Prairie**
Walk to the trailhead—indicated by a signboard with a trail map and background information on the area—at the southern edge of the site's main parking lot, the more northerly of two. Ascend gradually on the unnamed gravel trail as it switchbacks through a grassy area before leveling off, after 0.1 mile, at an open prairie on the crest of a ridge, where you'll enjoy unimpeded views of the Wallowa Mountains to the east; the views don't let up for the duration of the hike.

▶ **MILE 0.1-0.7: Ridgeline Prairie to Knight's Pond Loop**
From atop this ridgeline prairie, follow the trail as it hugs **Silver Lake Ditch**, which joins the Wallowa River and flows into Wallowa Lake a half mile south. You'll walk past a small forest dotted with cottonwood, ponderosa pine, and Douglas fir; keep an eye out here for fox, elk, and deer. After 0.4 mile, you'll arrive at an unsigned junction. Head right for a flat, 0.2-mile loop around tranquil **Knight's Pond.** Here you might see lupine, sagebrush mariposa lily, and other wildflowers in late spring and summer.

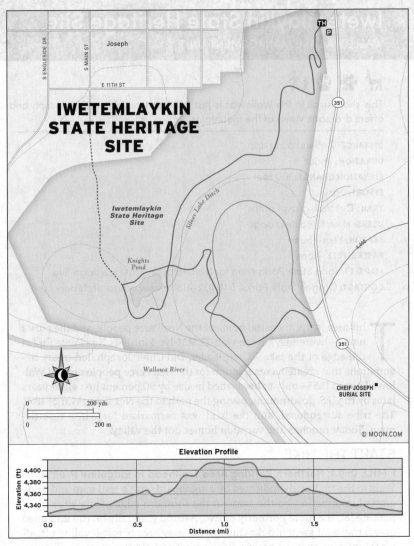

IWETEMLAYKIN
STATE HERITAGE
SITE

Iwetemlaykin
State Heritage
Site

Knights
Pond

Silver Lake Ditch

Joseph

S ENGLESIDE DR

S MAIN ST

E 11TH ST

351

4-409

351

Wallowa River

CHEIF JOSEPH
BURIAL SITE

0   200 yds

0   200 m

© MOON.COM

Elevation Profile

Elevation (ft)

4,400
4,380
4,360
4,340

0.0   0.5   1.0   1.5

Distance (mi)

▸ **MILE 0.7-1: Knight's Pond Loop to Southern Parking Area**

After completing the loop, turn right to head east, crossing a footbridge over Silver Lake Ditch, ascending the grassy hillside. Several social trails also wend up the hill, but stay on the gravel path to protect the park's fragile ecology. Traversing this hill offers the hike's best views, with no nearby houses or trees to block the imposing peaks. The mountains look especially majestic April-May, when they're still covered in snow; you can understand why they're nicknamed the "Swiss Alps of Oregon." The trail ends in 0.3 mile at the park's unmarked southern parking area.

Return the way you came.

▲ WALLOWA MOUNTAINS

▶ **OPTIONAL ADD-ON HIKE (0.2 MILE): Old Chief Joseph Gravesite**
Add 0.2-mile round-trip to your hike by visiting the **gravesite of Old Chief Joseph** before returning the way you came. His remains, originally buried elsewhere, were relocated in 1926 to a plot overlooking Wallowa Lake. From the end of the Iwetemlaykin State Heritage Site trail, turn right to walk south on the paved cycling and walking path along Highway 351, remaining on the west side of the road. In 0.1 mile, turn right at a sign for the gravesite, and follow the footpath to the grave. An interpretive panel details Old Chief Joseph's life and provides context for a dark chapter of American history.

DIRECTIONS

Drive south on Main Street through downtown Joseph, following the road for one mile as it curves to the left and becomes East 8th Street and then Highway 351. Turn right into the park's main (northern) parking lot, just 0.2 mile past South College Street, at the sign for Iwetemlaykin State Heritage Site.

GPS COORDINATES: 45.34297, –117.22349 / N45° 20.5782′ W117° 13.4094′

BEST NEARBY BITES

Fuel up for your hike at **Old Town Cafe** (8 S. Main St., Joseph, 541/432-9898, 8am-2pm Thurs.-Tues.). The cozy eatery serves filling, home-style breakfasts and lunches. Locals love the fist-sized cinnamon rolls and loaded breakfast burritos, ideally consumed on Old Town's sunny patio. From the trailhead, the 0.8-mile drive north via Main Street and East 8th Street takes 2 minutes. Or you can walk from one to the other in 15 minutes.

Imnaha River to Blue Hole

WILD AND SCENIC IMNAHA RIVER

Hike through an alpine forest and a landscape scarred by wildfire to Blue Hole, where the jade-hued Imnaha River emerges from a river gorge.

DISTANCE: 4.6 miles round-trip
DURATION: 2.25 hours
ELEVATION CHANGE: 230 feet
EFFORT: Easy
TRAIL: Dirt trail, rocks, gravel
USERS: Hikers, leashed dogs, horseback riders
SEASON: June-November
PASSES/FEES: Northwest Forest Pass
MAPS: USGS topographic map for Deadman Point
CONTACT: Wallowa-Whitman National Forest, 541/426-5546, www.fs.usda.gov

START THE HIKE

▶ **MILE 0-0.25: Indian Crossing Trailhead to Imnaha River Overlook**
Start at the **Indian Crossing Trailhead,** wedged between the restrooms and an informational signboard at the western edge of the parking area, following a sign for the Blue Hole and Twin Lakes onto the **South Fork Imnaha Trail.** It parallels the Imnaha River, but a shady forest of fir trees and lodgepole pine keeps it hidden—at least until you emerge, after 0.25 mile, at a small **overlook** at a break in the trees above its banks. The river originates in the Eagle Cap Wilderness and the Wallowa-Whitman National Forest and, for roughly 70 miles, follows a geologic fault line before flowing into the Snake River along the Oregon-Idaho border.

▶ **MILE 0.25-2.1: Imnaha River Overlook to Twin Lakes Trail**
From here you'll ascend gradually for the next 0.25 mile, gaining just over 100 feet along the way. The trail levels out after this initial ascent, and you'll trade forest canopy in another 0.5 mile for a sea of charred, toothpick-like snags—the result of a 1996 wildfire. The lack of tree cover on this stretch means you'll enjoy expansive views of the surrounding Imnaha River basin and Eagle Cap Wilderness. Plants and wildlife thrive here along the river. You might see goldenrod, red paintbrush, and dazzling pink fireweed in the summer. Surrounding aspen groves deliver fiery foliage displays every autumn. Keep an eye out for elk, butterflies, and birds, including Cassin's finches, yellow-rumped warblers, Steller's jays, and pileated woodpeckers. In spring, anglers enjoy fishing this stretch of the Imnaha—occasionally visible, to your left, through the snags—for Chinook salmon, Oregon's official state fish. You'll come to a fork in the trail in

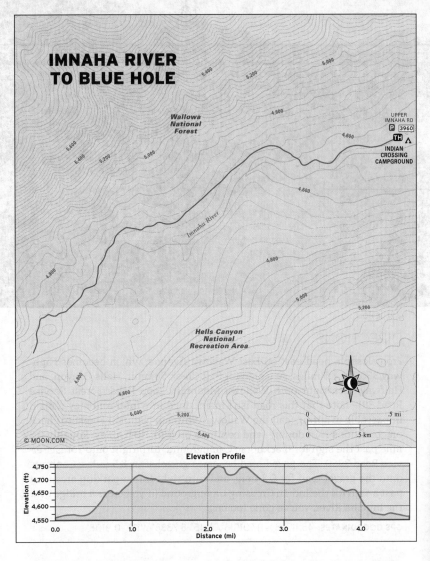

IMNAHA RIVER
TO BLUE HOLE

Wallowa
National
Forest

UPPER
IMNAHA RD
P 3960
TH Λ
INDIAN
CROSSING
CAMPGROUND

Imnaha River

Hells Canyon
National
Recreation Area

© MOON.COM

0   .5 mi
0   .5 km

Elevation Profile

another 1.1 miles; following a sign for the Blue Hole and Twin Lakes, turn left onto the **Twin Lakes Trail.**

▶ **MILE 2.1–2.3: Twin Lakes Trail to Imnaha River and Blue Hole**
You'll lose a bit of elevation before ending in a few hundred feet at the banks of the **Imnaha River.** Wade in during midsummer—this is a popular, if chilly, swimming hole—but exercise caution when the river runs high in spring. To your right you can see the **Blue Hole,** a teal-hued pool, emerging from a rocky, 50-foot river gorge just upstream, but you can also scramble up some rocks to the west for even better views of the pool, as well as a wider panorama of the burned-out river basin.

Return the way you came.

▲ BLUE HOLE

DIRECTIONS

From Joseph, head east on East Wallowa Avenue, which becomes Highway 350, for 8.5 miles. At a sign for Salt Creek Summit, Hells Canyon, and Halfway, turn right onto Wallowa Mountain Loop Road (Forest Service Road 39)—note that this road isn't maintained in winter and may remain impassable in spring (call the Wallowa-Whitman National Forest to check on conditions if in doubt)—and continue on it for 30.5 miles. Roughly 0.5 mile past the sign for Blackhorse Campground, turn right onto Forest Service Road 3960. The paved road becomes gravel after 8.5 miles. Continue onto the gravel road for 0.3 mile, and turn right into a parking area, just past a sign for the Indian Crossing Campground (if you cross a bridge over the Imnaha River, you've gone too far).

GPS COORDINATES: 45.11223, –117.01518 / N45° 6.7338′ W117° 0.9108′

BEST NEARBY BREWS

The Blue Hole trailhead is in a remote area of the Wallowas, so the closest options are in Joseph, and **Embers Brew House Restaurant and Pub** (204 N. Main St., Joseph, 541/432-2739, 11am-9pm daily) makes a satisfying stop if you're returning through the town. Embers offers a hearty selection of regional craft beer, burgers, pizzas, and outdoor seating with views of the surrounding mountain peaks. From the trailhead, the 38-mile drive northwest takes 1.75 hours via Wallowa Mountain Loop Road and Highway 350.

Hike past alpine lakes, through wildflower meadows, and in the shadow of granite peaks—all in just a few miles.

DISTANCE: 3.2 miles round-trip

DURATION: 1.5 hours

ELEVATION CHANGE: 490 feet

EFFORT: Easy

TRAIL: Gravel and dirt paths, rocks

USERS: Hikers, leashed dogs

SEASON: June–October

PASSES/FEES: $4 per vehicle

MAPS: USGS topographic map for Anthony Lakes

CONTACT: Wallowa-Whitman National Forest, 541/523-6391, www.fs.usda.gov

START THE HIKE

▶ **MILE 0-0.5: Parking Area to Hoffer Lakes Trail**

From the parking area, head south into the forest from the unsigned trailhead to shortly arrive at the shore of **Anthony Lake** and an unsigned junction. Enjoy the first of many dramatic views along this trail; visible from here are, from east to west, Gunsight Mountain, Angell Peak, and Lees Peak. Turn left onto the **Anthony Lake Shoreline Trail** to begin the hike's clockwise loop. Follow the shoreline as it cuts through subalpine fir forests and summertime wildflowers including purple asters and pink heather. After 0.3 mile, you'll cross a stone boat dock and, in a couple hundred feet, turn right onto a wide gravel path. After a mostly flat 0.2 mile, turn left onto the **Hoffer Lakes Trail.**

▶ **MILE 0.5-1.4: Hoffer Lakes Trail to Hoffer Lakes**

Soon after, you'll encounter a faint, unsigned Y-shaped junction. Keep left again to remain on the Hoffer Lakes Trail. Follow the rocky trail along **Parker Creek,** ascending steadily and gaining 320 feet before arriving, after 0.6 mile, at a signed junction announcing your arrival at **Hoffer Lakes.** Walk the short distance to the shore of the smaller of the two lakes for dramatic views, with Lees Peak towering above it. Then take the quick jaunt east from the junction on the 0.25-mile round-trip **spur trail.** This flat path brings you to the larger of the two Hoffer Lakes, which butts up against granite crags. You may see false hellebore and red paintbrush blooming along this trail.

WALLOWA MOUNTAINS AND BLUE MOUNTAINS

Anthony Lake to Hoffer Lakes

303

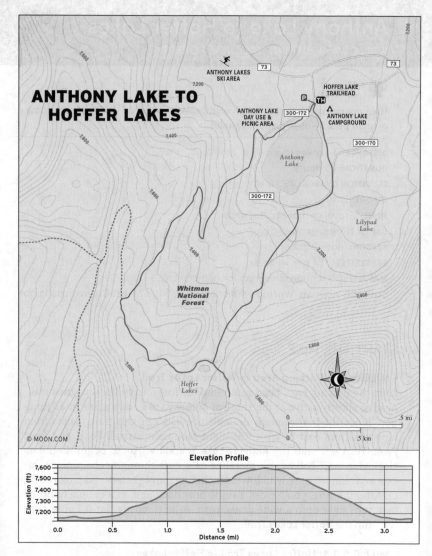

ANTHONY LAKES
SKI AREA

HOFFER LAKE
TRAILHEAD

ANTHONY LAKE
DAY USE &
PICNIC AREA

P

TH

ANTHONY LAKE
CAMPGROUND

ANTHONY LAKE TO
HOFFER LAKES

300-172

Anthony
Lake

300-170

300-172

Lilypad
Lake

Whitman
National
Forest

Hoffer
Lakes

© MOON.COM

0   .5 mi

0   .5 km

Elevation Profile

Elevation (ft): 7,600 / 7,500 / 7,400 / 7,300 / 7,200

Distance (mi): 0.0   0.5   1.0   1.5   2.0   2.5   3.0

▶ **MILE 1.4–1.9: Hoffer Lakes to Forest Road 5185**

Back at the junction, follow the Hoffer Lakes Trail as it heads west, following the smaller lake's shoreline before gently yet steadily ascending into open alpine meadows. These fields are littered with purple monkeyflower, northern mule-ears, bigleaf lupine, and other wildflowers late spring-early summer. You'll arrive at the unsigned **Forest Road 5185** in 0.5 mile. Turn right onto the road to start looping northeast. Lees Peak and Gunsight Mountain occasionally peek through the trees to your right.

▶ **MILE 1.9–3.2: Forest Road 5185 to Parking Area**

In 1 mile, you'll arrive at a Y-junction; head right onto the hard-packed dirt road as it curves south, back toward Anthony Lake, and continue on as it becomes gravel. After about 350 feet, you'll arrive at an unsigned

T-junction; to your left is the road to the guard station and trailhead parking area, but continue 150 feet straight ahead, and look to the left for an unsigned trail that leads to day-use sites and reconnects with the **Anthony Lake Shoreline Trail.** In summer, the purple blossoms of Jeffrey's shooting star line this stretch. You'll also pass a **gazebo,** built in the 1930s by the Civilian Conservation Corps, off to your left. Several other unmarked paths crisscross the day-use area here—you can follow any of them east and, in about 0.2 mile, you'll complete the loop, arriving back at the original junction. Turn left to return to the parking area.

DIRECTIONS

From La Grande, head east on I-84 for 23.3 miles. Take exit 285, and continue west on River Lane for 4 miles. Turn left onto Ellis Road, continuing on it for 0.7 mile. Turn right onto Anthony Lakes Highway, which becomes Forest Road 73 after 7.7 miles at a Y-shaped junction; follow the road as it curves to the right and, after another 7.9 curvy miles, turn left at a fork to follow a sign for Anthony Lake Campground. You'll soon pass the Anthony Lake Guard Station on the right. A small parking area is to your left, just across the road from a restroom.

GPS COORDINATES: 44.96147, -118.23091/ N44° 57.6882′ W118° 13.8546′

ONE OF THE HOFFER LAKES ▶

BEST NEARBY BITES

Kick back with pizza, burgers, salads, and a regional craft beverage at **Summer at the Starbottle** (Anthony Lakes Rd., North Powder, 541/856-3277, http://anthonylakes.com/summer-at-the-starbottle, 11am-6pm Fri.-Sun. July-early Sept.). Nestled in the lodge at Anthony Lakes Mountain Resort, the seasonal restaurant prides itself on using locally sourced ingredients and offers plenty of outdoor seating with views of the surrounding Elkhorn Mountains. From the trailhead, the 0.3-mile drive west takes one minute—or five minutes of walking—via Forest Road 73.

National Historic Oregon Trail Interpretive Center

BAKER CITY, VALE DISTRICT

✿ 🐾 🚶 ♿

Walk amid wagon ruts left in the Baker Valley by Oregon Trail pioneers.

BEST: Kid-Friendly Hikes

DISTANCE: 4.3 miles round-trip

DURATION: 2 hours

ELEVATION CHANGE: 480 feet

EFFORT: Easy

TRAIL: Dirt trail, paved path, gravel

USERS: Hikers, wheelchair users, leashed dogs

SEASON: Year-round

PASSES/FEES: $5-8 adults, $3.50-4.50 seniors, free for children 15 and younger

MAPS: Free trail map at the Historic Oregon Trail Interpretive Center

PARK HOURS: 9am-6pm daily Memorial Day weekend-October, subject to seasonal changes

CONTACT: Bureau of Land Management, 541/523-1843, www.blm.gov

Located atop Flagstaff Hill, the National Historic Oregon Trail Interpretive Center is a museum with interpretive panels, exhibits, and movies documenting the historic westward journey, as well as several miles of interpretive hiking trails.

START THE HIKE

▶ **MILE 0-0.9: Replica Wagon Train to Oregon Trail Ruts Loop**

Find the **replica wagon train** at the southern edge of the parking lot to begin this clockwise loop hike, following the wide, unmarked path known as the **Ascent Trail**; it's the steepest trail on the property and so much more fun to descend. The paved path soon transitions to gravel as you hike down toward the valley floor, passing all manner of vegetation—including sagebrush, bluebunch wheatgrass, buttercup, and fleabane—and views of the Blue Mountains open up. There's little shade along this westward route, so you'll appreciate the covered bench after 0.9 mile, at a four-way intersection. Take a left here onto the **Oregon Trail Ruts Loop,** where you'll find **Oregon Trail ruts** and a **covered wagon replica.**

▶ **MILE 0.9-2.3: Oregon Trail Ruts Loop to Rocky Outcrop Viewpoint**

After 0.1 mile, turn left onto the 0.7-mile round-trip **Auburn Burnt River Spur Trail,** an out-and-back gravel trail that takes you to the site of an **old wagon road** likely used by miners in the 1860s. Back on the Oregon Trail Ruts Loop, continue west for 0.1 mile, then take a left at the signed junction onto the gravel **Eagle Valley Railroad Grade Loop Trail.** In 0.5 mile,

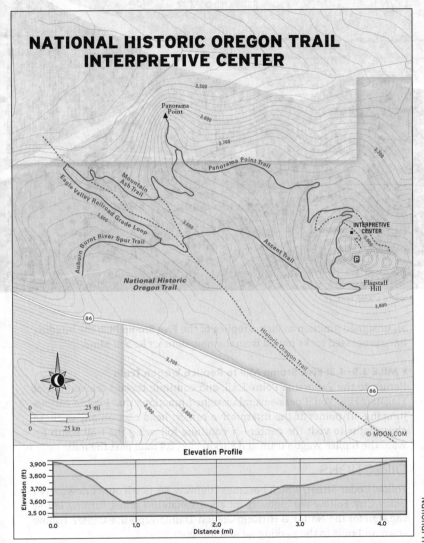

NATIONAL HISTORIC OREGON TRAIL INTERPRETIVE CENTER

Elevation Profile

you'll come to a **rocky outcrop** that offers 360-degree views of Flagstaff Hill behind you, wagon ruts cutting through the southern hillside, and Baker Valley and the Blue Mountains to the west. From here, you'll gradually ascend back to the museum and summit of Flagstaff Hill.

▶ **MILE 2.3-3.9: Rocky Outcrop Viewpoint to Five Stamp Mill**
In 0.25 mile, you'll arrive at an unsigned T-shaped junction; take a left onto the paved **Mountain Ash Trail**. Head left again in 0.4 mile at a junction for the 0.25-mile round-trip **Panorama Point spur trail**. In addition to covered benches, the point offers views of the broader Baker Valley. Back at the junction, follow the sign to head back east via the **Panorama Point Trail** for a gentle ascent to the summit of Flagstaff Hill. After 0.7 mile, turn left at

▲ FIVE STAMP MILL

an unsigned junction to visit a replica of the **Five Stamp Mill;** the building once processed rocks pulled from the now-defunct Rabbit Mine.

▶ **MILE 3.9–4.3: Five Stamp Mill to Replica Wagon Train**
Return to the Panorama Point Trail, and continue toward the summit of Flagstaff Hill. You'll pass several unsigned junctions that lead to various jumping-off points at the interpretive center; head east on any of these short paths to visit the center—or continue following the trail south toward the replica wagon train and parking lot, 0.4 mile past the mill.

DIRECTIONS

Follow Cedar Street, which becomes Highway 86, north out of downtown Baker City. Follow the highway for approximately 7 miles, turning left at the sign for the National Historic Oregon Trail Interpretive Center. Follow the road 1 mile to the parking lot and museum.

GPS COORDINATES: 44.813538, –117.728864 / N44° 48.8123' W117° 43.7318'

BEST NEARBY BITES AND BREWS

No trip to Baker City is complete without a stop at **Barley Brown's Beer** (www.barleybrownsbeer.com). Grab lunch, dinner, and beer in the **restaurant** (2190 Main St., Baker City, 541/523-4266, www.barleybrownsbeer.com, 4pm-10pm Mon.-Sat.), or sample an expanded selection of Barley Brown's award-winning beers across the street in the **taproom** (2200 Main St., Baker City, 541/523-2337, 2pm-close daily). From the trailhead, the 8.5-mile drive southwest takes 15 minutes via Highway 86.

NEARBY CAMPGROUNDS

NAME	DESCRIPTION	FACILITIES	SEASON	FEE
Wallowa Lake State Park	popular campground on the southern edge of Wallowa Lake	121 full-hookup sites, 88 tent sites, 2 yurts, restrooms	year-round	$20-75
Marina Lane, Joseph, 541/432-4185, http://oregonstateparks.org				
Hurricane Creek Campground	popular campground alongside Hurricane Creek	3 tent-trailer sites, 5 tent sites, restrooms	summer-fall	$6
Hurricane Creek Rd., Enterprise, 541/426-5546, www.fs.usda.gov				
Minam State Recreation Area	quiet campground along the Wallowa River	22 tent sites, restrooms	spring-fall	$10
Hwy. 82, Minam, 800/551-6949, http://oregonstateparks.org				
Catherine Creek State Park	remote campground along a rushing river	20 tent sites, restrooms	April-October	$10
Hwy. 203, Union, 541/983-2277, http://oregonstateparks.org				
Anthony Lake Campground	alpine campground in the Elkhorn Mountains	37 tent and trailer sites, restrooms	July-September	$10-50
Forest Rd. 73, North Powder, 541/894-2332, www.anthonylakes.com				

HIKING TIPS

Safety

BEFORE YOU GO

All too often, when hikers find themselves in distress, the trouble didn't start on the trail. It started in their living room. It's the seemingly tiny mistakes made at home that can compound into significant problems in the wilderness. Forgetting to let somebody know where you're going. Not checking the weather or time of nightfall. Forgetting to pack rain gear, food, water, or extra batteries. Maybe even (and, yes, at least one of us has done this) forgetting your entire day pack. You have a map and compass, but do you know how to use them? Were you honest about your limitations and fitness level (your current fitness level) when you selected the hike?

Safe and fun hikes start during the preparation process. Here's what you need to get ready for your day hike:

The 10 Essentials

Since 1974, when it was formalized by the Seattle-based outdoor group The Mountaineers, the 10 Essentials has been widely regarded as the standard list of gear hikers and climbers need to stay safe and respond to an emergency when traveling in the backcountry.

1. Extra food: Pack more than you think you'll need.

2. Extra water: Carry more than you think you'll need or, if there are water sources along your route, carry a water purification system.

3. First aid: In a waterproof bag, carry a first-aid kit with items to care for yourself and those depending on you (including pets). Don't forget insect repellent, foot care, and medications.

4. Emergency shelter: Take a lightweight bivy, waterproof tarp, or an oversized and durable plastic bag.

5. Insulation: Pack extra clothes for warmth and protection from the elements.

6. Illumination: A headlamp and/or flashlight and extra batteries.

7. Fire: A stove, waterproof matches, or lighter and tinder.

8. Sun protection: Bring a hat and sunglasses and always use sunscreen (even on overcast days).

9. Navigation: Start with a map and compass. Consider carrying a GPS device (more resistant to weather than phones), an altimeter, and a personal locator beacon (capable of sending an emergency signal from outside cell coverage). Bring battery backup for electronic devices. While your phone is a wonderful tool, don't treat it as a lifeline: Phones are fragile, and cell coverage in the backcountry is not a given.

10. Repair kit and tools: A multipurpose tool, knife, duct tape, zip ties, safety pins, and a sewing kit are great for solving problems on the trail.

HIKING APPS

Whether you want to identify a bird or a mountain, need help finding your way, or just need directions and the weather forecast, your phone can help. There are numerous apps that can enhance your outdoor excursion. Here are some of our favorites:

- **CAIRN** (www.cairnme.com, Android, IOS, free with in-app purchases) shares your location with friends and family of your choosing and alerts them if you're overdue. The app also helps find cell coverage, records your route, and offers topographical maps to download for offline use.
- **DARK SKY WEATHER** (www.darksky.net, Android, free with in-app purchases; IOS, $3.99) and **WEATHER UNDERGROUND** (www.wunderground.com, Andriod, IOS, free with in-app purchases) are good choices for staying abreast of weather forecasts in the area you're hiking.
- **FIRST AID - AMERICAN RED CROSS** (www.redcross.org, Android, IOS, free) helps diagnose and treat common injuries and ailments you might face on the trail. Videos and written directions offer expert advice on dealing with sprains, heat stroke, hypothermia, and more.
- **GAIAGPS** (www.gaiagps.com, Android, IOS, free with in-app purchases) lets you navigate the wilderness, record your hike, download maps, check weather forecasts, and search for trails.
- **MERLIN BIRD ID** (www.merlin.allaboutbirds.org, Android, IOS, free) helps you identify more than 3,000 bird species by snapping a photo or answering questions. The app then gives you in-depth info on the bird and even lets you listen to birdsongs.
- **PEAKFINDER AR** (www.peakfinder.org, Android, IOS, $4.99) and **PEAKVISOR** (www.peakvisor.com, Andriod, $4.49, IOS, free with in-app purchases) are excellent apps for identifying peaks. Just point your phone's camera at the mountain in question: The apps use augmented reality to overlay a rendering of the peak so you can determine its name.
- **ALLTRAILS** (www.alltrails.com, Andriod, IOS, free with in-app purchases) is a valuable tool for hikers, complete with hiking suggestions and trip reports with details about current trail and road conditions.

Hiking Prep

With the right gear and preparation, you're ready to hit the trail.

Tell a friend: If you get lost or need help, will rescuers know to look for you? It's vital to make sure a friend or family member knows where you are going and understands your itinerary.

Check the forecast: Be prepared for what the weather is supposed to be like, but remember the weather is unpredictable. So, also be ready for sudden and dramatic changes. Check with a ranger station or land manager before your trip to confirm the trail is open, whether you can reach the trailhead (or get close enough to walk). And don't forget to check the avalanche forecast.

Go old school with directions: Siri is a wealth of information, but she doesn't seem to hike much. Follow directions to trailheads provided in this guide.

Check yourself before you wreck yourself: A mountaintop, five miles from your car, is a bad place to come to the realization that your athletic glory days are behind you. Be honest about your fitness level and how much stress your joints can handle before they turn on you. If it's been a while since you hiked, start slow.

Double-check: Make sure your gear is in working order and double-check that you have everything you need before pulling out of the driveway.

Get trailhead-ready: Opportunistic burglars love trailheads. Lock your car and never leave valuables inside. If you routinely keep stuff in your car, consider leaving those items at home. And if you do leave items in your car, make sure they're out of sight. And don't forget to hang your parking pass.

On the Trail
WEATHER
For hikers, meteorologists are also stylists. They're talking about rain, snow, and high-pressure systems, but what we hear are guidelines for how to dress. After all, almost every day is perfect for hiking if you have the right gear. The Northwest might be famous for rain, but don't let gloomy forecasts get you down. Heading out in the rain can be a good way to avoid crowds. Plus, most rainy days have windows free of precipitation. To really dial in your forecast, head to www.weather.gov, where you can click on a location on a map and NOAA will serve up a personalized prediction.

Be sure to know what time the sun will set, especially in late summer and early fall when it's not uncommon for hikers to be surprised when darkness arrives earlier than they expected. In winter and early spring, check avalanche conditions on the Northwest Avalanche Center website (www.nwac.us).

Check for road closures and mountain pass conditions at www.tripcheck.com. It links to numerous webcams that help you better understand what you'll face during your drive.

WILDLIFE
Whether it's a squirrel scurrying up a tree or a black bear foraging in a trailside huckleberry bush, wildlife encounters are an exciting and inevitable part of hiking in the Pacific Northwest. These encounters are usually peaceful if hikers keep their distance, but there's a reason these animals are called wildlife. They are wild and unpredictable. You don't know what they will do if they are startled or feel cornered, and you don't want to find out.

Give the animals plenty of space and never feed them. Feeding animals conditions them to associate humans with food. This can be unsafe for people and the animals.

Bears

If you stumble across a bear while hiking in the Northwest, it's likely a black bear. Look for fresh scat, tracks, and clawed trees as you hike. Making noise by clapping your hands or talking loudly is often enough to keep bears away. Bears are attracted to scents like perfume, deodorant, and even toothpaste. If you're camping, hang everything that smells (except your hiking partner) at least 10 feet off the ground and at least 100 yards outside of camp.

If you stumble across a black bear, stop and try to stay calm as you assess the situation. If the bear doesn't notice you, slowly back away. If the bear approaches you, don't throw anything and avoid direct eye contact, which the bear could interpret as a threat. Instead, stand up, wave your hands, and talk to it in a low voice. If you are in a group, stand shoulder-to-shoulder and wave your arms to appear intimidating. If the bear charges you, fight the urge to run (bears can run 35 mph, about 7 mph faster than Usain Bolt). Stand your ground. It's likely bluff-charging. If the bear attacks, fight back.

Cougars

Cougars are solitary creatures who usually want nothing to do with humans. If you happen across one of these massive cats, they're likely to scram quicker than you can process what you saw. Attacks are rare. The best way to avoid cougars is to hike in a group, make noise to avoid surprising these beasts, and stay away from animal carcasses. Cougars might be saving these dead animals for their next meal.

If you encounter a cougar, do not run. Instead, keep eye contact and make yourself look as big as possible. Open your jacket, wave your arms, shout, and throw rocks to convince the animal you are a predator, not prey. Pick up small children. Assess the situation and back away slowly if it is safe to do so. If it attacks, fight back.

Mountain Goats

Mountain goats meandering across rocky slopes are a sight to behold, but get too close and they can be dangerous. Try to stay at least 50 yards away from these peaceful-looking creatures. Mountain goats have an insatiable appetite for salt and might follow you in hope of tasting your sweat and urine or scoring a snack. Never feed them. If a goat won't leave you alone, try to scare it off by hollering, waving your arms, and throwing small rocks. They might look harmless, but if a mountain goat charges you it can be deadly.

Rattlesnakes

They slither, they're venomous, and they'll get your adrenaline pumping, but rattlesnakes aren't likely to bite if you give them plenty of space. Found east of the Cascades, rattlesnakes are most active in late spring and summer and usually shake their rattles to warn you of their presence. Don't let them scare you off the trail. Be mindful of where you step—especially when crossing scree fields, logs, and rocks—and where you put your hands (don't reach under rocks). Keep pets and kids close. And wear hiking boots to protect your feet. Rattlesnake bites are rare, but if you end up on the unlucky side of the odds, here's what the Red Cross recommends: Call 9-1-1, gently wash the wound, and keep it lower than your heart. Stay calm and, unless necessary, avoid walking.

Ticks

Ticks hang out on grass and leaves and will latch on to a human or animal if given the chance. Don't be a good host. Wearing a long-sleeve shirt, pants, and lightweight gaiters (or tucking your pants into your socks) makes it hard for these bugs to attach to you. Avoiding overgrown trails and wearing insect repellent with DEET also helps avoid these pests.

Ticks burrow into your skin and, like tiny eight-legged vampires, they want to drink your blood. If a tick attaches to you, use tweezers and grasp the bug as close to your skin as possible and slowly pull it out. Wash the bite area and apply an antibiotic ointment. You can save the tick so your doctor can test it for Lyme disease. Remember to also inspect your pet for ticks. The Red Cross warns against myths regarding removing ticks. Do not try to remove ticks by burning them or applying petroleum jelly or nail polish.

Hazardous Plants

Learning to identify and avoid poison ivy and poison oak is a good way to avoid an itchy situation. Both grow as shrubs or vines with green leaves that turn red in the fall. Poison ivy leaves have three leaflets while poison oak leaves vary in shape. Both can cause an itchy rash that will spoil your hike.

Wearing pants and a long-sleeve shirt will protect your skin. Avoid overgrown trails. If you come in contact with these plants, wash your skin. The oil emitted by the plants can linger on your gear, clothes and pets, so they'll need to be washed too. Anti-itch cream, an ice pack, and a cool shower can give you some relief.

Wildfire

The biggest summer bummer for Northwest hikers in recent years has been wildfires. Local forest fires coupled with smoke blowing in from fires in California and British Columbia have led to a lousy air quality and poor visibility on many popular trails. Visit www.airnow.com to view the air-quality index. Be sure to check the forecast and call or visit a ranger station in the area where you plan to hike to determine if your plans are safe. Don't be shy about changing plans. You can always return at another time. Wildfires are unpredictable.

PROTECT THE ENVIRONMENT

Whether you're looking for inspiring views, a challenging workout, a few hours of solitude, or memories that last a lifetime, the trails of the Pacific Northwest will take care of you. All they need in return is for you to take care of them. Here are some tips for minimizing your impact:

Dirt won't hurt: Too often, hikers walk around the perimeter of trail-blocking puddles, but this often tramples vegetation and creates wide spots in the trails. Hiking through the puddle is usually the best move.

HIKING WITH DOGS

Your dog probably loves playing in the outdoors as much as you, but just like you and your human hiking companions, things can go wrong if you aren't prepared. Here are some recommendations for making sure everything goes smoothly for you and your best friend:

- **KNOW THE RULES:** Don't leave the house before finding a destination where dogs are allowed. They are permitted in many areas, but some places (like national parks and wildlife refuges) don't allow pets.

- **FIRST-AID UPGRADE:** Make sure your first-aid kit has items than can help tend to an injured dog. Duct tape, vet wrap, wound closure strips, and antibiotic ointment are a good idea. Ask your vet about carrying an antihistamine in case of bee sting. Apply canine sunscreen to exposed skin (and don't forget the nose).

- **PAY ATTENTION TO YOUR DOG:** If your dog is panting excessively, drooling, or unsteady on its feet, it's probably overheated. Blue, purple, or bright red gums are also a sign the dog needs to cool off. Get the dog in the shade, off hot surfaces such as rocks and asphalt, and get it water to drink. Put wet towels behind its neck and on its paws, groin, and armpits.

- **FLEA AND TICK PROTECTION:** A flea and tick collar or medication helps keep these pests away. But a tick puller (or tweezers) is a good addition to your first-aid kit.

- **REIGN IT IN:** Always keep your dog on a leash, no matter how well trained it is. A leash can keep your dog from unwanted encounters with wildlife and hikers who might not love dogs as much as you. Ask before letting your dog interact with another hiker's pet.

- **GEAR UP:** Doggy jackets, booties, and sunglasses can keep your pet safe and comfortable. Plus, they're super adorable. A body harness is likely to be most comfortable for your dog. Buy one with pockets so they can carry their own food, water, and doggy doo.

Don't cut switchbacks: It's horrible for the trail and vegetation. Even if you aren't traipsing through vegetation, these shortcuts can change the way water flows in the area and erode the slope and the trail.

Leave nothing, take nothing: Be prepared to pack out all your trash. Bonus points for collecting garbage you find along the way. Don't collect rocks, pick flowers, or take anything else. If you need a souvenir, take a picture. Don't carve initials or anniversary dates in trees or benches. It's not romantic. It's vandalism.

Be a super pooper: If you can't make it back to a trailhead or to a pit toilet, dig a hole at least six inches deep and at least 200 feet from the trail and the nearest water source. Cover the hole when you are done, but don't bury toilet paper. Pack it out. Or use natural TP like grass, leaves, or pinecones. And never bury your business in the snow. Snow melts. Pack it out.

Don't feed the animals: Feeding animals trains them to associate people with food. You don't want bears seeing you as walking beef jerky, so give other hikers the same courtesy.

Be considerate: In a 2017 interview, Ben Lawhon, educational director at Leave No Trace, told me speakers blasting music don't keep bears away (a common excuse). They are just giving users a false sense of security and spoiling the serenity for others. And it might unnecessarily scare other wildlife, he said.

Yield like a boss: Always yield to horses and uphill hikers. Don't step off the trail, if possible.

Volunteer: Several organizations give hikers the chance to give back to the trails that give them so much. Call your favorite park or check www.volunteer.gov for more opportunities.

PASSES, PERMITS, AND FEES

At popular Northwest trailheads, it's somewhat common to see cars with a collection of parking passes spread out on their dashboards. For some hikers, it's confusing determining who manages the land they're parking on and which pass to use. It's easier just to lay out everything in the glovebox. Generally, you'll be covered if you have passes for state, national forest, and national park land. Here's what you need to legally park at the trailheads for every hike in this book.

A **Northwest Forest Pass** (discovernw.org, $5 per day, $30 annual pass) is required at developed Forest Service recreation sites in Oregon. Passes are available at Forest Service offices, through hundreds of vendors, and online at www.store.usgs.gov/forest-pass.

An **Oregon State Parks Permit** ($5 per day, $30 annual pass, $50 two-year pass when not camping at that park) is required at the 25 Oregon state parks that charge a day-use fee; it can be purchased online and at kiosks within the parks.

National Parks

At **Crater Lake National Park,** it's $30 per vehicle in summer (May 22-Oct. 31), $20 per vehicle in winter (Nov. 1-May 21); $25 per motorcycle in summer (May 22-Oct. 31), $20 per motorcycle in winter (Nov. 1-May 21); $15 per cyclist or pedestrian; and $55 for an annual pass. Non-annual passes are good for seven days.

Purchase passes in advance at www.yourpassnow.com.

America the Beautiful Passes

A must for outdoor lovers, America the Beautiful Passes (888/275-8747, www.nps.gov) cover entry and amenity fees on lands managed by six federal agencies: the National Park Service (national parks), U.S. Forest Service (national forests and grasslands), U.S. Fish and Wildlife Service (national wildlife refuges), Bureau of Land Management, Bureau of Reclamation, and U.S. Army Corps of Engineers. You have several options:

Annual Pass: Buy this $80 pass at a federal recreation site, by phone at 888/275-8747, or online at store.usgs.gov/pass.

BEERS MADE BY WALKING

Beer enthusiast Eric Steen believes in the connection between the great outdoors and good beer. So in 2011, he founded **Beers Made By Walking** (www.beersmadebywalking.com) to bring together those seemingly disparate worlds. Every spring and summer, Steen plans a series of interpretive hikes throughout the United States, where hikers and local brewers learn about the medicinal and edible characteristics of plants they encounter.

Following the hike, the brewers turn those ideas into new beers and hold tasting events to show off the finished products. Since the first Beers Made By Walking event, these brewers have developed ales and lagers with, for example, stinging nettles, huckleberries, pine needles, sagebrush, prickly pear cactus fruit, and dozens of other ingredients. Each beer release generally raises money for conservation efforts and local nonprofits.

Beers Made By Walking is present throughout the Pacific Northwest, with events in Portland, Bend, Eugene, and Corvallis. Hikes are usually free and open to the public, and end-of-season celebrations vary by city; Portland-area brewers have, in recent years, held tapping events at participating breweries. Check the website in spring to see the upcoming list of cities, sign up for a hike, and stay up-to-date on tasting events.

Military Pass: Free for current U.S. military members and dependents; obtain a pass by showing a Common Access Card or military ID at a federal recreation site.

4th Grade Pass: Kids and their families get free access to federal recreation lands during the student's fourth-grade year. Fourth-grade teachers and those at organizations serving fourth-graders (youth group leaders, camp directors, etc.) are also eligible. Visit www.everykidinapark.gov for details.

Senior Pass: U.S. citizens and permanent residents 62 and older may buy a lifetime interagency pass for $80 or an annual pass for $20. Passes may be purchased online at www.store.usgs.gov/pass, through the mail, or, to avoid a $10 processing fee, in person at a federal recreation site. Note that Golden Age Passports are no longer sold but are still honored.

Access Pass: Free to U.S. citizens and permanent residents with permanent disabilities. Documentation of permanent disability is required. Passes are available at federal recreation sites and by mail; ordering by mail requires a $10 processing fee.

Volunteer Pass: Once you volunteer 250 hours with federal agencies participating in the Interagency Pass Program, you're eligible for a free pass. Contact your local federal recreation site for specifics. Find volunteer opportunities at www.volunteer.gov.

HIKING WITH CHILDREN

It's you and nature vs. Netflix and the Xbox in a battle to capture your kids' imagination, and the odds aren't in your favor. Not only does it take significantly more energy to ready the little ones for an excursion, but it can also be intimidating. But if you want to pass along your love of the outdoors, the sooner you start hiking the better. Here are some tips for keeping it fun (and safe):

- **PLAN:** Your hands are going to be full on hike day, so ready maps, driving directions, gear, food, water, and pass information the night before.
- **START EASY AND INTERESTING:** The joy of testing your toughness on hard trails is usually lost on kids. Choose something you know will be easy on their little legs. And pick something with ponds, big trees, beaches, or other things that will hold their attention.
- **GO AT THEIR PACE:** Give yourself plenty of time to finish the hike. Those puddles, flowers, and ladybugs you didn't even notice are mesmerizing to kids.
- **GEAR UP:** On short, easy trails, tennis shoes are usually fine hiking footwear for kids. But making sure the youngsters are dressed appropriately for the conditions can be the difference between misery and an outing that launches a lifelong love for the outdoors. A comfortable child-carrier backpack is ideal for babies and toddlers who might need to split time between riding and walking.
- **PLAY GAMES:** Don't give kids a chance for their attention to wane. Play games like I Spy, or count squirrels, birds, or mushrooms for an added layer of entertainment.
- **PACK PLENTY OF SNACKS AND WATER:** Take snack breaks along the way and maybe even save a special snack for the halfway point.
- **GO WITH FRIENDS:** No matter how old, hiking with friends enhances the adventure. Plus, having another parent around means extra help in dealing with emotional meltdowns and diaper blowouts. Looking for a kid-friendly hiking group? Hike it Baby (www.hikeitbaby.com), founded in Portland in 2013, is an excellent resource for finding family hiking meetups.
- **TEACH:** Use the outing to start teaching your kids about nature and trail and environmental etiquette.

BEST HIKES WITH KIDS:

- **WEST METOLIUS RIVER:** Follow a mostly flat footpath to the Wizard Falls Hatchery, which rears six species of trout and salmon and hosts open-air ponds and interpretive panels. For a quarter you can buy fish food out of on-site gumball machines (page 160).
- **CARROLL RIM TRAIL:** Your kids will get a kick out of this short hike to a summit offering expansive views of the surrounding Painted Hills (page 194).
- **NATIONAL HISTORIC OREGON TRAIL INTERPRETIVE CENTER:** Walk in the dusty footsteps of Oregon Trail pioneers, and head inside the interpretive center afterward for displays, movies, and more (page 306).

RESOURCES

CITY AND COUNTY PARKS

PORTLAND PARKS & RECREATION
1120 SW 5th Ave.
Portland, OR 97204
503/823-7529
www.portlandoregon.gov

BEND PARKS AND RECREATION DISTRICT
799 SW Columbia St.
Bend, OR 97702
541/389-7275
www.bendparksandrec.org

CITY OF ASHLAND PARKS DIVISION
1195 E. Main St.
Ashland, OR 97520
541/488-5340
www.ashland.or.us
www.whitmancounty.org

STATE PARKS AND FORESTS

OREGON STATE PARKS
725 Summer St. NE, Suite C
Salem, OR 97301
503/986-0707
www.oregonstateparks.org

OSWALD WEST STATE PARK
U.S. 101
Manzanita, OR 97102
503/368-3575
www.oregonstateparks.org

CAPE LOOKOUT STATE PARK
13000 Whiskey Creek Rd.
Tillamook, OR 97141
503/842-4981
www.oregonstateparks.org

TILLAMOOK STATE FOREST
45500 Wilson River Hwy.
Tillamook, OR 97141
866/930-4646
www.oregon.gov/ODF

HECETA HEAD LIGHTHOUSE STATE SCENIC VIEWPOINT
93111 U.S. 101
Florence, OR 97439
541/547-3416
www.oregonstateparks.org

ALFRED A. LOEB STATE PARK
99917 North Bank Chetco River Rd.
Brookings, OR 97415
541/469-2021
www.oregonstateparks.org

TRYON CREEK STATE NATURAL AREA
11321 SW Terwilliger Blvd.
Portland, OR 97219
503/636-9886
www.oregonstateparks.org

SILVER FALLS STATE PARK
20024 Silver Falls Hwy. SE
Sublimity, OR 97385
503/873-8681
www.oregonstateparks.org

GUY W. TALBOT STATE PARK
U.S. 30 (Historic Columbia River Highway)
Corbett, OR 97019
503/695-2261
www.oregonstateparks.org

THE COVE PALISADES STATE PARK
7300 Jordan Rd.
Culver, OR 97734
541/546-3412
www.oregonstateparks.org

SMITH ROCK STATE PARK
9241 NE Crooked River Dr.
Terrebonne, OR 97760
541/548-7501
www.oregonstateparks.org

NATIONAL PARKS AND MONUMENTS
CRATER LAKE NATIONAL PARK
PO Box 7
Crater Lake, OR 97604
541/594-3000
www.nps.gov/crla

OREGON CAVES NATIONAL MONUMENT & PRESERVE
19000 Caves Hwy.
Cave Junction, OR 97523
541/592-2100
www.nps.gov/orca

JOHN DAY FOSSIL BEDS NATIONAL MONUMENT
32651 Highway 19
Kimberly, OR 97848
541/987-2333
www.nps.gov/joda

NATIONAL FORESTS

U.S. FOREST SERVICE—PACIFIC NORTHWEST REGION
1220 SW 3rd Ave.
Portland, OR 97204
503/808-2468
www.fs.usda.gov/r6

SIUSLAW NATIONAL FOREST
3200 SW Jefferson Way
Corvallis, OR 97331
541/750-7000
www.fs.usda.gov/siuslaw

SIUSLAW NATIONAL FOREST—CAPE PERPETUA VISITOR CENTER
2400 U.S. 101
Yachats, OR 97498
541/547-3289
www.fs.usda.gov/siuslaw

ROGUE RIVER-SISKIYOU NATIONAL FOREST
3040 Biddle Rd.
Medford, OR 97504
541/618-2200
www.fs.usda.gov/rogue-siskiyou

COLUMBIA RIVER GORGE NATIONAL SCENIC AREA
902 Wasco Ave., Suite 200
Hood River, OR 97031
541/308-1700
www.fs.usda.gov/crgnsa

MOUNT HOOD NATIONAL FOREST
16400 Champion Way
Sandy, OR 97055
503/668-1700
www.fs.usda.gov/mthood

WILLAMETTE NATIONAL FOREST
3106 Pierce Parkway, Suite D
Springfield, OR 97477
541/225-6300
www.fs.usda.gov/willamette

DESCHUTES NATIONAL FOREST
63095 Deschutes Market Rd.
Bend, OR 97701
541/383-5300
www.fs.usda.gov/deschutes

OCHOCO NATIONAL FOREST
3160 NE 3rd St.
Prineville, OR 97754
541/416-6500
www.fs.usda.gov/ochoco

KLAMATH NATIONAL FOREST
1711 S. Main St.
Yreka, CA 96097
530/842-6131
www.fs.usda.gov/klamath

FREMONT-WINEMA NATIONAL FOREST
1301 S. G St.
Lakeview, OR 97630
541/947-2151
www.fs.usda.gov/fremont-winema

WALLOWA-WHITMAN NATIONAL FOREST
1550 Dewey Ave., Suite A
Baker City, OR 97814
541/523-6391
www.fs.usda.gov/wallowa-whitman

OTHER RESOURCES
BUREAU OF LAND MANAGEMENT OREGON-WASHINGTON
1220 SW 3rd Ave.
Portland, OR 97204
503/808-6001
www.blm.gov

THE MOUNTAINEERS
www.mountaineers.org

THE NATURE CONSERVANCY—OREGON
821 SE 14th Ave.
Portland, OR 97214
503/802-8100
www.nature.org

FRIENDS OF THE COLUMBIA GORGE
www.gorgefriends.org

TRAILKEEPERS OF OREGON
www.trailkeepersoforegon.org

**OREGON DEPARTMENT OF TRANSPORTATION
TRIPCHECK TRIP-PLANNING TOOL**
www.tripcheck.com

CRATER LAKE HOSPITALITY
www.travelcraterlake.com

OREGON NATURAL DESERT ASSOCIATION
www.onda.org

OREGON WILD
www.oregonwild.org

TRAVEL OREGON
www.traveloregon.com

NATIONAL WEATHER SERVICE
www.weather.gov

NORTHWEST AVALANCHE CENTER
www.nwac.us

AIRNOW AIR QUALITY INDEX
www.airnow.gov

TIDES AND CURRENTS
www.tidesandcurrents.noaa.gov

INDEX

PHOTO CREDITS

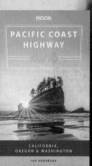  

MOON ROAD TRIP GUIDES

MOON
BLUE RIDGE PARKWAY
Road Trip

(INCLUDING SHENANDOAH & GREAT SMOKY MOUNTAINS NATIONAL PARKS)

JASON FRYE

MOON
CALIFORNIA
Road Trip

SAN FRANCISCO, YOSEMITE, LAS VEGAS, GRAND CANYON, LOS ANGELES, & THE PACIFIC COAST HIGHWAY

STUART THORNTON

MOON
NASHVILLE TO NEW ORLEANS
Road Trip

NATCHEZ TRACE PARKWAY · MEMPHIS · TUPELO · MISSISSIPPI BLUES TRAIL

MARGARET LITTMAN

MOON
NEW ENGLAND
Road Trip

BOSTON, ACADIA NATIONAL PARK, WHITE MOUNTAINS, BERKSHIRES, NEWPORT, AND CAPE COD

JEN ROSE SMITH

MOON
NORTHERN CALIFORNIA
Road Trip

DRIVES ALONG THE COAST, REDWOODS, AND MOUNTAINS WITH THE BEST STOPS ALONG THE WAY

STUART THORNTON & KAYLA ANDERSON

MOON
PACIFIC COAST HIGHWAY

CALIFORNIA, OREGON & WASHINGTON

IAN ANDERSON

MOON
PACIFIC NORTHWEST
Road Trip

SEATTLE, VANCOUVER, VICTORIA, THE OLYMPIC PENINSULA, PORTLAND, THE OREGON COAST & MOUNT RAINIER

ALLISON WILLIAMS

MOON
ROUTE 66
Road Trip

JESSICA DUNHAM

MOON
SOUTH FLORIDA & THE KEYS
Road Trip

WITH MIAMI, WALT DISNEY WORLD, TAMPA & THE EVERGLADES

JASON FERGUSON

Share your adventures using **#travelwithmoon**

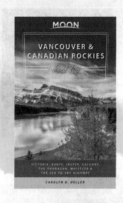

MOON NATIONAL PARKS

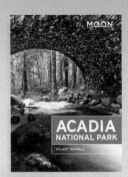

In these books:

- Full coverage of gateway cities and towns
- Itineraries from one day to multiple weeks
- Advice on where to stay (or camp) in and around the parks

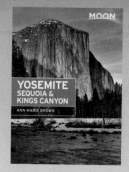

TRAILS AT A GLANCE

PAGE	HIKE NAME	DISTANCE	DURATION
PORTLAND AND THE WILLAMETTE VALLEY			
26	Lower Macleay Trail to Pittock Mansion	6.4 mi rt	3 hr
29	Marquam Trail to Council Crest	3.9 mi rt	2 hr
32	Tryon Creek State Natural Area Loop	4.5 mi rt	2 hr
35	Trail of Ten Falls	9.3 mi rt	4.5 hr
38	Table Rock	8.2 mi rt	4 hr
41	Bagby Hot Springs	3.3 mi rt	1.5 hr
44	Opal Pool and Jawbone Flats Loop	8.5 mi rt	4.5 hr
47	Battle Ax Mountain	6.8 mi rt	3 hr
50	Marys Peak	6.9 mi rt	3.5 hr
53	North Fork River Walk	7 mi rt	3.5 hr
COLUMBIA RIVER GORGE			
60	Latourell Falls Loop	3.1 mi rt	1.5 hr
63	Angel's Rest	4.9 mi rt	2.5 hr
66	Wahkeena Falls–Multnomah Falls Loop	5.9 mi rt	3 hr
70	Larch Mountain Crater Loop	7.1 mi rt	3.5 hr
73	Beacon Rock	2 mi rt	1 hr
76	Dry Creek Falls	5 mi rt	2.5 hr
79	Dog Mountain	6.9 mi rt	4 hr
82	Coyote Wall (Labyrinth Loop)	6.3 mi rt	3.5 hr
85	Mosier Plateau	3.7 mi rt	1.5 hr
88	Tom McCall Point Trail	3.8 mi rt	2 hr
MOUNT HOOD			
96	Lost Lake Butte	4.4 mi rt	2 hr
99	Vista Ridge to Owl Point	5.4 mi rt	2.5 hr
102	Ramona Falls	8.1 mi rt	4 hr
105	Salmon River	8.2 mi rt	4.5 hr
108	Elk Meadows	6.9 mi rt	3.5 hr

DIFFICULTY	SEASONAL ACCESS	WILDLIFE	WATER-FALLS	DOG-FRIENDLY
Easy/moderate	Year-round	X		X
Easy/moderate	Year-round			X
Easy	Year-round	X		X
Moderate/strenuous	Year-round		X	X
Moderate	June-Nov.			X
Easy	June-Oct.			X
Moderate	Mar.-Nov.		X	X
Moderate	June-Oct.			X
Moderate	Apr.-Nov.			X
Easy/moderate	Year-round			X
Easy/moderate	Year-round		X	X
Moderate	Year-round		X	X
Moderate	Year-round		X	X
Easy/moderate	June-Oct.			X
Easy/moderate	Year-round	X		
Moderate	Year-round		X	X
Moderate/strenuous	Mar.-Dec.	X		X
Easy/moderate	Year-round	X	X	X
Easy/moderate	Year-round	X	X	X
Easy/moderate	Mar.-Oct.	X		
Easy/moderate	May-Oct.	X		X
Easy/moderate	July-Oct.	X		X
Moderate	Apr.-Oct.		X	X
Moderate	Apr.-Nov.			X
Easy/moderate	June-Oct.			X

TRAILS AT A GLANCE (continued)

PAGE	HIKE NAME	DISTANCE	DURATION
OREGON COAST			
116	Saddle Mountain	5.9 mi rt	3.5 hr
119	Cape Falcon	5.8 mi rt	3 hr
122	Neahkahnie Mountain	5.9 mi rt	3 hr
125	Kings Mountain	5.4 mi rt	3 hr
128	Cape Lookout	5.5 mi rt	2.5 hr
131	Cascade Head	5.2 mi rt	2.5 hr
134	Drift Creek Falls	4.4 mi rt	2 hr
137	Cape Perpetua	5.8 mi rt	2.5 hr
141	Heceta Head to Hobbit Trail	5 mi rt	2.5 hr
144	Cape Sebastian	3.8 mi rt	2 hr
147	River View Trail to Redwood Nature Trail	3.3 mi rt	1.5 hr
BEND AND THE CENTRAL OREGON CASCADES			
154	McKenzie River Trail to Tamolitch (Blue Pool)	4.6 mi rt	2.5 hr
157	Little Belknap Crater	5.3 mi rt	3 hr
160	West Metolius River	5.7 mi rt	3 hr
163	Black Butte	4.8 mi rt	2.5 hr
166	Tam-a-láu Trail	7.1 mi rt	3.5 hr
169	Misery Ridge-River Trail Loop	4.2 mi rt	2.5 hr
172	Tumalo Mountain	4.4 mi rt	2.5 hr
175	Shevlin Park Loop	4.8 mi rt	2 hr
178	Flatiron Rock	6.3 mi rt	2.75 hr
181	Paulina Peak	4.7 mi rt	2.5 hr
JOHN DAY RIVER BASIN			
188	Steins Pillar	4.5 mi rt	2.25 hr
191	Lookout Mountain	7.7 mi rt	4 hr
194	Carroll Rim Trail	1.7 mi rt	1 hr
197	Sutton Mountain	7.5 mi rt	4 hr
200	Blue Basin Overlook	3.4 mi rt	1.75 hr

DIFFICULTY	SEASONAL ACCESS	WILDLIFE	WATER-FALLS	DOG-FRIENDLY
Moderate	Mar.-Nov.			X
Easy/moderate	Year-round	X	X	X
Easy/moderate	Year-round			X
Moderate	Mar.-Nov.			X
Moderate	Year-round	X		X
Easy/moderate	Year-round	X		X
Easy/moderate	Year-round		X	X
Easy/moderate	Year-round			X
Easy/moderate	Year-round	X		X
Easy/moderate	Year-round	X		X
Easy/moderate	Year-round	X		X
Easy	Feb.-Dec.		X	X
Easy/moderate	Summer-early fall			X
Easy/moderate	Year-round	X		X
Moderate	June-Oct.			X
Easy/moderate	Mar.-Nov.	X		X
Easy/moderate	Year-round	X		X
Moderate	June-Oct.	X		X
Easy	Mar.-Nov.			X
Easy/moderate	Year-round	X		X
Moderate	June-Oct.			X
Easy/moderate	Apr.-Nov.			X
Easy/moderate	May-Nov.	X		X
Easy	Year-round			X
Moderate	Year-round	X		X
Easy/moderate	Year-round			X

TRAILS AT A GLANCE (continued)

PAGE	HIKE NAME	DISTANCE	DURATION
CRATER LAKE NATIONAL PARK			
208	Boundary Springs	5.5 mi rt	2.5 hr
211	Cleetwood Cove and Wizard Island	4.9 mi rt	3 hr
214	Garfield Peak	3.4 mi rt	1.5 hr
217	Plaikni Falls	2.2 mi rt	1.5 hr
220	Mount Scott	4.6 mi rt	2.5 hr
ASHLAND AND THE ROGUE VALLEY			
228	Rainie Falls	4.4 mi rt	2.5 hr
231	Mount Elijah	5.7 mi rt	3 hr
234	Lower Table Rock	4.8 mi rt	2.5 hr
237	Grizzly Peak	5.6 mi rt	3 hr
240	Siskiyou Mountain Park	4.9 mi rt	2 hr
243	Mount Ashland (via the Pacific Crest Trail)	8.1 mi rt	4 hr
246	Soda Mountain	4.5 mi rt	2.5 hr
SKY LAKES WILDERNESS AND KLAMATH BASIN			
254	Horseshoe Lake	6.1 mi rt	3 hr
257	Brown Mountain Lava Flow	6.1 mi rt	3 hr
260	Sky Lakes Basin via Cold Springs Trail	7.2 mi rt	3.5 hr
263	Puck Lakes via Nannie Creek Trail	5.4 mi rt	2.5 hr
266	OC&E Woods Line State Trail	4.7 mi rt	2.5 hr
STEENS MOUNTAIN AND ALVORD DESERT			
274	Riddle Brothers Ranch and Little Blitzen River	5.8 mi rt	2.5 hr
277	Big Indian Gorge	8.1 mi rt	4 hr
280	Wildhorse Lake	2.8 mi rt	2 hr
283	Pike Creek Canyon	6.5 mi rt	3 hr
286	Borax Lake Hot Springs	2 mi rt	1 hr

DIFFICULTY	SEASONAL ACCESS	WILDLIFE	WATER-FALLS	DOG-FRIENDLY
Easy/moderate	June-Nov.	X	X	
Easy/moderate	June-Sept.	X		
Easy/moderate	July-Oct.	X		
Easy	July-Oct.		X	
Easy/moderate	July-Oct.	X		
Easy/moderate	Year-round	X	X	X
Easy/moderate	June-Nov.			X
Easy/moderate	Year-round	X		
Easy/moderate	June-Nov.			X
Easy/moderate	Year-round	X		X
Moderate	June-Nov.	X		X
Easy/moderate	June-Oct.	X		X
Easy/moderate	June-Oct.	X		X
Easy/moderate	June-Nov.	X		X
Easy/moderate	July-Oct.			X
Easy/moderate	July-Oct.	X		X
Easy	Year-round	X		X
Easy/moderate	May-Nov.	X		X
Moderate	June-Nov.	X		X
Easy/moderate	July-Oct.	X		X
Moderate	Apr.-Nov.	X		X
Easy	Year-round	X		

TRAILS AT A GLANCE (continued)

PAGE	HIKE NAME	DISTANCE	DURATION
WALLOWA MOUNTAINS AND BLUE MOUNTAINS			
294	Hurricane Creek to Slick Rock Gorge	7.5 mi rt	3.5 hr
297	Iwetemlaykin State Heritage Site	2 mi rt	1 hr
300	Imnaha River to Blue Hole	4.6 mi rt	2.25 hr
303	Anthony Lake to Hoffer Lakes	3.2 mi rt	1.5 hr
306	National Historic Oregon Trail Interpretive Center	4.3 mi rt	2 hr

DIFFICULTY	SEASONAL ACCESS	WILDLIFE	WATER-FALLS	DOG-FRIENDLY
Easy/moderate	June–Oct.	X	X	X
Easy	Year-round	X		X
Easy	June–Nov.	X		X
Easy	June–Oct.			X
Easy	Year-round			X

MOON OREGON HIKING

Avalon Travel
Hachette Book Group
1700 Fourth Street
Berkeley, CA 94710, USA
www.moon.com

Editor: Kristi Mitsuda
Acquiring Editor: Nikki Ioakimedes
Series Manager: Sabrina Young
Copy Editors: Brett Keener, Kelly Lydick
Graphics Coordinator: Ravina Schneider
Production Coordinator: Ravina Schneider
Cover Design: Kimberly Glyder Design
Interior Design: Megan Jones Design
Moon Logo: Tim McGrath
Map Editor: Mike Morgenfeld
Cartographers: Lohnes+Wright, Brian
    Shotwell, Karin Dahl
Proofreader: Ann Seifert
Editorial Assistance: Samia Abbasi
Indexer: Greg Jewett

ISBN-13: 9781640495043
Printing History
1st Edition — March 2021
5 4 3 2 1

Text © 2021 by Matt Wastradowski.
Maps © 2021 by Avalon Travel.
Some text, photos, and illustrations
    are used by permission and are the
    property of the original copyright
    owners.

Front cover photo: Cape Perpetua. ©
    Lynne Nieman | Alamy Stock Photo
Back cover photo: Mount Hood. ©
    Josemaria Toscano | Dreamstime.com

Printed in China by RR Donnelley

ICON AND MAP SYMBOLS KEY

- PCT PCT
- Wildlife
- Wildflowers
- Waterfalls
- Dog-friendly
- Kid-friendly
- Wheelchair accessible
- Public transportation

——— Expressway	——— Feature Trail	♠ Park
——— Primary Road	---------- Other Trail	✦ Unique Feature
——— Secondary Road	——— Contour Line	⬊ Waterfall
- - - - Unpaved Road	🅿 Parking Area	∧ Camping
- - - - Rail Line	TH Trailhead	▲ Mountain
		○ City/Town
		★ Point of Interest
		▪ Other Location
		✈ Airport
		⛷ Ski Area

QUICK-REFERENCE CHART: TRAILS AT A GLANCE